EU Criminal Justice

Tommaso Rafaraci • Rosanna Belfiore

Editors

EU Criminal Justice

Fundamental Rights, Transnational
Proceedings and the European Public
Prosecutor's Office

 Springer

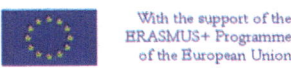 With the support of the
ERASMUS+ Programme
of the European Union

Editors
Tommaso Rafaraci
Department of Law
University of Catania
Catania, Italy

Rosanna Belfiore
Department of Law
University of Catania
Catania, Italy

ISBN 978-3-319-97318-0   ISBN 978-3-319-97319-7   (eBook)
https://doi.org/10.1007/978-3-319-97319-7

Library of Congress Control Number: 2018959223

This Springer imprint is published by the registered company Springer Nature Switzerland AG
The registered company address is: Gewerbestrasse 11, 6330 Cham, Switzerland

Preface

This book is a collection of updated and thoroughly revised presentations from three international conferences organised within the Jean Monnet project entitled "Three Conferences on EU Criminal Justice: Fundamental Rights, Investigation Measures and the Future European Public Prosecutor's Office – EUJuCo" by the University of Catania, between September 2015 and February 2017, at the Department of Law and the Siracusa International Institute for Criminal Justice and Human Rights.

In line with the project—for the benefit of scholars, students and practitioners of law—this book presents, first of all, some contributions dedicated to the Directives, and their domestic implementation, which have progressively reinforced the cornerstone of procedural rights of suspects and defendants in criminal proceedings in the EU Member States so as to facilitate judicial cooperation (Part I). So, it is in this necessary framework that the following contributions must be placed concerning investigative measures and evidence in transnational criminal proceedings, which have to be seen as a cross section of the current state of judicial cooperation in the area of freedom, security and justice, with the related issues of efficiency, coordination, settlement of conflicts of jurisdiction and guarantees (Part II). Lastly, the contributions in the final part concern emblematically the prospect of a supranational justice system, presenting the legislative proposal for the establishment of the European Public Prosecutor's Office and its developments. By the time this Jean Monnet project had already been concluded, the proposal, by means of "enhanced cooperation", took the form of EU Regulation 2017/1939, which the contributions naturally take into account (Part III).

The editors trust that these essays, also thanks to the proven expertise of their authors, might stimulate critical reflection on a protean and continually evolving subject.

Catania, Italy
Catania, Italy
20 April 2018

Tommaso Rafaraci
Rosanna Belfiore

Contents

Part III   The Establishment of the European Public Prosecutor's Office: Steps Forward *Versus* National Resistances

**Defence Areas and Limits in the Investigations of the European Public
Prosecutor**.. 205

Ezechia Paolo Reale

List of Contributors

Rosanna Belfiore University of Catania, Catania, Italy

Martin Böse University of Bonn, Bonn, Germany

Gabriella Di Paolo University of Trento, Trento, Italy

Mitja Gialuz University of Trieste, Trieste, Italy

Mar Jimeno-Bulnes University of Burgos, Burgos, Spain

André Klip University of Maastricht, Maastricht, The Netherlands

Cristina Mauro Public Prosecutor, Paris, France

Former Professor of Criminal Law and Procedure, University of Poitiers, Poitiers, France

Daniele Negri University of Ferrara, Ferrara, Italy

Lucia Parlato University of Palermo, Palermo, Italy

Tommaso Rafaraci University of Catania, Catania, Italy

Ezechia Paolo Reale The Siracusa International Institute for Criminal Justice and Human Rights, Siracusa, Italy

Francesca Ruggieri University of Insubria, Como, Italy

Fabrizio Siracusano University of Catania, Catania, Italy

Francesco Testa Chief Prosecutor, Court of Chieti, Chieti, Italy

Former Legal Adviser to the Permanent Mission of Italy to the International Organisations, Vienna, Austria

Marianne L. Wade University of Birmingham, Birmingham, UK

Part I
Rights and Guarantees of Suspects and Defendants in Criminal Proceedings: The EU Directives and Their Impact on National Laws

Fair Trial Rights in the European Union: Reconciling Accused and Victims' Rights

André Klip

Contents

Abstract After many years of concentrating on legislation with a repressive component, the EU has finally embraced the defence. Since 2010, it has legislated various defence rights as part of a road map for more citizen's rights. What are these rights and to which extent are they different than the rights already guaranteed by the ECtHR? How do these rights compete or balance with the rights given the victims? This paper brings all these developments together and sketches the steps towards building up the rights-component of European criminal law.

1 Introduction

After more than 60 years of regulatory influence of the ECHR only, the EU is now gradually taking defence rights seriously. Step by step, every aspect of the right to a fair trial is addressed in a Directive harmonising the law of the Member States. However, the approach is not pro-defence only, but encompasses also strengthening the position of the victim. The major challenges are thus three-fold: (1) realising minimum rights for the defence throughout the EU; (2) strengthening victims' rights; (3) reconciling victims' rights with those of the accused. This contribution explores the specific fair trial rights of the accused under Union law. It further raises the

A. Klip (✉)
University of Maastricht, Faculty of Law, Maastricht, The Netherlands
e-mail: andre.klip@maastrichtuniversity.nl

© Springer Nature Switzerland AG 2019
T. Rafaraci, R. Belfiore (eds.), *EU Criminal Justice*,
https://doi.org/10.1007/978-3-319-97319-7_1

question to what extent the European Union context creates fair trial rights of a different shape than those found in the ECHR and other international human rights instruments.

2 Harmonisation of Criminal Procedure in the European Union

How does the EU reach harmonisation in the area of criminal law? It does so via the legal mandate to adopt legal instruments that may harmonise or approximate the legal systems of the Member States. Both Articles 82 and 83 TFEU mention *minimum rules*, the former relates to procedural criminal law with the aim to facilitate the mutual recognition of judgments and judicial decisions,[1] and the latter focuses on substantive criminal law for the purposes of combating serious crime on a common European basis. Articles 82 and 83 TFEU delineate the areas in which approximation may take place. They concern:

- mutual admissibility of evidence between the Member States;
- the rights of individuals under criminal procedure;
- the rights of the victims of crime;
- any other specific aspects of criminal procedure added by a decision of the Council;
- minimum rules concerning the definition of criminal offences and sanctions.

What amounts to a "minimum rule" with regard to procedural rules? Whereas Recital 32 of *Directive 2010/64 on Interpretation and Translation* makes it clear that the character of the Directive is to set minimum rules, it also provides us with the perspective from which this should be considered: it is the citizens' right to a fair trial.[2] Recital 8 of *Directive 2013/48 on the Right of Access to a Lawyer* states that common minimum rules should not only increase confidence in the criminal justice systems of all Member States and promote a fundamental rights culture in the European Union, these should also remove obstacles to free movement of citizens. However, the picture is inconsistent. Whereas it is clear that *Directive 2014/42 on Freezing Proceeds of Crime* contains minimum rules,[3] its perspective (instrumentality or rights) is unclear as both the creation of more possibilities to confiscate as well as safeguards for property owners are explicitly dealt with in the Directive.

[1]See Recital 10 *Directive 2012/13 on the Right to Information*: "Common minimum rules should lead to increased confidence in the criminal justice systems of all Member States, which, in turn, should lead to more efficient judicial cooperation in a climate of mutual trust."

[2]Recital 11 of *Directive 2012/29 on Victim's Rights* also allows for a higher level of protection for victims.

[3]See Recital 22: "This Directive lays down minimum rules. It does not prevent Member States from providing more extensive powers in their national law, including, for example, in relation to their rules on evidence."

The idea behind these minimum rules is that they contribute to the mutual trust Member States will have in each other when cooperating. In addition, mutual trust is a legal obligation. Member States must trust each other, so that, when goods are placed on the market in one Member State, the other Member States must have confidence that verifications to check compliance with Union law have been genuinely undertaken by that Member State.[4] As a consequence, if goods are legally placed on the market in one Member State, other Member States may not subject them to further checks or formalities.[5] This finds its basis in the general rule that Member States mutually trust each other.[6] The Court held in answer to questions by the Latvian Augstākās tiesas Senāts that: "the rules on recognition and enforcement laid down by that regulation are based on mutual trust in the administration of justice in the European Union. Such trust requires that judicial decisions delivered in one Member State are not only recognised automatically in another Member State, but also that the procedure for making those decisions enforceable in that Member State is efficient and rapid."[7] Mutual trust is defined by the Court as follows: "Thus, when implementing EU law, the Member States may, under EU law, be required to presume that fundamental rights have been observed by the other Member States, so that not only may they not demand a higher level of national protection of fundamental rights from another Member State than that provided by EU law, but, save in exceptional cases, they may not check whether that other Member State has actually, in a specific case, observed the fundamental rights guaranteed by the EU."[8]

Whereas mutual trust can be regarded as a broad principle,[9] mutual recognition is of a much more specific nature. Mutual trust implies that one Member State will have jurisdiction to make decisions and that other Member States will trust the outcome and not review the assessment made by the first court.[10] Mutual trust presumes a division of responsibilities between the authorities of the Member States,[11] it is mutual trust that may have enabled Member States to adopt a Regulation and set up a compulsory system of jurisdiction.[12]

---

[4]11 May 1989, Case 25/88, *criminal proceedings against Esther Renée Bouchara, née Wurmser, and Norlaine SA.*

[5]8 July 1975, Case 4-75, *Rewe-Zentralfinanz eGmbH* v. *Landwirtschaftskammer* ; 22 September 1988, Case 286/86, *Ministère public* v. *Gérard Deserbais.*

[6]Mutual trust is occasionally also referred to as "mutual confidence". See 21 December 2011, Joined Cases C-411/10 and C-493/10, *N. S. (C-411/10)* v. *Secretary of State for the Home Department and M. E. (C-493/10), A. S. M., M. T., K. P., E. H.* par. 79. There is no indication whatsoever that it was intended to create new and different terminology.

[7]6 September 2012, Case C-619/10, *Trade Agency Ltd* v. *Seramico Investments Ltd*, par. 40.

[8]18 December 2014, Opinion 2/13, par. 192.

[9]In the fourth preambular paragraph of *Directive 2013/48 on the Right of Access to a Lawyer* it is stated that: "The implementation of the principle of mutual recognition of decisions in criminal matters presupposes that Member States trust in each other's criminal justice systems."

[10]15 July 2010, Case C-256/09, *Bianca Purrucker* v. *Guillermo Vallés Pérez* , par. 72–74.

[11]1 July 2010, Case C-442/08, *Commission* v. *Germany*, par. 70–71.

[12]26 April 2012, Case C-92/12 PPU, *Health Service Executive* v. *C. and C.*, par. 103.

In a similar way this was expressed in Recital 4 of the preamble of *Directive 2010/64 on Interpretation and Translation*: "Mutual recognition of decisions in criminal matters can operate effectively only in a spirit of trust in which not only judicial authorities but all actors in the criminal process consider decisions of the judicial authorities of other Member States as equivalent to their own, implying not only trust in the adequacy of other Member States' rules, but also trust that those rules are correctly applied."

Mutual trust and mutual recognition are not unlimited. This is expressed by the repeated reference in all legal instruments on mutual recognition to the effect that: "Nothing in this Framework Decision should be interpreted as prohibiting refusal to execute a decision when there are objective reasons to believe that the sentence was imposed for the purpose of punishing a person on the grounds of his or her sex, race, religion, ethnic origin, nationality, language, political opinions or sexual orientation, or that that person's position may be prejudiced on any one of those grounds."[13]

3   Defence Rights in the European Union

European Union law recognizes various defence rights to apply in criminal proceedings. Some have a general applicability in the sense that they are relevant at all stages. A few rights are typical pre-trial rights and some apply during trial only. Some of the rights were specifically formulated in a Directive, other are based on case law of the Court, deriving from general principles of Union law, the Charter or the ECHR.

3.1   Fair Trial and the Rights of the Defence

The case law of the Court distinguishes between the general right to a fair trial, also known as the rights of the defence, and more specific rights.[14] Observance of the rights of the defence is a general principle of Union law and must be complied with.[15] With regard to the rights of the defence, the leading cases are *Hoechst* and *Dow*, in which the obligations of the defendant to co-operate with the Commission during investigations into competition law violations were discussed. Both companies applied to the Court, alleging that the Commission had violated their respective rights. The Court referred to the rights of the defence which had already been

---

[13]Recital 13 *Framework Decision 2008/909 on Custodial Sentences.*

[14]This case law has been codified in the Charter. Article 47 Charter stipulates the general right to a fair and public hearing. Article 48, paragraph 2, Charter, reads: "Respect for the rights of the defence of anyone who has been charged shall be guaranteed".

[15]10 May 2007, Case C-328/05 P, *Appeal of SGL Carbon AG* , par. 59.

recognised in earlier judgments, but then proceeded to elaborate on those in far greater detail,[16] during which it extended the scope of application of the rights of the defence under Union law to the stage of investigations: "it is also necessary to prevent those rights from being irremediably impaired during preliminary inquiry procedures including, in particular, investigations which may be decisive in providing evidence of the unlawful nature of conduct (. . .)."[17]

In a similar manner to the ECtHR in its case law, the Court has held that the right to a fair trial or fair hearing is not a static right, but one that may be balanced with the rights and interests of others.[18] In *Pupino*, the Court emphasised the importance of both the ECHR and the fundamental rights that result from the constitutional traditions of the Member States.[19] The relevant Framework Decision also referred to the compatibility with the basic legal principles of the Member State concerned. The obligations deriving from Article 6 ECHR require that the accused's right to a fair trial be balanced with the rights of vulnerable victims.[20]

The specific rights found in the case law, or in the Charter, include the right to be informed of the charge, the right of access to the file, the right to liberty and security, the right to privacy, the right to legal representation, the lawyer-client privilege, the right to be tried within reasonable time, the right to an effective remedy, the right to be tried by an impartial tribunal, and the presumption of innocence. This list is not regarded as exhaustive.[21] It was drawn up upon the basis of the specific rights recognised in the case law of the Court and those stipulated in the Charter. However, it is conceivable that other rights recognised in the ECtHR case law might be applied as specific rights under the *chapeau* of a fair trial for the accused, or under the rights of the defence.

3.2 Access to a Lawyer

With *Directive 2013/48 on the Right of Access to a Lawyer* the European legislator wishes to further strengthen the rights of the defence. This Directive is part of a package of defence rights, to which *Directive 2010/64 on Interpretation and Translation, Directive 2012/13 on the Right to Information, Directive 2016/343 on the Presumption of Innocence* and *Directive 2016/800 on Procedural Safeguards for*

---

[16]7 June 1983, Joined Cases 100 to 103/80, *SA Musique Diffusion française and others* v. *Commission* , par. 10–11.

[17]21 September 1989, Joined Cases 46/87 and 227/88, *Hoechst AG* v. *Commission* , par. 15; 17 October 1989, Case 85/87, *Dow Benelux NV* v. *Commission* , par. 26.

[18]14 February 2008, Case C-450/06, *Varec SA* v. *Belgian State*.

[19]16 June 2005, *criminal proceedings against Maria Pupino*, Case C-105/03 par. 57 and 58.

[20]Opinion of Advocate General Kokott of 11 November 2004, Case C-105/03, *criminal proceedings against Maria Pupino*, point 67.

[21]21 September 1989, Joined Cases 46/87 and 227/88, *Hoechst AG* v. *Commission* , par. 16; 17 October 1989, Case 85/87, *Dow Benelux NV* v. *Commission* , par. 27; 18 May 1982, Case 155/79, *AM & S Europe Limited* v. *Commission* . See further Klip (2016), pp. 260–284.

Accused Children also belong. As appears from its first preambular paragraph, Directive 2013/48 must be seen in the context of the right to a fair trial as embodied in Article 47 Charter, Article 6 ECHR and Article 14 International Covenant on Civil and Political Rights.[22] All these Directives set minimum standards concerning the right of suspects and accused persons in all criminal proceedings, regardless of whether they relate to eurocrimes or whether there is a link with free movement. The Directives are applicable in all criminal proceedings, as well as to European arrest warrant proceedings.[23] This is a point where the human rights protection under Union law goes further than under the ECHR. The ECtHR has always rules that extradition proceedings do not fall within the notion of a fair trial.[24] All Directives apply to both suspects and accused. None of the Directives define these terms.

Directive 2013/48 on the Right of Access to a Lawyer applies from the moment that a person is made aware that he is suspected or accused of having committed a criminal offence (Article 2, paragraph 1 Directive 2013/48).[25] The application is irrespective of whether the person is deprived of liberty and will continue until the final determination of guilt as well as possible legal remedies. Article 2, paragraph 2 Directive 2013/48 applies the Directive to requested persons under the arrest warrant proceedings from the time of their arrest in the executing Member State. The Directive does take into consideration the fact that persons in their contact with the police or any other law enforcement authority may become a suspect or accused person. If that is the case, the Directive will also apply from that moment onwards. This rule relates to the right to be protected against self-incrimination (Recital 21).

The Directive does not apply in respect of minor offences that will be adjudicated by administrative proceedings for which there is an appeal to a criminal court, as well as to minor offences for which deprivation of liberty cannot be imposed (Article 2, paragraph 4).[26] This exclusion is not absolute and subject to the right of a fair trial. The last sentence of paragraph 4 of Article 2 reiterates that "In any event, this

---

[22]The general human rights character of the legal instrument is also reflected in clauses such as legal aid (Art. 11), effective remedies (Art. 12), vulnerable suspects and accused (Art. 13) and non-regression (Art. 14).

[23]Article 1 Directive 2013/48 specifically refers to Framework Decision 2002/584. This raises the question whether the Directive is applicable in proceedings other than the arrest warrant, such as the mutual recognition of judgments, transfer of supervision of detention on remand or the European protection order. All of these have in common the fact that they do not deal with the determination of the nature of the charge, which is the decisive criterion for considering a proceeding a criminal proceeding. However, as the character of the proceedings is similar to the arrest warrant proceedings, and they deal with the consequences of a suspicion, charge or sentence, the right of access to a lawyer should exist on an equal level. Article 2 Directive 2013/48 also indicates that the scope encompasses full proceedings.

[24]ECtHR, 7 October 2008, *Monedero v. Spain*, Appl. 41138/05.

[25]The Directive is in the end the codification of a new step in the case law of the ECtHR that started with its judgment of 27 November 2008, *Salduz* v. *Turkey*, Application 36391/02.

[26]Recital 13 also excludes disciplinary proceedings in prison facilities and with regard to military offences. See further Recitals 16–18.

Directive shall fully apply where the suspect or accused person is deprived of liberty, irrespective of the stage of the criminal proceedings."

Article 3 elaborates the details of the basic right of access to a lawyer.[27] Paragraph 1 obliges Member States to ensure that suspects and accused persons have the right of access to a lawyer in such time and in such a manner as to allow the persons concerned to exercise their rights of defence practically and effectively. This makes clear not only that it is not a symbolic right, but also that it must be respected as early as possible and without undue delay. Access to a lawyer must be realised at any of the points in time, whichever is the earliest:

- before the accused is questioned by the police or by another law enforcement or judicial authority;
- upon the carrying out by investigating or other competent authorities of an investigative or other evidence-gathering act;
- without undue delay after deprivation of liberty; or
- where the accused has been summoned to appear before a court having jurisdiction in criminal matters, in due time before they appear before that court.

What does access to a lawyer consist of? This is regulated in paragraph 3 of Article 3. Suspects and accused are entitled to meet with their counsel in private, including prior to questioning by the police or by any other authority. The right to communicate with the lawyer representing the accused may also be effected through means of communications technology. There is a right to have the lawyer present and participate effectively when questioned. That is the basic European notion of this specific right. What this participation effectively means is further regulated by national law (Article 3, paragraph 3 (b)). The right relates to questioning, not checking the identity of the individual or the possession of weapons (Recital 20). The lawyer must also be given the opportunity to attend identity parades, confrontations and reconstructions of the scene of a crime. In exceptional circumstances applicable in the pre-trial stage temporal derogation of the rights of paragraph 3 may take place. There are only two compelling reasons that might justify that: (a) where there is an urgent need to avert serious adverse consequences for the life, liberty or physical integrity of a person; or (b) where immediate action by the investigating authorities is imperative to prevent substantial jeopardy to criminal proceedings (Article 3, paragraph 6).[28]

As a consequence of the existence of the right, Member States are also under the obligation to make general information available so as to facilitate the obtaining of a lawyer (Article 3, paragraph 4).[29] The right of access to a lawyer in criminal

---

[27]Recital 15: "The term 'lawyer' in this Directive refers to any person who, in accordance with national law, is qualified and entitled, including by means of accreditation by an authorised body, to provide legal advice and assistance to suspects or accused persons."

[28]See further Article 8 on rules applicable to derogations, underlining their exceptional and temporary character and taking into consideration proportionality and fair trial demands.

[29]This also relates to *Directive 2012/13 on the Right to Information*.

proceedings found in Articles 3 and 10 can be waived, if such a waiver complies
with the conditions of Article 9. These conditions, formulated in paragraph 1, can be
summarised as requiring informed, voluntary and unequivocal consent. The waiver
can be made either in writing or orally. At any point during the criminal proceedings,
the waiver may be revoked by the suspect or accused. The revocation does not affect
the lawfulness of procedural acts carried out during the period that the right
concerned was waived (Recital 41).

3.3   Free Choice of Defence Counsel

Accused persons are entitled to a lawyer of their own choice to represent them. In
principle, any lawyer admitted within the European Union may be chosen. It is
therefore relevant to look at the applicable conditions for lawyers providing services
in another Member State, or for those who wish to establish themselves in another
Member State.

Member States may, in issues relating to the representation of a client in legal
proceedings, require to work with a local lawyer (Article 5 *Directive 77/249 on
Lawyers' Freedom*). This might result in a decision not to admit a lawyer qualified in
another Member State. However, the Court has held that, in proceedings for which
national legislation does not make representation by a lawyer mandatory, foreign
lawyers may not be refused.[30] Although national law may (for security reasons)
require that visits to persons in custody take place in conjunction with a local lawyer,
other forms of corresponding with the person in custody may not be subject to
restrictions.[31]

Article 47 Charter stipulates that legal aid shall be made available to those who
lack sufficient resources, in so far as such aid is necessary to ensure effective access
to justice. Thus, a right to legal aid for citizens of the European Union applies on the
same basis as is applicable to nationals. The provision in the Charter seems to give
more than the mere reference in Article 11 *Directive 2013/48 on the Right of Access
to a Lawyer*: "This Directive is without prejudice to national law in relation to legal
aid, which shall apply in accordance with the Charter and the ECHR." There is no
EU right to legal aid.

3.4   Lawyer-Client Privilege

Article 4 *Directive 2013/48 on the Right of Access to a Lawyer* now provides for a
general confidentiality of communication between suspects or accused and their

---

[30]25 February 1988, Case 427/85, *Commission* v. *Germany*.

[31]25 February 1988, Case 427/85, *Commission* v. *Germany*, par. 29–32.

lawyer. In a case brought by various *Bar associations* against the *Council of Ministers of Belgium,* the confidential relationship between lawyer and client was specifically considered.[32] In his Opinion, Advocate General Poiares Maduro opined that the professional secrecy of lawyers has obtained a rank of fundamental status in the majority of Member States.[33] The Court subsequently acknowledged the special position of the lawyer in criminal matters.[34] Unlike the Commission, which wished to limit the exemption granted to lawyers to the stage of representation before courts, the Court also recognised that lawyer-client privilege should be protected in the advice stage "as to the manner of instituting or avoiding judicial proceedings".[35] However, in another decision, the Court did not acknowledge a legal professional privilege with respect to in-house lawyers, despite their enrolment with a Bar or Law Society.[36]

3.5 Access to File

The right of access to the materials of the case free of charge is further regulated in Article 7 *Directive 2012/13 on the Right to Information.* Arrested and detained persons must have access to documents related to the specific case in the possession of the competent authorities which are essential to effectively challenging, in accordance with national law, the lawfulness of the arrest or detention (Article 7, paragraph 1). Article 7, paragraph 2 contains a disclosure obligation for the prosecution to grant access to the defence of all material evidence in their possession. Paragraph 4 entails a derogation to the accessibility when it would endanger the life of others, important public interest or national security. However, even in those situations it may not prejudice the right to a fair trial.

---

[32] 26 June 2007, Case C-305/05, *Ordre des barreaux francophones et germanophone, Ordre français des avocats du barreau de Bruxelles, Ordre des barreaux flamands, Ordre néerlandais des avocats du barreau de Bruxelles* v. *Conseil des Ministres.*

[33] Opinion of Advocate General Poiares Maduro, 14 December 2006, Case C-305/05, *Ordre des barreaux francophones et germanophone, Ordre français des avocats du barreau de Bruxelles, Ordre des barreaux flamands, Ordre néerlandais des avocats du barreau de Bruxelles* v. *Conseil des Ministres,* par. 39.

[34] 22 October 2002, Case C-94/00, *Roquette Frères SA* v. *Directeur général de la concurrence, de la consommation et de la répression des fraudes and the Commission,* par. 46.

[35] 26 June 2007, Case C-305/05, *Ordre des barreaux francophones et germanophone, Ordre français des avocats du barreau de Bruxelles, Ordre des barreaux flamands, Ordre néerlandais des avocats du barreau de Bruxelles* v. *Conseil des Ministres,* par. 34.

[36] 14 September 2010, Case C-550/07 P, *Akzo Nobel Chemicals Ltd, established in Hersham (United Kingdom), Akcros Chemicals Ltd, established in Hersham* v. *Commission,* par. 43–47.

3.6 The Right to Liberty and Security

The right to liberty and security is guaranteed in Article 6 Charter. Regarding the right to liberty, one may refer to the *acquis* that was developed by the ECtHR under Article 5 ECHR. *Framework Decision 2009/829 on Supervision Measures* has been adopted to ensure the right to liberty and offers alternatives to pre-trial detention, whilst respecting the interests of the general public. The right to security is a new right on the horizon. The question arises as to what its contents are, and to what extent it relates to the security that is offered to citizens in the area of freedom, security and justice.

As such, national rules as to which offences, and what degree of suspicion, justify keeping a suspect in detention on remand, also apply to other EU nationals. However, most Member States apply criteria that relate to the risk of absconding should a suspect be provisionally or conditionally released. This risk is often regarded as higher when the suspect has no domicile in the country. Should a Member State, for instance, apply criteria that directly relate to nationality, or indirectly by using domicile as a relevant criterion, there is a real possibility that this would be incompatible with the prohibition under Union law to discriminate on the basis of nationality (Article 18 TFEU). These negative effects will be somewhat limited by *Framework Decision 2009/829 on Supervision Measures* which states in an illuminating fifth Recital: *"As regards the detention of persons subject to criminal proceedings, there is a risk of different treatment between those who are resident in the trial state and those who are not: a non-resident risks being remanded in custody pending trial even where, in similar circumstances, a resident would not. In a common European area of justice without internal borders, it is necessary to take action to ensure that a person subject to criminal proceedings who is not resident in the trial state is not treated any differently from a person subject to criminal proceedings who is so resident."*

In an effort to enhance the right of liberty and the presumption of innocence, the Framework Decision has as its objective the promotion of non-custodial measures as an alternative to provisional detention. Whilst Article 2, paragraph 2 states that the Framework Decision does not confer any right on a person to the use of a non-custodial measure as an alternative to custody, it certainly does make it much more difficult to be stricter with regard to a foreign accused than towards accused who are nationals. Recital 18 of *Framework Decision 2009/829 on Supervision Measures* reiterates that the Framework Decision should be applied in conformity with the right to move within the EU and reside freely in another Member State.

From the Court's case law, it is clear that European Union nationals who make use of free movement rights, but also commit crimes, may not be regarded as waiving their freedoms. Since none of the freedoms is absolute, European Union nationals may also be subjected to restrictions, on suspicion or conviction of having committed offences. With both restrictions, the proportionality requirement applies. With regard to accused persons who are not finally convicted, the presumption of innocence also applies. This means that the offence, and the facts supporting the suspicion, must be very strong. In applying these criteria, European Union nationals may not be placed in a less favourable position than nationals of the Member State where they find themselves, with regard to provisional release and bail. In addition, the risk of not being available for trial has been significantly reduced by the establishment of the European Arrest Warrant mechanism. It will be even further reduced when *Framework Decision 2009/829 on Supervision Measures* is implemented in practice.

3.7   Presumption of Innocence

Directive 2016/343 on the Presumption of Innocence elaborates in detail on the general provision of Article 48 Charter: "1. Everyone who has been charged shall be presumed innocent until proved guilty according to law." Applicable in all stages of criminal proceedings "suspects and accused persons are presumed innocent until proved guilty according to law." (Article 3). This right not only entails a formal recognition at the hearing but also implies that public references to guilt are not made, for as long as the accused has not been proved guilty (Article 4). The authorities that must refrain from such public statements are not only those involved in the criminal proceedings, but also those from another public authority, such as ministers and other public officials (Recital 17). The Directive precludes both verbal references that violate the presumption of innocence as well as non-verbal conduct. This is expressed in Recitals 20 and 21: "The competent authorities should abstain from presenting suspects or accused persons as being guilty, in court or in public, through the use of measures of physical restraint, such as handcuffs, glass boxes, cages and leg irons, unless the use of such measures is required for case-specific reasons, either relating to security, including to prevent suspects or accused persons from harming themselves or others or from damaging any property, or relating to the prevention of suspects or accused persons from absconding or from having contact with third persons, such as witnesses or victims. The possibility of applying measures of physical restraint does not imply that the competent authorities are to take any formal decision on the use of such measures.

Where feasible, the competent authorities should also abstain from presenting suspects or accused persons in court or in public while wearing prison clothes, so as to avoid giving the impression that those persons are guilty." Article 5 symbolises an approach that underlines respect for the accused's dignity and aims at preventing stigmatisation.

Article 6 stipulates the most important provision which relates to the burden of proof: "1. Member States shall ensure that the burden of proof for establishing the guilt of suspects and accused persons is on the prosecution. This shall be without prejudice to any obligation on the judge or the competent court to seek both inculpatory and exculpatory evidence, and to the right of the defence to submit evidence in accordance with the applicable national law. 2. Member States shall ensure that any doubt as to the question of guilt is to benefit the suspect or accused person, including where the court assesses whether the person concerned should be acquitted."

3.8 Right to Remain Silent

Also as a further elaboration of Article 48 Charter, Article 7 *Directive 2016/343 on the Presumption of Innocence* recognizes the right to remain silent. This right has two main elements: the right to remain silent and the right not to incriminate oneself. The exercise of the right not to incriminate oneself shall not prevent the competent authorities from gathering evidence which may be lawfully obtained through the use of legal powers of compulsion and which has an existence independent of the will of the suspects or accused persons. Recital 27 makes clear that the interpretation as given in the case law of the ECtHR is leading.

3.9 Right to Privacy: The Inviolability of the Home

Articles 7 and 8 Charter provide for respect for private and family life, as well as the protection of personal data.[37] The fact that investigations into competition violations by the Commission find their basis in a competition Regulation complies with the requirements of Article 8, paragraph 2 ECHR, which states that any interference into private life must be in accordance with the law.[38] In *Hoechst* and in *Dow*, the Court held that the right to privacy is limited to natural persons, and that undertakings are not protected by it.[39] On this issue, the interpretation of the ECHR by the Court deviated from that of the ECtHR. A few years after the Court had pronounced its judgments in *Hoechst* and *Dow*, the ECtHR recognised the inviolability of non-private homes as a right under Article 8 ECHR.[40]

---

[37] A specific Directive stipulates the rules applicable on data protection in cooperation in criminal matters. See Directive 2016/680 on the protection of natural persons with regard to the processing of personal data by competent authorities for the purposes of the prevention, investigation, detection or prosecution of criminal offences or the execution of criminal penalties, and on the free movement of such data, and repealing Council Framework Decision 2008/977.

[38] 26 June 1980, Case 136/79, *National Panasonic (UK) Limited* v. *Commission* , par. 19–20.

[39] 21 September 1989, Joined Cases 46/87 and 227/88, *Hoechst AG* v. *Commission* , par. 17–18; 17 October 1989, Case 85/87, *Dow Benelux NV* v. *Commission* , par. 28–29. However, Advocate General Mischo had advocated a fundamental right to the inviolability of business premises. See Joined Opinion of 21 February 1989, Joined Cases 46/87 and 227/88, *Hoechst AG* v. *Commission* , and Case 85/87, *Dow Benelux NV* v. *Commission*, point 103.

[40] ECtHR, 16 December 1992, *Niemietz* v. *Germany*, Series A-251B.

3.10 Interpretation and Translation

In a multilingual Union like the EU, fair trial issues often circle around being able to understand the proceedings. *Directive 2010/64 on Interpretation and Translation* lays down rules concerning the right to interpretation and translation in criminal proceedings, as well as proceedings for the execution of a European Arrest Warrant. The right applies to suspects or accused from the moment of an official notification up to and including the resolution of any appeal (Article 1, paragraph 2 *Directive 2010/64 on Interpretation and Translation*). It applies to criminal proceedings before investigative and judicial authorities, during police questioning, all court hearings and any necessary interim hearings (Article 2, paragraph 1). Paragraph 2 of Article 2 obliges Member States to ensure that interpretation is available for communication between accused and their legal counsel. Most rights of this Directive are drafted in such a clear and unequivocal manner that their invocation does not depend on implementation into national law. The Court has ruled that, when national law entitles its own citizens to choose in which of the national languages proceedings will be conducted, this right must also be given to other EU nationals.[41]

In the first case in which the Court had the opportunity to interpret *Directive 2010/64 on Interpretation and Translation*, it distinguished the meaning of Article 2 from the one for Article 3: "As regards Article 2 of Directive 2010/64, which governs the right to interpretation, it follows from the actual wording of that article that, unlike Article 3 of that directive, which concerns the written translation of certain essential documents, Article 2 of the directive refers to the oral interpretation of oral statements. Thus, in accordance with Article 2(1) and (3) of that directive, only suspected or accused persons who are unable to express themselves in the language of the proceedings, whether that be due to the fact that they do not speak or understand that language or the fact that they have hearing or speech impediments, are able to exercise the right to interpretation."[42] The Court regarded the rights of the accused in the context of safeguarding the fairness of the proceedings. The result of which is, that when the accused is called upon to make oral statements himself, he is entitled to do so in his own language, or as expressed by Advocate General Bot "linguistic assistance under Article 2 of that directive may be requested by the defence 'not only in order to understand, but also to be understood'."[43]

However, when it comes to the translation of documents *produced* by the defence, there is no right to the translation thereof. In this context the Court stated:

---

[41] 11 July 1985, Case 137/84, *criminal proceedings against Robert Heinrich Maria Mutsch*. Belgian law provided that, in the German speaking part of the country, Belgian nationals could choose between German and French, yet it refused this to Mutsch, a worker from Luxembourg. In 24 November 1998, Case C-274/96, *criminal proceedings against Horst Otto Bickel and Ulrich Franz* , the Court held that if Italian law entitles German-speaking Italians to have criminal proceedings conducted in German, this right should also be given to German-speaking non-Italians.

[42] 15 October 2015, Case C-216/14, *criminal proceedings against Gavril Covaci*, par. 30 and 31.

[43] Opinion of Advocate General Bot of 7 May 2015, Case C-216/14, *criminal proceedings against Gavril Covaci*, point 60.

"However, to require Member States, as suggested inter alia by Mr Covaci and the German Government, not only to enable the persons concerned to be informed, fully and in their language, of the facts alleged against them and to provide their own version of those facts, but also to take responsibility, as a matter of course, for the translation of every appeal brought by the persons concerned against a judicial decision which is addressed to them would go beyond the objectives pursued by Directive 2010/64 itself."[44] The right to interpretation provided for in Article 2 of Directive 2010/64 concerns the translation by an interpreter of the oral communications between suspected or accused persons and the investigative and judicial authorities or, where relevant, legal counsel, to the exclusion of the written translation of any written document produced by those suspected or accused persons. The idea behind Article 3 of the Directive is that the accused must know what the charges against him are. It does not cover a right to have all writings of the accused translated.

More discussion will inevitably flow from the right given in Article 3 to translation of essential documents. Member States must provide the accused, within a reasonable time, a translation of essential documents. Article 3, paragraph 2 stipulates that essential documents include any decision depriving a person of his liberty, any charge or indictment, and any judgment. Other documents may be regarded as essential, subject to a decision by the competent authorities. Another provision that will also lead to many discussions in court is paragraph 4 of Article 3, stipulating that irrelevant passages do not need to be translated. Member States shall meet the costs of interpretation and translation (Article 4) and will take measures to ensure that interpretation and translation meet prescribed quality standards (Article 8).

3.11 Impartiality

The right to a fair trial embodies the right to an independent and impartial tribunal. The Court has held that there are two aspects of impartiality: "(i) the members of the tribunal themselves must be impartial, that is, none of its members must show bias or personal prejudice, there being a presumption of personal impartiality in the absence of evidence to the contrary; and (ii) the tribunal must be objectively impartial, that is to say, it must offer guarantees sufficient to exclude any legitimate doubt in this respect."[45] With reference to the case law of the ECtHR, the Court has stated that this does not preclude the same judge from sitting in two chambers and hearing and determining the same case in succession.

---

[44] 15 October 2015, Case C-216/14, *criminal proceedings against Gavril Covaci*, par. 38.

[45] 1 July 2008, Case C-341/06P and C-342/06P, *Chronopost SA (C-341/06 P), La Poste, (C-342/06 P), Union française de l'express (UFEX), established in Roissy-en-France (France), DHL Express (France) SAS, formerly DHL International SA, established in Roissy-en-France, Federal express international (France) SNC, established in Gennevilliers (France), CRIE SA, in liquidation, established in Asnières (France)* v. *Commission* , par. 54 (references omitted).

3.12   Right to Information

With the advent of *Directive 2012/13 on the Right to Information* the Union legislature confirmed its wish to strengthen the rights of suspects and accused in national criminal proceedings and of those persons that are subject to a European Arrest Warrant. Article 2, paragraph 1 *Directive 2012/13 on the Right to Information* clearly states its scope: it "applies from the time persons are made aware by the competent authorities of a Member State that they are suspected or accused of having committed a criminal offence until the conclusion of the proceedings, which is understood to mean the final determination of the question whether the suspect or accused person has committed the criminal offence, including, where applicable, sentencing and the resolution of any appeal." The Directive is also applicable to administrative proceedings in which an appeal may be lodged before a criminal court.

The right to information about rights entails:

(a) the right of access to a lawyer;
(b) any entitlement to free legal advice and the conditions for obtaining such advice;
(c) the right to be informed of the accusation;
(d) the right to interpretation and translation;
(e) the right to remain silent.

Article 3 stipulates that this information must be provided promptly and in manner that allows those entitled to exercise their right effectively. It further allows Member States to give the information orally or in writing, in simple and accessible language, taking into account any particular needs of vulnerable suspects or vulnerable accused persons. This highlights immediately some of the weak elements of the right as envisaged in the Directive. Can we expect all accused that have been told about their rights to understand? This has been compensated for by the introduction of the Letter of Rights in Article 4. This Letter must be given in a written form and the accused shall be allowed to keep it in possession. Article 4, paragraph 2 extends the rights with: "(a) the right of access to the materials of the case; (b) the right to have consular authorities and one person informed; (c) the right of access to urgent medical assistance; and (d) the maximum number of hours or days suspects or accused persons may be deprived of liberty before being brought before a judicial authority." Paragraph 3 of Article 4 adds that the Letter of Rights must also give basic information about any possibility of challenging the lawfulness of the arrest; obtaining a review of the detention or making a request for provisional release. It must be noted that both Article 3 and Article 4 do not create new rights under national law, but only create a right to information about these specific rights as they apply under national law. However, the level of protection may never fall below the standards provided by the case law of the ECtHR.[46] The Directive sets minimum rules. Member States may extend the level of protection. Member States must make

---

[46]See Recital 40 *Directive 2012/13 on the Right to Information*.

sure that they draft the Letter of Rights in simple and accessible language. In an annex to *Directive 2012/13 on the Right to Information*, published in the Official Journal, a suggested model Letter of Rights has been published.[47]

The right to information about the accusation and its subsequent changes is further explained in Article 6. Any accused is entitled to prompt information about the criminal act they are suspected or accused of (Article 6, paragraph 1). For those detained, they must also be informed of reasons for their arrest or detention (Article 6, paragraph 2). At the latest on submission of the merits of the accusation to a court, detailed information is provided on the accusation, including the nature and legal classification of the criminal offence, as well as the nature of participation by the accused person (Article 6, paragraph 3).

3.13   The Right to Inform Others of Arrest

Article 5 *Directive 2013/48 on the Right of Access to a Lawyer* gives suspects and accused the right to have at least one person informed of their deprivation of liberty without undue delay. The legislator had a relative or employer in mind. However, it is the arrestee, who nominates. Temporary derogation is provided when: (a) where there is an urgent need to avert serious adverse consequences for the life, liberty or physical integrity of a person; (b) where there is an urgent need to prevent a situation where criminal proceedings could be substantially jeopardised (Article 5, par. 3). A right to communicate with at least one third person, nominated by the suspect or accused exists on the basis of Article 6. This right may only be limited "in view of imperative requirements or proportionate operational requirements."

Suspects and accused that are deprived of their liberty and who are non-nationals have the right to have the consular authorities of their state informed (Article 7).[48] If they wish, they have the right to communicate with those authorities. As a consequence of this information and communication right, paragraph 2 of Article 7 provides in the right to be visited by their consular authorities. In addition, there is the right to converse and correspond with them and the right to have legal representation arranged for by their consular authorities, subject to the agreement of those authorities and the wishes of the suspects or accused persons concerned.

---

[47]OJ 2012, L 142/8, similarly for persons arrested on the basis of a European Arrest Warrant, OJ 2012, L 142/8.

[48]This right already exists on the basis of Article 36 of the 1963 Vienna Convention on Consular Relations.

3.14   Right to Be Present/Represented and in Absentia Proceedings

Directive 2016/343 on the Presumption of Innocence also contains more details on a right provided in more general terms in Article 47 of the Charter reads: "Everyone shall have the possibility of being advised, defended and represented". Article 8, paragraph 1 Directive 2016/343 stipulates the general rule: "Member States shall ensure that suspects and accused persons have the right to be present at their trial." Whilst recognising the general rule, Article 8, paragraph 2 of the Directive at the same does allow for an exception, provided that:

(a) the suspect or accused person has been informed, in due time, of the trial and of the consequences of non-appearance; or

(b) the suspect or accused person, having been informed of the trial, is represented by a mandated lawyer, who was appointed either by the suspect or accused person or by the State.

Similar to the format applicable in Article 4a *Framework Decision 2002/584 on the European Arrest Warrant*, Article 8 *Directive 2016/343 on the Presumption of Innocence* emphasizes the due diligence as to the summons or other manner of informing the accused of the upcoming or pending trial. The right to a fair trial of an accused person, as guaranteed in Article 6 ECHR, forms the main reason to harmonise the application of the right of the accused to appear in person. The Framework Decision starts from the presumption that the right of the accused to appear in person at the trial is not absolute, and that under certain conditions he may, of his own will, expressly or tacitly—but unequivocally—waive that right.

The Framework Decision reduces the possibilities to refuse warrants when a national court has complied with the common rules on trials at which the accused was not present. These conditions relate to obligations for the state to make sure that the accused is informed of the trial, as well as obligations and rights of the accused to a new trial. This is expressed in Article 4a *Framework Decision 2002/584 on the European Arrest Warrant*. To a certain extent one may characterise this provision as the expression that the accused has no right to block the continuation of the criminal proceedings against him through his absence. However, if the conditions of Article 8, paragraph 2 *Directive 2016/343 on the Presumption of Innocence* were not met, the accused has "a right to a new trial, or to another legal remedy, which allows a fresh determination of the merits of the case, including examination of new evidence, and which may lead to the original decision being reversed." (Article 9).

In addition, there is the right to be represented.[49] The right to legal presentation has been recognised by the Court as part of the rights of the defence.[50] It is rather strange that *Directive 2016/343 on the Presumption of Innocence* does not refer to the right to be represented. A simple statement made by a member of the bar of one

---

[49]This is further reinforced by *Framework Decision 2009/299 on In Absentia*.

[50]22 October 2002, Case C-94/00, *Roquette Frères SA* v. *Directeur général de la concurrence, de la consommation et de la répression des fraudes and the Commission* , par. 46.

of the Member States, who, as a barrister, is subject to a code of professional conduct, that he represents a client, is sufficient to determine that he has the power of attorney.[51]

3.15 Reasonable Time

Article 47 Charter entitles everyone to a fair and public hearing within a reasonable time by an independent and impartial tribunal. In various competition law cases, the Court has dealt with the reasonableness of the period of the legal process. This must be assessed "in the light of the specific circumstances of each case and in particular, the importance of the case for the person concerned, its complexity and the conduct of the applicant and of the competent authorities."[52]

3.16 Effective Remedy

Article 47 Charter requires an effective remedy, as well as that proceedings be conducted before an impartial tribunal. The right to appeal, or to lodge any other legal remedy, must apply without discrimination. A specific right to an effective remedy has been stipulated in Article 12 *Directive 2013/48 on the Right of Access to a Lawyer* and Article 10 *Directive 2016/343 on the Presumption of Innocence.* Article 8 *Directive 2014/42 on Freezing Proceeds of Crime* gives specific safeguards to persons affected by freezing and confiscation. Member States shall take the necessary measures to ensure that the freezing order is communicated to the affected person as soon as possible after its execution. Such communication shall indicate, at least briefly, the reason or reasons for the order concerned. When it is necessary to avoid jeopardising a criminal investigation, the competent authorities may postpone communicating the freezing order to the affected person.

3.17 Special Safeguards in Case of Accused Children

Directive 2016/800 on Procedural Safeguards for Accused Children provides a series of specific rules that could be summarised as providing a child-friendly justice.

---

[51] 18 January 2007, Case C-229/05, *Osman Ocalan (PKK) and Serif Valy (KNK) appellants, Council, defendant* , par. 116–122.

[52] 2 October 2003, C-194/99 P, *Thyssen Stahl AG* v. *Commission* 1, par. 155; 25 January 2007, Joined Cases C-403/04 P and C-405/04, *Sumitomo Metal Industries Ltd and Nippon Steel Corp.* v. *Commission*, pp. 116–122.

The Directive specifically addresses the weak spots of this particular vulnerable accused. The Directive applies throughout the criminal proceedings, until the final determination of guilt, including sentencing and the resolution of any appeal (Article 2). For this specific category of accused, the Directive provides rights in more detail than already provided: right to information (Article 4), the assistance by a lawyer (Article 6), right to protection of privacy (Article 14), right of the child to be accompanied by the holder of parental responsibility during the proceedings (Article 15), right of children to appear in person at, and participate in, their trial (Article 16).

However, there are also rights not found in the generally applicable defence rights Directives: The right of the child to have the holder of parental responsibility informed (Article 5); the obligation to provide audio-visual recording of questioning (Article 9). More strict than concerning adults is the obligation to limit deprivation of liberty when relating to children (Article 10) and the obligation to see whether it is possible to have recourse to alternatives to detention (Article 11). Found in other legal instruments, but stipulated in the Directive again is the obligation to detain children separate from adults (Article 12) and to treat their cases in a timely and diligent manner (Article 13).

Really new is the provision of Article 7 on the right to an individual assessment, by which it must be ensured "that the specific needs of children concerning protection, education, training and social integration are taken into account." This must be done with a view to "serve to establish and to note, in accordance with the recording procedure in the Member State concerned, such information about the individual characteristics and circumstances of the child as might be of use to the competent authorities when:

(a) determining whether any specific measure to the benefit of the child is to be taken;
(b) assessing the appropriateness and effectiveness of any precautionary measures in respect of the child;
(c) taking any decision or course of action in the criminal proceedings, including when sentencing."

Another new right is found in Article 8 and relates to the right to a medical examination.

4 Victim's Rights in the Context of Rights of the Accused

Directive 2012/29 on Victim's Rights refers to the general context in which the rights of the victim must be placed and its relationship with the fairness of the proceedings. Whilst the Directive does recognise the relationship between the rights of the defence and the rights of the victim, it leaves significant ambiguity as to which rights in the end prevail. For instance, Article 7, paragraph 6 deals with the issue that an oral summary or translation may be provided instead of a written translation on the condition that such oral translation or summary does not prejudice the "fairness of the proceedings". This raises the question whether fairness to the victim or to the accused is meant here. Article 7, paragraph 8 provides that interpretation and translation may not unreasonably prolong the criminal proceedings. This obviously is an interest of all parties involved, and may relate to the accused's right to be tried within reasonable time, as well as to mere efficiency.

More clear are other references to the "rights of the defence" that may not be prejudiced when taking specific measures in the interests of the victim. They relate to making use of technology when interpreting or translating for victims (Articles 7, paragraph 2), protective measures for victims (Article 18, paragraph 1), protection of victims during criminal investigations (Article 20, paragraph 1) and protection of victims with special needs (Article 23, paragraph 1). All of these references presume a primacy of the rights of the defence over the right of the victim. The rights of the defence at stake are not further specified. There are no cross-references from the other side: The victim is not mentioned at all in the Directives on the rights of the accused.[53]

The Directive is silent on how by whom and when a person is recognised as a victim. Article 2 does give a definition of the concept victim, but does not state whether there must be a link with an accused, and if so what kind of link. A victim is a person who has suffered harm directly caused by a *criminal offence*. This means that in the recognition of a person as a victim a criminal offence must be identified.[54] This does not require the identification of an accused that committed that offence. That is logical in the sense that a victim may already make himself known quite some time before the identity of a perpetrator might be disclosed or before the trial against a specific accused may be held. The Directive does not explicitly require the existence of a causal link between the criminal offence committed against the victim and the accused before admitting a victim to the criminal proceedings.

There is a presumption in the Directive that the victim is the victim of the accused standing trial, or at least the victim of a crime. The question is whether or not this may violate the presumption of innocence of the accused and affect the fairness of the proceedings, as the accused will be confronted with an additional accuser on top of the prosecution. Nowhere in the Directive is it reflected that an alleged victim might not be (the) victim of this accused.[55] What would be the consequence if, at the end of the proceedings, it becomes clear that the alleged victim is:

- not a victim at all;
- not a victim of the accused standing trial; or

---

[53]That means *Directive 2010/64 on Interpretation and Translation, Directive 2012/13 on the Right to Information* and *Directive 2013/48 on the Right of Access to a Lawyer.*

[54]Directive 2012/29 does not state how, when and by whom such a finding should be taken. Is this the national criminal court, it may amount to a violation of the presumption of innocence if the finding that the person is a victim coincides with the finding that the victim is a victim of the accused?

[55]Many authors advise not to use the term alleged victim, because the effects are negative for the victim. See for instance Brienen and Hoegen (2000), p. 1169.

– not a victim of the counts for which the accused stood trial and was convicted of?

The Directive demonstrates a certain bias towards the victim. In Recital 12 the offender is defined as a convicted person, as well as a suspected or accused person. There is not a similar provision on the victim, as a person for whom there is a final judgment stating that s/he is a victim. Apparently, the decision to recognise somebody as a victim cannot be challenged, neither by the accused nor by anyone else. Where for the accused the allegations are tested at regular intervals by an impartial judiciary (especially when the accused is in detention), the status of the victim seems to be decision made once and for always, and it is unclear which authority should take that decision. What are the criteria to find somebody a victim before the criminal proceedings have been finalised with a judgment?

It is interesting to see that the need for victims' rights is regarded as self-evident. It is said that victims are forgotten and neglected and that their voice must be heard.[56] There is no explanation or rationale given for victims' rights, other than reference to the fact that it is one of the Union's priorities. Groenhuijsen already identified a victim fatigue, and stated that the attention paid to victims' rights went too far on some points.[57] That may be so for practitioners, but certainly not for legislators and politicians. However, it is relevant to raise the question of what exactly the purpose of victims' rights is in the context of a criminal trial. Only if we know its purpose will it be possible to match it with the other rights that are at stake in a criminal proceeding.[58] For the defence that purpose has been clearly stated: individual rights serve the ultimate goal of a fair trial for the accused as well as the protection of human rights.

The consequences of victims playing an increasing role in criminal proceedings are manifold. It requires significant efforts by the authorities in terms of logistics (informing victims, assisting victims, giving time to speak during the hearing), it may lead to more time-consuming criminal trials. At the International Criminal Court, the increased participation of victims has led to a lot of frustrations and delay, especially in view of the rather large numbers of victims in those proceedings.[59] In addition to the large numbers, the real victims are not present at the ICC hearings, but are represented by their counsel. The mass participation of victims contributes to further delay to proceedings that are already quite complex. In 2008, the Appeals Chamber of the ICC accepted that to be admitted as a victim under the ICC Statute, it is not necessary for it to have been proven that the victim is a victim of the accused and that one of the counts with which the accused is charged with relates

---

[56]Braun (2013), pp. 1889–1908.

[57]Groenhuijsen (2014), p. 42.

[58]The Directives on rights of the defence clearly state that the general purpose of the instruments is to be conducive to a fair trial. See Recital 1 *Directive 2013/48 on the Right of Access to a Lawyer*, Recital 5 *Directive 2010/64 on Interpretation and Translation* and Recital 5 *Directive 2012/13 on the Right to Information*.

[59]See Tonellato (2012), pp. 315–359.

to this victim.[60] The ICC has thus shaped victim participation into something that may not have any relation at all to the accused standing trial.

A further issue that the Directive does not address is what the consequences are if one of the rights of the victim has not been respected. Does that mean that the proceedings will be suspended until the violation has been repaired? Does it lead to a dismissal of the case, or would it lead to a right for the victim to be (financially) compensated? Directive 2012/29 has created the conditions for rather chaotic and unclear situations in criminal proceedings in which it is likely that expectations of victims and other participants will be heavily disappointed. From the accused's side a greater role for alleged victims may be regarded as being confronted with a second prosecutor and lead to three-party proceedings. The victim's increasing role in criminal proceedings raises some more existential questions as to what the purpose of this is and whether that purpose could be served within the scope of a criminal trial without affecting the rights of an accused still presumed innocent. Only if this becomes clear will it be possible to respect all interests involved.

There are many challenges ahead of us in the development of a fair trial notion under Union law. In comparison to the ECHR, it is important to note that fair trial in the EU is part of a broader context of individual rights, predominantly free movement rights. More so than the Court on the ECHR, the ECtHR has refrained from stating anything on Union law. This may be due to the more clearly defined jurisdiction of the ECtHR, which exclusively deals with the interpretation of the ECHR. By contrast, the ECHR is part of the general principles that the Court has to interpret. This also justifies the conclusions that the Court will gradually emerge as the paramount human rights court in the Union. Only the Court is competent to reconcile the ECHR and the Charter with the obligations from the treaties. In addition, the ECtHR supervisory mechanism suffers from an increasing back-log of cases. The Council of Europe has as yet been unable to effectively regulate the workload of the ECtHR.

The fact that within the EU cooperation in criminal matters takes place on a large scale contributes to enhancing the rights of the accused and convicted persons. The more integrative approach under the law of the Union, placing fair trial in the context of free movement rights, building mutual trust among the Member States and facilitates mutual recognition, will lead to different interpretation of basic rights we thought that were more or less clear for quite some time. Being a party to the ECHR, so experience shows "does not always provide a sufficient degree of trust in the criminal justice system of other Member States" (Recital 5 *Directive 2016/343 on the Presumption of Innocence* and Recital 3 *Directive 2016/800 on Procedural Safeguards for Accused Children)*. Whatever the exact outcome will be, the EU made the choice to have common norms applicable in all Member States. In

---

[60]See ICC, 11 July 2008, Judgment on the appeals of The Prosecutor and The Defence against Trial Chamber I's Decision on Victims' Participation of 18 January 2008, *Prosecutor* v. *Thomas Lubanga Dyilo*, A.Ch., ICC-01/04-01/06, OA9OA10, Klip and Freeland (2013), par. 66: "neither rule 85 of the Rules nor the Rome Statute framework has the effect of restricting the participation of victims to the crimes contained in the charges confirmed by the Pre-Trial Chamber."

addition, these norms are tailor made for the specific circumstances of the Union that endanger fair trial rights: a multilingual Union, in which people freely circulate and in which Member States assist each other to such a degree when conducting criminal proceedings that it is often difficult to tell in which Member State the proceeding is running.

References

Braun K (2013) Giving victims a voice: on the problems of introducing victim impact statements in German criminal procedure. German Law J 14(9):1889–1908

Brienen MEI, Hoegen EH (2000) Victims of crime in 22 European criminal justice systems. Wolf Legal Productions, Nijmegen

Groenhuijsen MS (2014) The development of international policy in relation to victims of crime. Int Rev Victimol 20(1):31–48

Klip A (2016) European criminal law - an integrated approach, 3rd edn. Intersentia, Cambridge

Klip A, Freeland S (2013) Annotated leading cases of international criminal tribunals, vol 40. Intersentia, Antwerpen

Tonellato M (2012) The victim's participation at a crossroads: how the international criminal court could devise a meaningful victim's participation while respecting the rights of the defendant. Eur J Crime Crim Law Crim Just 20(3):315–359

The Implementation of the Directive on Linguistic Assistance in Italy, Between Changes to the Code of Criminal Procedure and Case-Law Resistance

Mitja Gialuz

Contents

Abstract With Directive 2010/64/EU, the European Union has inaugurated a new season of awareness for the fundamental rights of the accused. It delineates a priority fundamental right compared to any other subjective position. Italy has implemented it with an incomplete manoeuvre which is particularly unsatisfactory as regards the service of interpreting and translation: on one hand, there are no guarantees on the professionalisation of language 'experts'; on the other, no effective remedies have been introduced in criminal proceedings. The result is the Italian judiciary seems not to have recognised the reform's importance by continuing the restrictive interpretation of the right to linguistic assistance.

1 Analysing the 2010/64/EU Directive

The 2010/64/EU Directive on the right to interpretation and translation in criminal proceedings[1] is a historic step in the evolution of the European Union's area of freedom, security and justice.

---

[1]On this Directive, see: Amalfitano (2011), p. 83; Aragüena Fanego (2011a), p. 1; Aragüena Fanego (2011b), p. 269; Balsamo (2014), p. 115; Bargis (2013), p. 96; Bazzocchi (2013), p. 170;

M. Gialuz (✉)
University of Trieste, Department of Law, Language, Interpretation and Translation, Trieste, Italy
e-mail: gialuz@units.it

© Springer Nature Switzerland AG 2019　　　　　　　　　　　　　　　　　　27
T. Rafaraci, R. Belfiore (eds.), *EU Criminal Justice*,
https://doi.org/10.1007/978-3-319-97319-7_2

For the first time, after having agitated for ten years over reinforcing European citizens' rights, the EU has passed a law aimed at guaranteeing a fundamental right of defendants: this is the "first EU fair trial law",[2] said the EU Parliament rapporteur. The Commission Vice-President emphasised its fundamental scope: "we are going in a direction which aims to achieve (. . .) the same high level of rights for all EU citizens wherever they are, whatever their problem. It does not matter whether they are traveling for study, for business or for leisure: they should feel at home, and have the same rights as they have at home, wherever they find themselves in Europe".[3]

The Directive is part of a very real system to protect rights, generally known as 'the Stockholm Directives'. These are a series of legal instruments outlined in the 'Stockholm roadmap',[4] which, in a step-by-step approach, has seen the adoption of a number of Directives relating to single rights.

Since the failure of the proposal for a Framework Decision on certain procedural rights in 2004,[5] this gradual approach[6] has moved from the one guarantee that during political discussion proved to be less problematic.

The Directive on interpretation and translation is without doubt the most ambitious, including those adopted in subsequent years, because it is not limited to just codifying the case-law of the European Court of human rights concerning Arts. 5 and 6 of the ECHR, but goes well beyond the standards of Strasbourg. The salient sections of Directive no. 64 are five: the quality and effectiveness of the guarantee; its gratuity; the onus of the authority to check for any linguistic shortfall; extending the right to an interpreter to meetings with defence lawyers; and finally the exact individuation of the acts to be translated in the criminal proceedings.

Beauvais (2011), p. 642; Biondi (2011), p. 2422; Cras and De Matteis (2010), p. 153; Gialuz (2011), p. 9; Gialuz (2012a), p. 1193; Iermano (2011), p. 335; Izzo (2012), p. 313; Kalb (2012), p. 344; Katschinka (2014), p. 105; Monjean-Decaudin (2011), p. 763; Monjean-Decaudin (2012); Rafaraci (2013), p. 336; Romoli (2012), p. 32; Troisi (2014), p. 109.

[2]See Sarah Ludford, in the sitting of the European Parliament of 14 June 2010 (http://www.europarl.europa.eu/sides/getDoc.do?pubRef=-//EP//TEXT+CRE+20100614+ITEM-022+DOC+XML+V0//EN).

[3]Litterally, V. Reding, in the sitting of the European Parliament of 14 June 2010 (http://www.europarl.europa.eu/sides/getDoc.do?pubRef=-//EP//TEXT+CRE+20100614+ITEM-022+DOC+XML+V0//EN).

[4]Resolution of the Council of 30 November 2009 on a Roadmap for strengthening procedural rights of suspected or accused persons in criminal proceedings (2009/C 295/01), in OJ, 4 December 2009, C 295, then recognized in The Stockholm Programme—An open and secure Europe serving and protecting citizens (2010/C 115/01), in OJ, 4 May 2010, C 115.

[5]On the Proposal for a Council framework decision on certain procedural rights in criminal proceedings throughout the European Union (COM(2004)328 def.), see, among others: Arangüena Fanego (2008), p. 3042; Morgan and Csonka (2011), p. 147; Nascimbene (2011), p. 133.

[6]During the preliminary debate, Erik Hertog spoke of "*salami approach*"; the same expression was then used by the head of the Department of Criminal Justice, Peter Csonka (see *Impact Assessment Accompanying the Proposal for a Framework Decision on the right to interpretation and to translation in criminal proceedings*, SEC (2009) 915, 8 July 2009, pp. 58 and 62).

One of the most important innovations of Directive no. 64, especially in relation to Strasbourg case-law, is without doubt on the quality of linguistic assistance. It should be quite rightly noted that already a reference to 'quality' instead of 'adequacy'—generally referred to by the European Court of human rights—, would seem to suggest a much higher standard than the usual required within the Council of Europe' Parties.[7]

The Directive validates the very real meaning of linguistic assistance: as regards interpretation (Art. 2, para. 8), as well as translation (Art. 3, para. 9), the Directive clarifies that texts translated from the original "shall be of a quality sufficient to safeguard the fairness of the proceedings, in particular by ensuring that suspected or accused persons have knowledge of the case against them and are able to exercise their right of defence". If there is no quality, you could hardly take linguistic assistance seriously.[8] Consistently, the Directive requires Member States to ensure the right to challenge a decision finding that there is no need for interpretation and, when interpretation has been provided, the possibility to complain that the quality of the interpretation is not sufficient to safeguard the fairness of the proceedings (Art. 2, para. 5, and Art. 3, para. 5).

Moreover, quality is not only guaranteed from a procedural perspective: according to analyses of 'disappointing experiences in the EU' and a study of experiences outside the EU, the conclusion is that quality can only be guaranteed by a professional interpreter/translator. In this light, the result of scholars, professional associations and jurists consists in two documents of different types.

These are the *Final Report of the Reflection Forum on Multilingualism and Interpreter Training* (2009) which is the best summary of research into interpreting[9]; and the *Proposal for a Resolution of the Council and of the Governments of the Member States meeting within the Council fostering the implementation by Member States of the right to interpretation and to translation in criminal proceedings* (2009), on which Member States unanimously agreed in October 2009.[10]

The accompanying non-binding instrument attached to the Directive had never been adopted. However, in part some of its content has appeared in Art. 5, paras. 2 and 3 which touches on the breadth of the debate in the 2000s.

Firstly, it prescribes that "in order to promote the adequacy of interpretation and translation and efficient access thereto, Member States shall endeavour to establish a register or registers of independent translators and interpreters who are appropriately qualified" (Art. 5, para. 2). Secondly, paragraph 3 of Art. 5 establishes that "Member States shall ensure that interpreters and translators be required to observe

---

[7]Brannan (2012), p. 145.

[8]According to Falbo (2013), p. 17, "the quality of interpretation and translation seems to join the inherent features of linguistic assistance in criminal proceedings".

[9]The document is available at http://ec.europa.eu/dgs/scic/docs/finall_reflection_forum_report_en.pdf.

[10]See the Council document no. 14793/09, 23 October 2009. It must be reminded that, in summer 2010, the resolution was proposed to be adopted in the form of a recommendation at the same time as the Directive (Council document no. 11471/10, 24 June 2010, pp. 2 and 3).

confidentiality regarding interpretation and translation provided under this Directive". The value of that confidentiality recognised by all ethical codes provides for a very real binding rule with sanctions for any breach and procedural guarantees where translators or interpreters must testify.

The other essential feature of linguistic assistance to be guaranteed in criminal proceedings can be deduced from Art. 4, Directive no. 64/2010, which says that any costs of interpretation and translation should be met by the Member States.

The issue of language service fees was dealt with by the Court of Strasbourg very rigorously. Since the judgment of *Luedicke, Belkacem and Koç v. Germania*, 1978, the Court has clarified that the dispositions of Art. 6, para. 3, e) ECHR, which is different from the one under c), explains an absolute guarantee: "free" and "*gratuitement*" "denote neither a conditional remission, nor a temporary exemption, nor a suspension, but a once and for all exemption or exoneration".[11]

This means that linguistic assistance should be paid by the public authority independently of the trial outcome. Objectively, the Strasbourg Court had already specified that making the accused pay would breach the basis of Art. 6, para. 3, e) ECHR.

On one hand, the difference between those who do not speak or understand the language and those who do, that the rule is trying to avoid, would remain unaltered; on the other hand, there would be a risk of prejudicing the effectiveness of the guarantee since the fear of financial repercussions could influence the choice of the accused.[12]

So, the Directive has echoed more or less literally the intention of the Strasbourg Court. However, it has left out a certain subjectivity. Nevertheless, on close reading, it can be deduced that the European Legislator has excluded that the gratuitous linguistic assistance can be subordinated to the accused's financial standing.[13]

The third great novelty is the explicit provision of the onus being on the authority to ascertain linguistic competence: Art. 2, para. 4 requires Member States to "ensure that a procedure or mechanism is in place to ascertain whether suspected or accused persons speak and understand the language of the criminal proceedings and whether they need the assistance of an interpreter". Furthermore, Recital 21 of the Preamble specifies that "such a procedure or mechanism implies that competent authorities verify in any appropriate manner, including by consulting the suspected or accused persons concerned, whether they speak and understand the language of the criminal proceedings and whether they need the assistance of an interpreter". What is important is that the Directive, according to a model improved in the subsequent

---

[11]ECrtHR, 28 November 1978, *Luedicke, Belkacem and Koç v. Germania*, § 46; ECrtHR, 21 February 1984, *Öztürk v. Germania*, § 58; as well as, ECrtHR, 20 November 2008, *Isyar v. Bulgaria*, §§ 45-49, and ECrtHR, 21 March 2011, *Hovanesian v. Bulgarie*, §§ 48-52. On the unconditional nature of free linguistic assistance in the ECHR, see Chiavario (1969), p. 330; Trechsel (2005), pp. 331–332.

[12]ECrtHR, 28 November 1978, *Luedicke, Belkacem and Koç v. Germania*, § 42; and ECrtHR, 19 December 1989, *Kamasinski v. Austria*, § 86.

[13]On this point, see Gialuz (2012a), pp. 1198–1199.

Directive 2012/29/EU on victims' rights, imposes an individual assessment to decide if the defendant requires linguistic assistance, given that linguistic ability leading to assistance may vary whether communication is oral or written.

Another absolutely innovative section of the Directive is extending linguistic assistance to the meetings between the accused and his defence. Strasbourg case-law had never provided for this before.

Thus, the Directive goes well beyond the Strasbourg standards.

The main idea can be deduced from the central motivation of the Directive: if the rationale for linguistic assistance is to allow the suspected or accused persons who do not speak or understand the language "fully to exercise their right of defence and safeguarding the fairness of the proceedings" (Recital 17 of the Preamble), then it should also be recognised in the communication between the accused and his defence lawyer, since the accused must be able to "explain their version of the events to their legal counsel, point out any statements with which they disagree and make their legal counsel aware of any facts that should be put forward in their defence" (Recital 19 of the Preamble).

On these bases, Art. 2, para. 2 provides that interpretation is available for communication between suspected or accused persons and their legal counsel, albeit to a twofold condition.

On one hand, the guarantee is limited to the hypothesis that assistance is necessary "for the purpose of safeguarding the fairness of the proceedings"; on the other, it is limited to only those communications "in direct connection with any questioning or hearing during the proceedings or with the lodging of an appeal or other procedural applications".

The last component is recognition of the right to translation of written documents for the suspected or accused persons who do not understand the language. According to Art. 3 of Directive no. 64/2010, "Member States shall ensure that suspected or accused persons who do not understand the language of the criminal proceedings concerned are, within a reasonable period of time, provided with a written translation of all documents which are essential to ensure that they are able to exercise their right of defence and to safeguard the fairness of the proceedings". This is a rule of historical import because it is the first instance at a European level of the right to translation. Compared to the *American Convention on Human Rights* which expressly recognises the translator alongside the interpreter,[14] the European Convention only refers explicitly to the right to interpretation [Art. 6, para. 3, e)].

So, the Directive provides for the translation of essential documents which are of two types. One concerns the essential documents representing the absolute assumption of the necessity of translation to guarantee fairness in the proceedings, according to Directive no. 64 or other sources. It concerns any decision depriving a person of

---

[14]See Art. 8, para. 2: *"During the proceedings, every person is entitled, with full equality, to the following minimum guarantees: a. the right of the accused to be assisted without charge by a translator or interpreter, if he does not understand or does not speak the language of the tribunal or court".*

his liberty, any charge or indictment, and any judgment. The other concerns those documents which may be essential and may be identified as essential by the national authority in relation to the concrete case (Art. 3, para. 3). While the first set concerns acts directed to the accused, the second set, as specified by the Court of Justice, may be acts produced by the accused.[15]

2 Transposing the Directive Into the Italian Legal Order with Legislative Decree No. 32/2014

The Directive has been transposed into national legal orders in various Member States by specific legislation (Austria, Bulgaria, Cyprus, Croatia, Finland, France, Germany, Greece, the UK, The Republic of Ireland, Lithuania, The Netherlands, Poland, The Czech Republic, Romania, Slovakia, Sweden),[16] whereas others did not need to change national law (eg. Portugal).

As for Italy, it should be noted that until a few months before the deadline, the implementation of the Directive had been assigned entirely to the Judiciary who, despite resistance, had started the process of interpreting Art. 143 of the Code of criminal procedure in compliance with the Directive, with particular reference to the issue of translating judgments.[17]

With just the Law of delegation 2013 (Law no. 96, 6th August, 2013), the Government was delegated to transpose Directive 2010/64/EU (Art. 1, para. 1, attachment B). By proxy, Parliament implemented also two other Directives: 2012/13/EU on the right to information in criminal proceedings, and 2012/29/EU establishing minimum standards on the rights, support and protection of victims of crime, and replacing Council Framework Decision 2001/220/JHA. Both of these EU sources contain regulations on linguistic assistance: the first sets out that information on rights—the so-called Letter of Rights—must be given in a language suspects or accused persons understand (Art. 4, para. 4); the second recognises—for the first time in clear terms—a very real right of the victim of crime to interpretation and translation (Art. 7).

So, it would have been reasonable to simultaneously implement these Directives, as happened in Germany and Romania with Directive no. 13, 2012. Such an approach would have facilitated gathering all the systemic connections within a complex subject, especially as regards the victim's right to linguistic assistance.

---

[15]See ECrtHR, 15 October 2015, C-216/14, *Covaci*, in *Cassazione penale*, 2016, p. 740, annotated by Biondi (2016), p. 745. See also Gialuz (2015), p. 100.

[16]See http://eur-lex.europa.eu/search.html?type=advanced&qid=1399314513886&or0=DN% 3D72010L0064*,DN-old%3D72010L0064*&page=1. For an overview at the expiring of the deadline (27 October 2013), see Gialuz (2013a).

[17]See Gialuz (2012b), p. 434; Gialuz (2013b), p. 2188.

Unfortunately, the Government chose the route of split implementation. In the sitting of 28th February 2014, it approved Legislative Decree no. 32, which only implemented Directive no. 64.

From the point of view of the quality and effectiveness of the guarantee, it might be said that it was a missed opportunity.

In the debate prior to adopting the text, it was hoped that the legislator would bear in mind foreign experiences and use the proxy to seriously deal with the professionalisation of legal interpreting: experience from abroad shows how the quality of interpreting/translating can only be guaranteed by a professional service which has been properly trained and accredited, officially registered and required to adhere to an ethical code.[18]

As regards the adequacy of linguistic assistance in Italy, "we are almost in the *stone age*".[19] At the Public Prosecutor's Office and the Courts of Law, there are unofficial lists of 'expert linguists': in reality, they are not qualified with a certified professional training but nearly always mere 'language acquaintances', known directly by the authority and nominated in the belief that they are reliable or more likely available to provide their services without notice, and that they are experienced.[20] Since there is no monitoring of the professional competences of these people, anybody could be called in to be an interpreter.[21]

Despite widespread awareness of the gravity of the Italian position regarding the quality of the interpreting and translation service, Legislative Decree no. 32 of 2014 is similarly disappointing. At procedural level, it does not cite a single redress for the quality of linguistic assistance. Equally disappointing are the choices made institutionally, those referring to professionalising the interpreter and translator.

On this point, the Government proposed a low-cost quasi-solution: they have lightened their conscience by modifying Art. 67 of the practical dispositions attached to the Code of criminal procedure ("disp. att. c.p.p.") which contemplates experts in "interpreting and translation" being listed in the register of experts at each Court of Law as per Art. 67 disp. att. c.p.p.

Apparently, this could be interpreted as a step forward: at least the interpreters are officially equivalent to other experts.

In reality, it risks being seen as merely a formal change. Indeed, the registers are not updated and there is no rigorous sifting of competences. Thereby, the risk is a tendency to decant the existing lists of "language experts" at the Secretary of the Prosecutor's Office and at the Court Clerks' Office into the official registers. Much will depend on the role played by the association's representatives at the national level of the unregulated professions, whose representatives will become part of the committee responsible for training the register's experts at the local level. Wherever

---

[18]See Ballardini (2012), p. 182; Garwood and Preziosi (2013), p. 79.

[19]Bargis (2013), p. 114. On the constant violation of European standards, see Falbo (2013), pp. 87 ss.; Garwood and Preziosi (2013), p. 79; Gialuz (2013c), p. 241.

[20]Curtotti Nappi (2002), p. 482; Garwood (2012), p. 173; Sau (2010), p. 216.

[21]Ballardini (2012), p. 164.

these associations make effective and permanent training a requirement of registration, there may be a guaranteed change for the better.

As regards the gratuity of the linguistic assistance, the Italian legislator has done his part.

To implement Art. 4 of Directive no. 64, Art. 3 of Legislative Decree no. 32, 2014 modifies Art. 5, d) of the text on Justice spending (Presidential Decree no. 115, 30 May 2002) in which after the words "magistrates auxiliary" come the words "except for nominated interpreters and translators in cases described in Art. 143 of the Code of criminal procedure". In effect, many scholars had underlined that the provision contrasted with that clearly outlined in Art. 4 of the Directive.[22] So, the Legislator has punctually intervened on this point with the result that the cost of linguistic assistance for the defence are unclaimable even if there is a conviction. This is perfectly in line with Art. 4 of Directive no. 64/2010.

They are however claimable when, in case of conviction, the costs refer not to linguistic assistance but to linguistic mediation for justice reasons. In fact, linguistic assistance does not cover the entire range of linguistic mediation in criminal proceedings. Alongside the right to linguistic assistance, there is room for interventions by interpreters and translators aimed at the use of influential evidence in the trial, like the interpretation of tapped conversations in foreign languages, or interpreting the hearing of a foreign witness, or even the translation of a document or legal text in a foreign language. So, the costs of such mediation for justice reasons are charged to the accused (foreign speaker or otherwise) on conviction.

With reference to the check on the conditions for the appointment of an interpreter or translator, by implementing Art. 2, para. 4 of Directive no. 64, the 2014 reform introduced some significant novelty establishing that "it should be carried out by the *judicial authority*" [italics added] (Art. 143, para. 4, of the Code of criminal procedure). Three fundamental consequences follow from this.

First of all, the check can be carried out only by the judicial authority. This means, according to most interpretations, the Public Prosecutor or the judge, and excludes the Police who are subordinate to the Public Prosecutor.[23]

The second consequence is the modification in the burden of proof: it is clear that it behoves the judicial authority to ascertain sufficient language knowledge and no longer the accused to prove his lack of knowledge.[24]

The last consequence stemming from the new Art. 143 is that in cases of any doubts over knowledge of Italian, the judicial authority should nominate an expert to ascertain such a level of knowledge and anyhow provide an interpreter.

As regards extending linguistic assistance to meetings with defence lawyers, in 2014 the Legislator intervened in two provisions.

In one, in the second part of Art. 143, para.1, he has specified that a defendant who does not know Italian "has an equal right to free linguistic assistance in

---

[22]Biondi (2011), p. 2425, footnote no. 49.

[23]Of this opinion, see Cocomello and Corbo (2014), p. 5.

[24]Curtotti Nappi (2014), p. 124; Iermano (2011), p. 343.

communications with his defence lawyer prior to any hearing, or in view of a request or a memorandum during the proceedings".

In the other, he has introduced paragraph 4-*bis* of Art. 104 which grants the non-speaking Italian detainee the right to a free interpreter for his first meeting with defence lawyer. This is probably a superfluous provision, given that the guarantee at the first meeting with the detained defendant could be inferred directly from the general regulation in Art. 143, para.1. This extends interpreting assistance to any meeting with defence lawyers which is instrumental in preparing for: (a) the questioning or cross-examination; (b) a "request" including re-examining either the decision on deprivation of liberty or the charge[25]; (c) a memorandum.

Finally, as regards the translation of acts, the new paragraphs 2 and 3 of Art. 143 implement Art. 3 of the Directive. The first paragraph covers acts which must always be translated within a deadline such as to allow the exercise of rights and the defence right. These concern 'notice of investigation', notice on the defence right, decisions applying personal precautionary measures,[26] notice on the conclusion of preliminary investigations, decrees on the preliminary hearing and summons to court, judgments and decrees for conviction.

As regards such a compulsory listing of the acts to translate, there are two considerations to be made.

One is that this list is full of gaps. Given that the EU directive refers to "any decision depriving a person of his liberty", it would have made sense to extend the obligation to translating the decision on validation of the arrest ("arresto") or preventive detention ("fermo"). Furthermore, it is hard to understand if the obligation only refers to the decision that for the first time applies the precautionary measure or also to subsequent ones. Given the reasoning behind the rule, it ought to support translating the decisions that apply precautionary measures and those that have a bearing on its content or, in other words, modify it for the worse (but also for the better).[27]

Another consideration is that the list seems long where it refers to precautionary measures. Even considering the need to limit translation costs, it would have been preferable to refer to custodial precautionary measures only, and to limit the other measures to translation upon request. This restriction would have been in line with a rigorous interpretation—even in light of the case-law of the Court of Strasbourg on Art. 5 ECHR—of the often repeated intent of the Directive: the EU refers exclusively to decisions which deprive the accused of personal liberty and not just limit their liberty. However, the Italian legislator has again been freer, unaware of the

---

[25]This provision will allow to go beyond the restrictive case-law that used to oblige the defendant to nominate a trusted interpreter to complete procedural acts (see Bargis (2009), p. 2024; Meloni (2010), p. 3683).

[26]Freezing orders and seizures are therefore excluded: see Court of Cassation, III, 28 May 2014, n. 33402, in *Diritto e giustizia*, 30 July 2014, which excluded the application of this provision to precautionary seizure.

[27]Legislative Decree no. 32, 4 March 2014, concerning interpretation and translation in criminal proceedings, cit., par. III, b.

circumstances that in Strasbourg and Brussels principles are less important than the effectiveness of rights.[28]

Alongside these essential provisions, Art. 143, para. 3, provides for ordering a free translation of "other acts or parts of them considered essential for informing the accused of what he is being charged of": the translation of these "essential acts" into the accused's language are laid down "even on request, by a motivated decision, which may be challenged together with the judgment". It should be noted that, compared to the second paragraph, the rule does not mention "written translation": thus, in such cases, translation may be oral.[29] However, this interpretation is not acceptable because "translation" means the transposition of a written text into another written one, unless expressly substituted for a translation on demand.

3 Case-Law Resistance

If the change of the law in 2014 presents several angles and a few shadows (especially on professionalising translators and interpreters), the same cannot be said of case-law. The Supreme Court seems to systematically disregard the import of the reform.

In terms of the effectiveness of the assistance, the case-law takes two approaches which both end up weakening the guarantee.

On one hand, given that Legislative Decree no. 32/2014 did not include any innovations on "consequences to the lack of translation of procedural acts", the lack of translation determines an intermediate nullity,[30] which could be remedied by simply challenging the judgment by the defence lawyer,[31] or, in the case of notice on the conclusion of preliminary investigations, by the mere presentation of a request for summary proceedings ("*giudizio abbreviato*")[32]: this would be quite debatable, given that the translation is aimed at exercising the right to challenge or the right to self-defence. Yet again, where the case-law—as it would seem from the first cases[33]—should confirm this approach, we are faced with an evident incompatibility

---

[28]See, for example, ECrtHR, 13 May 1980, *Artico v. Italia*, § 33.

[29]Bricchetti and Pistorelli (2014), p. 67.

[30]See Court of Cassation, II, 7 May 2014, n. 18781, in *Cassazione penale*, 2015, p. 2740.

[31]This has been sustained by Court of Cassation, III, 15 November 2007, n. 181, in *Ced. Cass.*, n. 238605: "the lack of translation, in the language known by the defendant who does not speak Italian, of the extract of the judgment, in case of trial *in absentia*, determines an intermediate nullity of general order, that can be remedied where the defendants appeals the merit of the judgment". Similarly, see Court of Cassation, II, 7 June 2011, n. 32555, in *Archivio della nuova procedura penale*, 2011, 654; Court of Cassation, V, 6 October 2004, n. 16185, in *Ced. Cass.*, n. 233642.

[32]Court of Cassation, V, 30 October 2013, n. 48782, in *Giurisprudenza italiana*, 2014, p. 714; Court of Cassation, sez. un., 26 September 2006, Cieslinsky, in *Cassazione penale*, 2007, p. 514.

[33]See Court of Cassation, II, 9 April 2014, n. 18781, cit., according to which Legislative Decree no. 32/2014 "has not brought about any novelty concerning the consequences following the lack of translation of procedural acts".

with the Directive; the automatic remedy—which results into a sort of implicit inadmissible waiver (*ex* Art. 3, para. 8 of the Directive)—in reality fails to grant an effective remedy which allows the defendant to censure the omitted translation: the solution in such a case might be that of a constitutional objection for violation of Art. 117, para. 1 of the Constitution, subject to a preliminary ruling by the Court of Justice.[34]

In other cases, the Court has held that the omitted translation does not invalidate *per se* the judgment, but only influences the deadlines for the appeal: it impedes the defendant from understanding the reasons behind his judgment and therefore fully exercising his right to a defence, which is also expressed through direct access to the motivations without any form of filtering by the technical defence, so as to be able to better evaluate the "*an*" and the "*quomodo*" of any further development in the proceedings.[35] The omitted translation therefore has the unique effect of suspending or postponing the deadline to appeal as long as the defendant is unable to know the act in a language he understands.[36]

As regards the duty of the prosecuting authority to ascertain the defendant's inability in Italian, the case-law does not seem to show any new sensitivity. It seems, in fact, to have neutralised the modified rule: it is as if Art. 143, para. 4 had never been changed; much less it considers an interpretation conforming to the Directive.

As a general rule, it often happens that the judge of preliminary investigations focuses entirely on the identification report compiled by the police: if the police certify that the foreigner speaks and understands Italian and that an interpreter is not required to explain anything, the judge excludes nominating an interpreter.

This procedure continues to be backed up by the Supreme Court according to which Art. 143, para. 4 literally does not imply that the judicial authority should proceed personally to verify language competence; indeed, where the legislator requires the personal participation of the judicial authority, it does so expressly, such as per Art. 103, para. 4 on inspections, searches and seizures at the offices of the defence lawyers.[37] This argument would seem very weak mostly because the two hypotheses are not analogous: one concerns an evidential act, whereas the other verifies if the defendant can stand before a court.

Even regarding the consequences following a doubt on linguistic inability, the Supreme Court—urged ever more frequently by the investigating authorities—seems not to have understood the profound innovation of the rule: the Court believed it an abnormal decision when a judge of the preliminary hearing invalidated the proceedings of the Public Prosecution and would not proceed unless all the proce-dural acts were translated into a language understood by the defendant.

---

[34]Of this opinion, see Recchione (2014), pp. 12, 19.

[35]Court of Cassation, VI, 29 September 2015, n. 45457, in *Ced. Cass.*, n. 265521.

[36]Court of Cassation, I, 11 February 2014, n. 23608, in *Ced. Cass.*, n. 259732; Court of Cassation, II, 5 July 2007, n. 32882, in *Ced. Cass.*, n. 237495; Court of Cassation, III, 19 November 2003, Kryczka in *Ced. Cass.*, n. 227849.

[37]Court of Cassation, V, 9 October 2014, n. 52245, in *Ced. Cass.*, n. 262101.

This judge had pointed out that the Border Police had identified the defendant through a multi-language module, whereas the report of election of domicile at an office defender had only been written in Italian; this gave rise to a real doubt that he had really understood that he was going to be tried or at least that the acts and related communications would have been sent to the elected domicile.

So, the Court felt that in this specific case the challenged decision was abnormal because there was a "'legitimate doubt' unaccompanied by any foundation of such a conclusion, and which was denied by the Police's report recalled by the Public prosecutor, which also revealed an aware interlocution with the defendant".[38]

Referring to extending the guarantee to meetings with defence lawyers, the Court established that violating Art. 104, para. 4-*bis* and Art. 143 can constitute an intermediate nullity *ex* Art. 178, para.1, c) "only if it concretely affects the right to linguistic assistance of the defendant, who must specify immediately the prejudice, including the impossibility to develop arguments or deductions, or other defense shortcomings as a result of a specific lack of information on the content of the accusation".[39]

From a substantive interpretation, the case-law has invented a totally unexpected requisite in this case of nullity. According to Italian law, nullity is formal: the diversity of the act as specified by law would be sufficient to trigger the sanction. This would appear to be completely reasonable given that evidence of the prejudice deriving from the lack of an interpreter at the meeting with the defence lawyer resembles a *probatio diabolica*.

Last but not least, the case-law has confirmed a restricted orientation concerning the translation of decisions on precautionary measures. It has been said that "even following the coming into force of Legislative Decree no. 32, 2014, which implemented the EU Directive 2010/64/EU on linguistic assistance, the written translation of a decision applying a precautionary measure issued at the conclusion of the hearing following the arrest at which the non-speaking Italian suspect had the regular assistance of an interpreter, is unnecessary since the accused has been made aware of the charges against him and is able to ask for a case review".[40]

It would seem to be a clear and unjustifiable misapplication of a provision which on this point leaves no leeway to the interpreter: the wording of Art. 143, para. 2 is in itself very clear but read in light of Art. 3, para. 2 of the Directive proves to be even more precise in affirming that all decisions applying precautionary measures should be translated and in no way differentiates by the context in which the decision was

---

[38]Court of Cassation, V, 26 October 2015, n. 11658, in *Ced. Cass.*, n. 266550, and Court of Cassation, V, 26 October 2015, n. 1136, in *Ced. Cass.*, n. 266069, with reference to cases decided before the entry into force of the new regime. Contrary to this approach, meaning that a similar decision of the judge of the preliminary hearing is not abnormal, see: Court of Cassation, V, 8 July 2015, n. 38109, in *Ced. Cass.*, n. 265007; Court of Cassation, II, 11 June 2015, n. 26241, in *Ced. Cass.*, n. 264012; Court of Cassation, I, 14 May 2014, n. 2263, in *Ced. Cass.*, n. 261998.

[39]Court of Cassation, I, 24 June 2015, n. 30127, in *Ced. Cass.*, n. 264488.

[40]Litterally, Court of Cassation, I, 8 October 2014, n. 48299, in *Cassazione penale*, 2015, p. 1502, annotated by Mari (2015), p. 1507.

issued. Besides, the logical-systematic argument used by the Court has no value. The validation of the arrest cannot be confused with the issuing of a decision applying a precautionary measure: they are autonomous decisions and therefore the participation of the non-speaking Italian suspect with the assistance of an interpreter at the questioning provided under art. 391, par. 2, allows him to understand the reason for the arrest; but the possible decision applying a precautionary measure issued after the validation order must also dwell on the required conditions for it, which the accused has heard via the Public Prosecution request, translated by the interpreter, without however being able to know if and in what measure the validation judge has applied them when the decision on the precautionary measure too is not translated.

The decision applying a precautionary measure should therefore be translated even when it has been issued after the hearing following the arrest.[41]

It is hoped that the Italian Supreme Court finally takes note of the paradigm alteration introduced by the Directive and its implementation. In the EU, where the citizens of its Member States circulate freely and where there is a growing number of migrants, there is a growing risk of proceedings against defendants who do not speak Italian. So, defendants who do not speak Italian must have the same privileges as those who understand the language so as not to violate Arts. 21 and 48 of the Nice Charter. Where Italian case-law does not abandon the substantial emptying of the guarantees provided for in Directive no. 64/2010, the Court of Justice may need to be called on.

References

Amalfitano C (2011) Unione europea e garanzie processuali: il diritto all'interpretazione e alla traduzione nei procedimenti penali. Studi sull'integrazione europea 1:83–110

Aranguena Fanego C (2008) Proposta di decisione quadro su determinati diritti processuali nei procedimenti penali nel territorio dell'Unione europea. Cassazione penale 7:3042–3059

Aranguena Fanego C (2011a) El derecho a la interpretación y a la traducción en los procesos penales. Comentario a la directiva 2010/64/UE del Parlamento Europeo y del Consejo, 20 de octubre de 2010. Revista General de Derecho Europeo 24:1–23

Aranguena Fanego C (2011b) Nuevas directivas sobre derechos procesales de sospechosos e imputados en el proceso penal. In: Aranguena Fanego C (ed) Cooperación judicial civil y penal en el nuevo escenario de Lisboa. Granada, Comares, pp 269–301

Ballardini E (2012) Traduire devant la justice pénale. L'interpréte traducteur dans les codes de procédure pénale italiens aux XIXe et XXe siècles. Bononia University Press, Bologna

Balsamo A (2014) Il contenuto dei diritti fondamentali. In: Kostoris RE (ed) Manuale di procedura penale europea, 2nd edn. Giuffrè, Milan, pp 109–171

Bargis M (2009) Inammissibile l'impugnazione redatta in lingua straniera: punti fermi e lacune di sistema dopo la pronuncia delle Sezioni unite. Cassazione penale 5:2016–2034

Bargis M (2013) L'assistenza linguistica per l'imputato: dalla Direttiva europea 64/2010 nuovi *inputs* alla tutela fra teoria e prassi. In: Bargis M (ed) Studi in ricordo di Maria Gabriella Aimonetto. Giuffrè, Milan, pp 91–117

---

[41]Similarly, see Mari (2015), p. 1514.

Bazzocchi V (2013) L'armonizzazione delle garanzie processuali nell'Unione europea: la direttiva sul diritto all'interpretazione e alla traduzione nei procedimenti penali. In: Civitarese Matteucci S, Guarriello F, Puoti P (eds) Diritti fondamentali e politiche dell'Unione europea dopo Lisbona. Maggioli, Rimini, pp 159–180

Beauvais P (2011) Droit pénal de l'Union européenne. Revue trimestrielle de droit européen 47 (3):637–658

Biondi G (2011) La tutela processuale dell'imputato alloglotta alla luce della direttiva 2010/64/UE. Cassazione penale 6:2412–2426

Biondi G (2016) Osservazioni a Corte Giustizia UE 15 ottobre 2015 n. 216. Cassazione penale 2:745–750

Brannan J (2012) Raising the Standard of Language Assistance in Criminal Proceedings: From the Rights under Article 6(3) ECHR to Directive 2010/64/EU. Cyprus Hum Rights Law Rev 1 (2):128–156

Bricchetti R, Pistorelli L (2014) Atti fondamentali scritti nella lingua dell'imputato. Guida al diritto 16:64–68

Chiavario M (1969) La Convenzione europea dei diritti dell'uomo nel sistema delle fonti normative in materia penale. Giuffrè, Milan

Cocomello A, Corbo A (2014) Attuazione della direttiva 2010/64/UE sul diritto all'interpretazione e alla traduzione nei procedimenti penali. https://www.penalecontemporaneo.it. Accessed 10 Apr 2014

Cras S, De Matteis L (2010) The directive on the right to interpretation and translation in criminal proceedings. Genesis and description. EUCRIM 4:153–162

Curtotti Nappi D (2002) Il problema delle lingue nel processo penale. Giuffrè, Milan

Curtotti Nappi D (2014) La normativa in tema di assistenza linguistica tra direttiva europea e nuove prassi applicative. Processo penale e giustizia 5:115–132

Falbo C (2013) La comunicazione interlinguistica in ambito giuridico. Temi, problemi e prospettive di ricerca. Edizioni Università di Trieste, Trieste

Garwood C (2012) Court interpreting in Italy. The daily violation of a fundamental right. Interpreters' Newsl 17:173–189

Garwood C, Preziosi I (2013) Un modello per un interpretariato giudiziario efficiente e di qualità in Italia: un approccio realistico all'applicazione della Direttiva 2010/64/UE. In: Rudvin M, Spinzi C (eds) Mediazione linguistica e interpretariato. Regolamentazione, problematiche presenti e prospettive future in ambito giuridico. Clueb, Bologna, pp 79–122

Gialuz M (2011) Novità sovranazionali. Processo penale e giustizia 2:9–13

Gialuz M (2012a) Il diritto all'assistenza linguistica nel processo penale. Direttive europee e ritardi italiani. Rivista di diritto processuale 5:1193–1206

Gialuz M (2012b) L'obbligo di interpretazione conforme alla direttiva sul diritto all'assistenza linguistica. Diritto penale e processo 4:434–440

Gialuz M (2013a) È scaduta la direttiva sull'assistenza linguistica. Spunti per una trasposizione ritardata, ma (almeno) meditata. https://www.penalecontemporaneo.it. Accessed 4 Nov 2013

Gialuz M (2013b) La Corte di cassazione riconosce l'obbligo di tradurre la sentenza a favore dell'imputato alloglotto. Cassazione penale 6:2188–2194

Gialuz M (2013c) La lingua come diritto: il diritto all'interpretazione e alla traduzione nel processo penale. In: Ruggieri F, Rafaraci T, Di Paolo G, Marcolini S, Belfiore R (eds) Processo penale, lingua e Unione europea. Cedam, Padua, pp 227–245

Gialuz M (2015) Dalla Corte di giustizia importanti indicazioni esegetiche in relazione alle prime due direttive sui diritti dell'imputato. Diritto penale contemporaneo-Riv Trim 4:100–107

Iermano A (2011) Verso comuni regole processuali europee: il diritto alla traduzione e all'interpretazione nei procedimenti penali. Diritto comunitario e degli scambi internazionali 50(2):335–358

Izzo I (2012) Spazio europeo di giustizia e cooperazione giudiziaria. In: Kalb L (ed) "Spazio europeo di giustizia" e procedimento penale italiano. Giappichelli, Turin, pp 313–343

Kalb L (2012) Il rafforzamento del diritto e gli effetti nell'ordinamento italiano. In: Kalb L (ed) "Spazio europeo di giustizia" e procedimento penale italiano. Giappichelli, Turin, pp 344–380

Katschinka L (2014) The impact of Directive 2010/64/EU on the right to interpretation and translation in criminal proceedings. In: Falbo C, Viezzi M (eds) Traduzione e interpretazione per la società e le istituzioni. Edizioni Università di Trieste, Trieste, pp 105–114

Mari A (2015) Il nuovo art. 143 c.p.p. e i vecchi problemi in tema di traduzione dell'ordinanza cautelare personale. Cassazione penale 4:1506–1514

Meloni S (2010) Niente di nuovo sul fronte della traduzione degli atti in ambito processuale: una storia italiana. Cassazione penale 10:3683–3691

Monjean-Decaudin S (2011) L'Union européenne consacre le droit à l'assistance linguistique dans les procédures pénales. Commentaire de la directive relative aux droits à l'interprétation et à la traduction dans les procédures pénales. Revue trimestrielle de droit européen 47(4):763–781

Monjean-Decaudin S (2012) La traduction du droit dans la procédure judiciaire. Contribution à l'étude de la linguistique juridique. Dalloz, Paris

Morgan C, Csonka P (2011) A European Union framework decision on procedural rights: the short history of a failure (so far). In: Pedrazzi M, Viarengo I, Lang A (eds) Individual guarantees in the European judicial area in criminal matters. Bruylant, Brussels, pp 147–152

Nascimbene B (2011) European judicial cooperation in criminal matters: what protection for individuals under the Lisbon Treaty? In: Pedrazzi M, Viarengo I, Lang A (eds) Individual guarantees in the European judicial area in criminal matters. Bruylant, Brussels, pp 123–135

Rafaraci T (2013) The rights of defence in EU judicial cooperation in criminal matters. In: Ruggeri S (ed) Transnational inquiries and the protection of fundamental rights in criminal proceedings. A study in memory of Vittorio Grevi and Giovanni Tranchina. Springer, Heidelberg, pp 331–343

Recchione S (2014) L'impatto della direttiva 2010/64/UE sulla giurisdizione penale: problemi, percorsi interpretativi, prospettive. https://www.penalecontemporaneo.it. Accessed 15 July 2014

Romoli F (2012) La direttiva 64/2010 sul diritto all'interprete e l'ordinamento italiano: prospettive su una zona d'ombra del diritto alla difesa. Diritto, immigrazione e cittadinanza 2:32–61

Sau S (2010) Le garanzie linguistiche nel processo penale. Diritto all'interprete e tutela delle minoranze riconosciute. Cedam, Padua

Trechsel S (2005) Human Rights in Criminal Proceedings. Oxford University Press, Oxford

Troisi P (2014) L'obbligo di traduzione degli atti processuali tra garanzie sovranazionali e resistenze interne. Processo penale e giustizia 1:109–123

Awareness of One's Own Rights and Knowledge of the Accusation: The Implementation of the Directive on the Right to Information in Italy

Daniele Negri

Contents

Abstract The contribution analyses some issues relating to the transposition into the Italian legal system of Directive 2012/13/EU on the right to information in criminal proceedings. The Author firstly examines the contents of the supranational measure and, afterwards, performs a critical evaluation of the national law aimed at implementing the European defence rights (d. lgs. 1 July 2014, no. 101). Some inconsistencies between the Directive and national law provisions are then highlighted, underlining how the internal legislator, instead of protecting the effectiveness of the right to information, only ensures a formal fulfilment of the obligations deriving from EU law.

D. Negri (✉)
University of Ferrara, Department of Law, Ferrara, Italy
e-mail: daniele.negri@unife.it

© Springer Nature Switzerland AG 2019
T. Rafaraci, R. Belfiore (eds.), *EU Criminal Justice*,
https://doi.org/10.1007/978-3-319-97319-7_3

43

1   The Essential Aims of the EU Directive on the Right to Information

The 2012/13/EU Directive sets out detailed regulations on the right to information in criminal proceedings which, in the context of the 'Stockholm Programme', reinforces the rights of suspects and defendants in criminal proceedings,[1] thus fulfilling the second of the *Roadmap* measures. The EU's declared objective is the principle of mutual recognition of judicial decisions in criminal matters which is only realisable by reinforcing reciprocal trust between Member States and their respective criminal justice systems so that they all guarantee homogeneous levels of protection of the right to defense.[2]

The Directive on the right to information, like others adopted after the Stockholm Programme, is minimally regulatory thereby not prejudicing the wider levels of protection eventually recognised by national legislations. This is clearly demonstrated by the non-regression clause in the Directive's Article 10. As regards its subjective application, the Directive concerns suspects and defendants in criminal proceedings, as well as those under EU arrest warrant (Art. 1). From an objective point of view, the Directive applies to criminal proceedings from the investigative phase to the final judgment (Art. 2, para. 1).

The Directive is divided into three levels, protecting the right to be informed of certain procedural prerogatives as established by national law; the right to know the limits of one's accusation; and the right to access the investigative materials of the case in the hands of the prosecuting authority.

On the first level, the guarantee is provided through an institute of general type and one of special type. Generally, suspects and defendants are provided with written and oral information about their essential rights to a fair proceeding. These prerogatives are identified in the first paragraph of Article 3 and concern the right to legal assistance, including the right to free legal aid, the right to be informed of the accusation, the right to translation and interpretation, as well as the right to silence. In order to guarantee the effective application of these rights, the information must be provided in simple and accessible language (Art. 3, para. 2), and it is essential to ensure prompt communication which should be given at the latest before the first interview by the police or other competent authority (as specified in Recital 19 of the Preamble).

Subsequently, there is a special discipline to reinforce the guarantee to be informed, which counter-balances the weak position of the person who is arrested or detained (Arts. 4 and 5 relating to the EU Arrest Warrant). Suspected or accused persons who are arrested or detained must be given a Letter of Rights, which they shall be allowed to keep in their possession throughout the time they are deprived of liberty, that details in simple and accessible language, besides the information on

---

[1]Resolution of the Council of 30 November 2009 (*OJ*, 4 December 2009, C-295, p. 1).

[2]For a more detailed analysis on this, see Rafaraci (2014), p. 1 ff.

rights under Art. 3, information about: the right of access to the materials of the case; the right to have consular authorities and someone else informed about their detention; the right of access to urgent medical assistance; the maximum number of hours or days suspects or accused persons may be deprived of liberty before being brought before a judicial authority; and any possibility, under national law, of challenging the lawfulness of the arrest, obtaining a review of the detention, or the right of making a request for provisional release. There is a form of Letter of Rights attached to the Directive in order to guide member States in guaranteeing homogeneity as far as possible.[3]

The second right arising from the Directive focuses on the information about the accusation (Art. 6). It specifies that all the elements of the charge necessary to guarantee the effective exercise of the right of defence and the right to a fair proceeding must be communicated. This means bringing to light all the factual details of the crime (including time and place), the hypothetical legal classification of the criminal acts and the supposed role of the accused. Where the accused is imprisoned, he should be told the reasons for his arrest or detention. The information about the charge must be sufficiently detailed, considering the phase of the proceedings in which the information is given. On this matter, the Directive creates a fundamental distinction. As close as possible to the interview, the accused must be informed of the accusation in such detail as to permit the effective exercise of his rights to defence. At the latest at the submission of the merits of the accusation to a court, all the elements must be communicated in detailed and specific terms.

The obligations upon the prosecuting authority regarding the right to be informed on charges are not limited to these provisions. The accusation drawn up initially in the proceeding is by its nature provisional and destined to change as more material is accumulated during the investigation. The accused must likewise be informed of all developments to the extent in which his position is "substantially affected" (Recital 29 of the Preamble). According to Article 6, para. 4, it is necessary to provide prompt information of "any changes" of the communicated accusation "where this is necessary to safeguard the fairness of the proceedings". This clause echoes Recital 29 of the Preamble, which requires any substantial modifications of the accusation to be communicated promptly. However, the Directive does not identify any specific terms, limiting itself to establish that effective defence must be assured.

The last right protected by the Directive is the right of access to the investigative materials of the case. This is a special provision in order to promptly provide the accused under arrest or detention and his lawyer with all the essential documents to effectively challenge the lawfulness of the arrest or detention (Art. 7, para. 1) at any stage of the criminal proceedings. The disclosure should take place prior to the judicial authority's decision on the legitimacy of the deprivation of the accused's liberty, in a time which allows the defence to challenge such legitimacy. This is clearly a hypothesis of a 'teleologically oriented' disclosure,[4] since the Directive

---

[3]See Ciampi (2012), p. 7.
[4]Ciampi (2013), p. 24; Ruggeri (2015), p. 18.

explicitly relates it to the need of allowing the defence to challenge the legitimacy of the restriction of liberty. The disclosure is not integral, but only regards the cognitive functional material to evaluate the foundation behind the deprivation of liberty. The authority has some discretion in selecting the investigative materials for consultation by the defence, since only the "essential" ones are disclosed. The grade of discretion depends on the interpretation of the ambiguous concept of 'essential'. It could lead to restrictive interpretations intended to limit the material justifying the detention to those which are 'most significant'. However, it should be noted that, given the overall spirit of the Directive, a broad interpretation would be preferable, leading to an integral disclosure of the material behind the detention order without arbitrary distinctions.

In addition to the hypothesis laid out in Art. 7, para. 1, and quite apart from any form of deprivation of liberty, is the unambiguous point which characterises the completeness of the disclosure. In paragraph 2 of the afore-mentioned Article, at the latest upon submission of the merits of the accusation to the judgment of a court, the defence must be granted with the right of access to all material evidence collected during the investigations. Where further material evidence comes into the possession of the competent authorities, access shall be granted in due time. This guarantees that when the merits of the accusation are at stake, the defence is able to question the accusation having all the investigative evidence at disposal, thereby excluding any accusation based on prosecution's 'hidden cards'.[5]

Such generalised access to evidence may be subject to certain derogations. According to Article 7, para. 4, access to certain materials is subject to restrictions if the access could lead to a serious threat to the life or the fundamental rights of another person or if the refusal is strictly necessary to safeguard an "important public interest" (Recital 32 of the Preamble). For example, Article 7 mentions the protection of an ongoing investigation or serious harm to the State's internal security. It should however be underlined that these clauses shall be interpreted in a restrictive way since they are exceptions to the general rule regarding investigative evidence (Recital 32 of the Preamble). Furthermore, such restrictions are only applicable after great consideration of the needs of those requiring protection and their defence rights, taking into account the phase of the proceedings at which the denial of access is invoked. The Directive, apropos, stipulates one jurisdictional reservation. The denial to access must be decided by a judicial authority, if not directly, it should however be subject to judicial review.

The compliance with the informational obligations of the Directive must be documented in the proceedings' acts. Furthermore, suspects or accused persons or their lawyers shall have the right to challenge the possible failure or refusal of the competent authorities to provide information in accordance with the Directive (Art. 8), either via a specific appeal procedure, or through specific procedural sanctions (Recital 36 of the Preamble).

---

[5]Ciampi (2012), p. 8.

2 Implementation of the Directive in the Italian Legal System: Banning Old Practices About the Right of the Accused to Be Informed of His Rights

In Italy, the Directive was implemented through Legislative Decree no. 101, 1st July 2014. As usual, in transposing European laws on the guarantees in criminal proceedings, the legislator's intervention is only limited to the adoption of minimal indispensable measures for obtaining some correspondence to supranational law. There is no attempt to innovate the national system, which, taking advantage of European law, may be able to resolve some of its own shortcomings regarding the right to information for persons under investigation and their defendants.

The first point that needs to be considered is the communication to the accused of his legal rights within criminal proceedings. In the background, there is the debatable orientation of the Italian Supreme Court whose obsolescence is laid bare by the novelties of European origin. On more than one occasion, the judges of the Supreme Court seemed to express that it was largely superfluous to provide information to persons under investigation or defendants relating their defence rights in certain procedural stages.[6] The decisions in question regarded in particular hearing notices ("avvisi di udienza") and especially the requirement to inform the defence on how to exercise personal defence. The general nature of the arguments behind such decisions nevertheless draws our attention to the topic under examination. Quite simplistically and swiftly, the Supreme Court observed that publishing the legislative text in the Official Journal is quite sufficient for informing all those involved on the procedural laws attributable to the defence. As a result of this, any eventual ignorance of procedural law cannot be invoked by the accused.

The intent behind the European law contributes to overcoming such archaisms. If the simple publication of procedural law were always appropriate to guarantee awareness, you would in no way be able to explain the informational obligations variously imposed by the prosecuting authority in favour of the accused, such as to bring him up to date with his procedural prerogatives. After all, whoever finds himself under accusation is nearly always unaware of the judicial regulations specifically governing the proceeding. Thus, it is inadmissible to criticise the accused of being ignorant; this is especially true if we consider that, as opposed to substantive criminal law, criminal proceedings do not protect judicial rights which are primary and inviolable at the level of social conscience and therefore within everyone's reach.[7]

The arguments for an overruling are contained in Directive 2012/13/EU as well as in the first decision of the Court of Justice on informational rights.[8] These rights

---

[6]Italian Court of Cassation, Sez. Un., 25 March 1998, D'Abramo, in *Cassazione penale*, 1998, p 2874. More recently, see Italian Court of Cassation, Sez. V, 20 September 2010, Perrotta, in *C.E. D. Cass.*, n. 248887.

[7]For a more detailed analysis, see Negri (2014), pp. 194 ff.

[8]ECJ, 15 October 2015, *Covaci*, C-216/14. See the annotation by Gialuz (2015), pp. 100 ff.

would not have any reason to exist if the mere publication of procedural law were sufficient to inform the defence of the accused. Furthermore, in the *Covaci* case, the attention of the Court of Justice was directed at emphasising the effectiveness of the rights recognised by the Directive. Even regarding the awareness of the accused, the Luxembourg judges were clear in interpreting the Directives clauses as prescribing an authentic awareness of the prerogatives of the defence. Therefore, merely formal presumptions of awareness are in no way compatible with EU law.[9]

3   The Informational Rights of Persons Under Arrest

Legislative Decree no. 101 of 2014 regulates the Letter of Rights for those whose personal freedom is restricted, interpolating numerous dispositions of the Code of criminal procedure.

More specifically, Art. 293 para. 1 and Art. 386 para. 1 have been modified, which respectively govern the application of custodial precautionary measure ("misura cautelare custodiale"), and arrest or temporary detention ("arresto o fermo"). According to such provisions, the detainee must receive written information indicating a series of rights relating to technical and personal defence (in particular informing about the right to silence, the right to an interpreter and translator, the right to be heard by the competent judicial authority within certain deadlines), making the accused aware of the accusation and indicating the documents justifying his detention. The ways to challenge the decision on the deprivation of liberty, the right to medical assistance and the right to inform a third party should also be mentioned. Alongside this, there should be a verbal communication, followed by the consignment of a written document to the accused who does not speak Italian, where a written communication in his mother tongue is not promptly available (Art. 293, para. 1-bis and Art. 386, para. 1-bis). Furthermore, in the case of custodial precautionary measures, an immediate communication to the defence lawyer should be provided (Art. 294, para. 1-bis), as already prescribed by Art. 386, para. 2 for arrest or temporary detention. According to Art. 293, para. 1-ter and Art. 386, para. 3, the submissions of such communications must be mentioned in the police report.

The effective and correct fulfilment of the informational duties is controlled at the time of the questioning following the custodial precautionary measure and at the time of the hearing following the arrest or temporary detention (Arts. 294, para. 1-bis and 391, para. 2). However, this control, rather than aimed at protecting the individual, seems to offer the judicial authorities the opportunity to amend previous shortcomings. Should information relating to defence rights have been wholly or partially omitted by the arresting authority, the judge is required to give it for the first time or to complete it. In this way the invalidity deriving from the violation of the

---

[9]Gialuz (2015), pp. 106–107.

rights of the defence because of the omission or defective communication to the arrested person can be regularised. However, it should be noted that, doing so, the role of the questioning *ex* Art. 294 and of the hearing following the arrest or temporary detention is shifted from that of a guarantee for the accused to that of an occasion useful to regularise invalidities caused by the non-fulfilment of activities imposed to the investigating authority. Despite such a solution assures formal respect for the informational guarantee, its most substantial significance—making sure the accused is aware of his rights in due time—remains futile.

The right of being informed about procedural rights for those who are not detained is ensured by Italian Code of criminal procedure under Art. 369-bis. This rule provides a written communication on self-defence and technical/professional assistance, including the right to legal aid for the less privileged.[10] This provision assures a higher level of protection than the European one, which allows a simple verbal communication.

Directive 2012/13/EU helps to solve doubts about the general scope of the information provided by Art. 369-bis. Some interpretations argued that information about powers and rights assigned by the law to the accused [Art. 369-bis, para. 2, a)] should be only given when acts at which the investigated person's defence counsel has the right to be present must be performed ('guaranteed acts').[11] The European source stipulates that the accused should be given all the information he is entitled to receive at least before the end of the preliminary phase.[12] The internal transposition of the European Directive confirms such formulation. The first paragraph of Art. 369-bis now states that the communication must take place "at the latest, together with the notice of the conclusion of preliminary investigations". This implies that the notification should take place independently from the completion of 'guaranteed acts', thereby dissolving the tie between the special function of each of these acts and the informational duties required prior to them.

Even though at first sight the all-inclusive nature of this communication might suggest greater protection for the accused, on a closer inspection this impression is debatable. The effective exercise of the whole gamut of defence rights depends on the pertinence of the information in relationship to each single act that has to be performed. That is to say that a general catalogue enumerating all the accused's prerogatives during the entire course of the proceeding weakens the real degree of awareness and disorients the layman.

A further change brought by Legislative Decree no. 101 of 2014 regards communication on the right to an interpreter and on the right to translation of fundamental acts [Art. 369-bis, para. 2, d-bis)]. This creates a connection with the preceding Directive 2010/64/EU, implemented in the domestic legal order by Legislative Decree no. 32 of 4th March 2014. It should be asked whether the fundamental rights to linguistic assistance are also outlined in the communication *ex* art.

---

[10]This provision has been introduced by Law no. 60, 6 March 2001.

[11]Nappi (2001), p. 696.

[12]For this opinion, see Cordova and D'Alterio (2001), p. 60; Ciampi (2010), pp. 472 ff.

369-bis. It would seem preferable to consider the necessity of listing in detail all the rights within this communication, nothing impeding it. To understand the wording of these rights, reference should be made to Art. 143 as modified by Legislative Decree no. 32 of 4th March 2014. Its greater detail makes it an essential reference.

In modifying Art. 369-bis, the legislator has however omitted to explain whether the communication shall contain also the information about the right to silence. The need for such information to be mentioned among the "rights attributable by law to the accused"—referred to in letter *a* of the mentioned Article—is sanctioned *expressis verbis* by Art. 3, para. 1, e) of Directive 2012/13/EU. By inserting such communication into the information given in view of 'guaranteed acts' and also in the invitation for questioning, the awareness of the guarantee of *nemo tenetur se detegere*, already subject to oral communication by the prosecuting authority at questioning [Art. 64, para. 3, b)], is anticipated and therefore increased.

Art. 369-bis also presents an aspect of dubious compatibility with the European Directive. At domestic level, the information of one's rights is only required when, in view of 'guaranteed acts" or upon notice of the conclusion of preliminary investigations, the counsel is appointed by the Court, but not when the accused has designated a trusted lawyer. However, the Directive does not cite any distinction on informational guarantees in relation to the existence of a trusting relationship on a professional level. There ought to be a legislative intervention since Art. 369-bis is sufficiently clear to exclude the admission of any operation aimed at extending its scope of application.[13] Lacking any *ad hoc* provision, it should anyway be asked if, at a national level, judicial authorities can directly apply Art. 3 of Directive 2012/13/UE. The answer may be yes. Although the Directive is an Act referring to all Member States which must be implemented by the respective national legislators, the Court of Justice already stated that under certain conditions EU legislation can have direct effects.[14] When Art. 3 is read in light of Recital 19 of the Preamble, it would seem to possess all the necessary requirements to unfold direct effects, given that it is an unconditional provision, sufficiently clear and precise, which the Member State has failed to implement when transposing Directive 2012/13/EU.

National rules do not expressly require the use of simple and accessible language for the communication specified in Art. 369-bis, but such obligation is clearly imposed to Member States by the Directive 2012/13/EU in Art. 3, para. 2, and Recitals nos. 22 and 38 of the Preamble.

As mentioned previously, an important novelty in Legislative Decree no. 101 of 2014 regards the need that information on the rights of defence is in any case notified at the latest together with the notice of the conclusion of preliminary investigations (Art. 415-bis). The provision tends to avoid the accused being excluded from the benefits of communication when, in the investigation stage, no 'guaranteed acts' were performed. If that were to happen, at the outcome of the investigations there would be the notification of a complex communication: the notices prescribed by

---

[13]Ciampi (2014), pp. 17–18.

[14]See ECJ, 4 December 1974, *Van Duyn*, C-41/74, and ECJ, 5 April 1979, *Ratti*, C-148/78.

Art. 415-bis, together with information provided under Art. 369-bis. So, any omission of the latter too, or anything missing from the list would be sufficient to invalidate the concluding act of the investigations, with catastrophic effects on the indictment as laid out in Art. 416.

It is worth adding that the range of information provided to the accused as per Art. 415-bis, particularly since it is so closely tied chronologically to the trial, ought to include a catalogue of the highlighted rights for any subsequent phase in the proceeding. So, for example, should the suspect become formally accused, he would be made aware of his right to be present at the trial.

4 In Particular: The Right to Be Informed of the Charge

As regards the right to be informed of the charges, the central provision of the national procedural system is Art. 369. It provides for 'notice of investigation' ("informazione di garanzia") when, during the preliminary investigations, a 'guaranteed act' must be carried out. Such information shall indicate the space-time coordinates of the facts and its provisional legal qualification.

If read as a 'monad' in the procedural system, the 'notice of investigation' does not cover the levels of protection required by Art. 6 of the 2012/13/EU Directive. A systematic interpretation of Art. 369 together with Arts. 335 and 415-bis is thus required. Legislative Decree no. 101 of 2014 reinforces and specifies the connection between 'notice of investigation' and the right set out in the third paragraph of Art. 335. Art. 369 par. 1-bis establishes that the 'notice of investigation' should include a notification of the right of access to the register of *notitiae criminis* (Art. 335). This prerogative allows the accused to be informed of the accusation at that moment in the proceeding. So then, where the defence exercises such right, it could be aware of any subsequent modifications in the charge. In any case, as the preliminary investigations are over, following the notification specified in Art. 415-bis, the accused and his defence should know the minutest details of the accusation as well as any eventual variations. In the notice of the conclusion of preliminary investigations, not only the provisions allegedly violated are indicated, the date and place of the facts reported, but also a detailed account of the facts according to the investigations' reconstruction.

As we have seen, the Directive requires Member States to guarantee that persons suspected or accused in criminal proceedings are promptly informed of any significant changes to the accusation. This communication must be made every time it "is necessary to safeguard the fairness of the proceedings" (Art. 6, para. 4), or, as specified in Recital 29 of the Preamble, whenever the accusation is changed, "to the extent that the position of suspects or accused persons is substantially affected". It is worth asking if providing the information on the accused's initiative falls within the EU Directive. The best answer would seem to be no.

The Directive sees the defence's role as merely passive, as an addressee of information relating to any significant change in the charge. Now, if nothing prohibits a Member State from providing informative mechanisms actuated by the accused or his defence by which they may be informed of unsubstantial modifications of the charge, it does not seem worth excluding any communication incumbent on the competent authority for all those changes significantly affecting the accused. This said, it does not seem possible to attribute any direct effects to Art. 6, para. 4 of the 2012/13/EU Directive.

This provision is necessarily conditioned by detailed internal rules which govern cases in which the information is due and those in which, by contrast, it is possible to update the crime records *ex* Art. 335, para. 2 without informing the defence. Yet again, it remains to be questioned whether the wording of the internal rule can be interpreted to fit the EU parameters.[15] However, the absence of any textual basis for identifying communication obligations which disregard defence initiatives leads to a negative answer.

The situation is further complicated considering the exceptions to the right of access to the register of *notitiae criminis* mentioned in Art. 335. These provisions are likely to cripple the right to know the accusation both from the start and, more so, as far as variations are concerned. In fact, the 'notice of investigation' is only due when the defence counsel has the right to be present.

Referring to the above derogations, as per the third paragraph of Art. 335, whenever the proceedings concern one of the serious crimes listed in Art. 407, para. 2, a), the rule of communicating any variation is automatically and without exception substituted by the rule of secrecy. The critical profile of this provision operates around its generality and invulnerability, meaning that it works quite apart from any reference to the single case which may impede communication *ex* Art. 335, for the only reason that the case concerns a crime listed in Art. 407, para. 2, a). It would seem dubious that this provision is compatible with the provisions of the EU Directive on the right to information, especially considering that the legal qualification of the criminal act allows the public prosecutor broad discretion. This is even more true at the initial stage of the proceedings, given the shortfall and precariousness of the investigative evidence. All things considered, there is a concrete risk that the required legal classification should result in arbitrariness where there is no guarantee of some form of jurisdictional control over it. There is no provision on this specific aspect in the Code of criminal procedure, and so the risk of forced legal definitions by the prosecutor—in order to classify the criminal act within the cases which impede access to the register of *notitiae criminis*, so as to paralyse defence rights—cannot be ruled out.[16]

The second derogation in communicating the charge is the case in which it is necessary to protect specific investigative requirements (Art. 335, para. 3-bis). It seems evident that there is ample room to manoeuvre for whoever decides to take

---

[15]On harmonious interpretation and the role of national judges, see Bontempelli (2014), pp. 82–84.
[16]Ciampi (2010), pp. 242–244.

advantage of secrecy about crime records. For this reason, it would have been more appropriate to attribute the competence on this point to the judge for preliminary investigations rather than to the public prosecutor.[17]

It should be highlighted that a fair exegesis of the internal rule limits its scope of application to the preceding moments of delivering the 'notice of investigation' or any other procedural act or judicial decision which discloses the accusation. From that moment on there is no justification for denying access to the register *ex* Art. 335.[18] Nevertheless, no procedural means can be used to challenge the refusal to access the crime records, despite the charge having been already communicated. After all, the legislator does not even worry about providing for redress in case of lack of response to the defence request of access as per Art. 335. From this point of view, the national rule cannot fully conform to the EU one. Art. 8, para. 2 of the 2012/13/EU Directive requires Member States to provide for the right to challenge the possible failure or refusal of the competent authorities to provide due information.

5 Continued: The Right of Access to the Materials of the Case

As far as the right of access to the investigative records is concerned, the legislator assumes that national rules comply with the standards of European protection. In effect, national rules provide a series of prerogatives each of which is applied at various stages of the criminal proceedings, and together protect the right of access to the investigative records.

As far as custodial precautionary measures are concerned, the combined effects of Art. 293, para. 3, and Art. 291, para. 1 allow the accused and his defence to access and copy the decision applying the precautionary measure, the request by the Public Prosecutor and the elements upon which the latter is founded together with the elements favouring the defence. As regards arrest and preventive detention, access to the records by the defence is covered by Arts. 386, 388 and 391. These dispositions allow the appointment of a defence lawyer, his swift involvement in the proceedings, as well as, in the case of questioning by the Public Prosecutor, the access to information regarding the accusation, the reasons behind the decision on the limitation of personal liberty, the charge and the related sources of evidence, excepting that which could prejudice the investigations; finally there is a jurisdictional check at the hearing following the arrest or temporary detention.

The Code of criminal procedure further provides a generalised and complete obligation to disclose the investigation acts in Art. 415-bis. After the investigative phase, should the Public Prosecutor be intentioned to prosecute, he must notify the

---

[17]Ciampi (2014), p. 8.
[18]Ciampi (2014), pp. 8–9.

notice of the conclusion of preliminary investigations, which specifies, among other things, that the defence has the right of access to all the investigative materials held by the secretary of the Public Prosecutor. Finally, various norms provide for the disclosure of the investigative materials after the indictment, thus guaranteeing access to the investigative materials in the trial. It is a well-articulated sequence of norms guaranteeing access to the investigative records both in ordinary proceedings and in special ones (Art. 416, para. 2, Art. 419, para. 2, Art. 450, para. 6, Art. 454, para. 2, Art. 457, and Art. 552, para. 4).

There is in effect a satisfactory level of protecting the right of the defence to be made aware of investigative acts previously covered by investigative secrecy. Nevertheless, the legislator might have taken advantage of the necessity to adapt internal rules to EU norms in order to modify certain critical aspects of this particular discipline.

As regards disclosure in the context of precautionary measures, for example, it should be noted that the selection of the materials to be presented to the judge is done unilaterally by the Public Prosecutor. Often, in identifying materials which are favourable to the suspect and which might hinder upholding a prosecution instance, the magistrate holds a significant and unchallengeable margin of appreciation.[19] The possibility that the Public Prosecutor omits to transmit certain elements which might negatively influence a judicial evaluation on the restriction of liberty does not seem to be subject to any procedural sanction.

Analogously, in relation to Art. 415-bis, one could ask what the consequences would be of a merely partial revelation of the investigative materials. Given that in such a case the Public Prosecutor's position would be unlawful since the lack of discretionary margin in depositing the investigative materials, the case-law is uniform in considering the unrevealed acts inadmissible.[20] Whereas, by virtue of the principle of exhaustiveness of the grounds for nullity (Art. 177), there is a tendency to exclude that, in the event in question, indictment is null. In truth, this defect is not due to a violation of a probative prohibition nor to a case of so-called 'physiological inadmissibility' due to separation between different stages of the proceedings.[21] Moreover, the consequences of exclusionary rule might lead to paradoxical results. Just imagine the case in which the failure to deposit investigative materials regards materials in favour of the defendant. This would lead to penalising the defence by a violation of Art. 415-bis put in place by the Public Prosecutor. This would also imply the risk that the Public Prosecutor may opportunistically ban from the proceedings acts favourable to the defence.[22]

---

[19]Illuminati (1996), pp. 100–101.

[20]See, for example, Italian Court of Cassation, Sez. IV, 8 November 2013, Stuppia and others, in *C. E.D. Cass.*, n. 259,121; Italian Court of Cassation, Sez. V, 22 April 2009, Abbruzzese and others, in *C.E.D. Cass.*, n. 243,899; Italian Court of Cassation, Sez. III, 15 October 2003, Spagnoletto and others, in *C.E.D. Cass.*, n. 226346.

[21]Ciampi (2014), pp. 27–28.

[22]For similar considerations, see Ciampi (2014), p. 29.

In hindsight, tracing back the hypothesis of a partial disclosure to a nullity, far from contrasting the current principle of exhaustiveness of the grounds for nullity, would seem to be the most appropriate option. The complete revelation of the materials imposed by Art. 415-bis allows real and effective defensive prerogatives, as covered by the subsequent third paragraph of the mentioned Article. Furthermore, the close connection between revealing the investigative materials and defence rights is confirmed by the dispositions in Directive 2012/13/EU. In the light of these rules, violating the obligation to deposit investigative materials results in a violation of the ability for the accused to intervene in the proceedings, which therefore constitutes an intermediate nullity, as laid out in Art. 178, c), and Art. 180. This invalidity reverberates on the indictment as per Art. 185. Consequently, when there is only partial disclosure of the investigative materials, the judge would have to call for a nullity, this determining a regression of the proceedings.

References

Bontempelli M (2014) Le garanzie processuali e il diritto dell'Unione europea fra legge e giudice. Processo penale e giustizia 3:80–92

Ciampi S (2010) L'informazione dell'indagato nel procedimento penale. Giuffrè, Milan

Ciampi S (2012) La direttiva del Parlamento europeo e del Consiglio sul diritto all'informazione nei procedimenti penali. http://www.penalecontemporaneo.it. 27 June 2012

Ciampi S (2013) Letter of Rights e Full Disclosure nella direttiva europea sul diritto all'informazione. Diritto penale e processo 1:21–27

Ciampi S (2014) Diritto all'informazione nei procedimenti penali: il recepimento low profile della direttiva 2012/13/UE da parte del d.lgs. 1° luglio 2014 n. 101. http://www.penalecontemporaneo.it. 24 Sept 2014

Cordova A, D'alterio A (2001) L'obbligo (oneroso) di comunicare facoltà e diritti con l'atto garantito. Diritto e giustizia 16:49–65

Gialuz M (2015) Dalla Corte di giustizia importanti indicazioni esegetiche in relazione alle prime due direttive sui diritti dell'imputato. Diritto penale contemporaneo 4:100–107

Illuminati G (1996) Presupposti delle misure cautelari e procedimento applicativo. In: Grevi V (ed) Misure cautelari e diritto di difesa nella l. 8 agosto 1995 n. 332. Giuffrè, Milan, pp 67–111

Nappi A (2001) Indagini preliminari (disposizioni generali). In: Enciclopedia del diritto, vol 5. Giuffè, Milan, pp 686–698

Negri D (2014) L'imputato presente al processo. Una ricostruzione sistematica. Giappichelli, Turin

Rafaraci T (2014) Diritti fondamentali, giusto processo e primato del diritto UE. Processo penale e giustizia 3:1–5

Ruggeri S (2015) Procedimento penale, diritto di difesa e garanzie partecipative nel diritto dell'Unione europea. http://www.penalecontemporaneo.it. 22 Sept 2015

The Right of Access to a Lawyer in the European Union: Directive 2013/48/EU and Its Implementation in Spain

Mar Jimeno-Bulnes

Contents

Abstract In light of the necessity to combine the EU pro-victim policy with that favouring the rights of the accused, striking a difficult balance between the two sides of criminal proceedings to ensure the quality of criminal justice as a whole, after the adoption of Directive 2012/29/EU which established minimum standards on the rights, support and protection of the victims of crime, the EU adopted different measures on the minimum procedural rights of defendants. In this paper, the Author focusses her attention on Directive 2013/48/EU, 22 October 2013, on the right of access to a lawyer and its implementation into the Spanish legal system.

The financial support of the Spanish Ministry of Economy and the European Commission is gratefully acknowledged (Research Projects 'A step forward in the consolidation of the European judicial area and its practical application in Spain: from the perspective of civil and criminal procedures', DER2015-71418-P and Best practices for EUROpean COORDination on investigative measures and evidence gathering, EUROCOORD, JUST-2015-JCOO-AG, 723198). Also thanks to Cristina Ruiz López for editing.

M. Jimeno-Bulnes (✉)
University of Burgos, Faculty of Law, Burgos, Spain
e-mail: mjimeno@ubu.es

© Springer Nature Switzerland AG 2019
T. Rafaraci, R. Belfiore (eds.), *EU Criminal Justice*,
https://doi.org/10.1007/978-3-319-97319-7_4

1   Introduction: In Defence of the Rights of the Accused

In recent times, it seems that the legislative landscape at both European and national levels has seen a shift to favour protecting the rights of victims in criminal proceedings. It is not necessary to recall here the adoption of Directive 2012/29/EU of the European Parliament and of the Council of 25 October 2012, establishing minimum standards on the rights, support and protection of victims of crime,[1] implemented in Spain by Law no. 4/2015, of April 27, on the Statute of the Victims of Crime[2] in the Spanish framework. This was adopted in response to the demand, by both scholars[3] and civil society, for a balanced position of the victim in criminal proceedings through the development of a "charter of guarantees".[4]

However, this pro-victim policy must be combined with one in favour of the rights of the accused since, undoubtedly, any increase in the level of protection of a party in the proceedings produces its impact on the level of protection of the counterparty (the accused, in a procedural system founded on a dual structure), and possibly jeopardise the very quality of criminal proceedings as a whole. This is the line of work undertaken both by the European Union, on the basis of various Directives on procedural rights, and by national legislations implementing them. Thus, Directive 2013/48/EU of 22 October 2013 on the right of access to a lawyer[5] seeks to maintain the difficult balance between the two sides in criminal proceedings.

The right of access to a lawyer is at the heart of the right to defence as a fundamental right (for some, a human right), which has been largely responsible for the great political difficulty in reaching the necessary agreement on procedural rights by the Member States of the Union. Certainly, the Directive does not deal exclusively with the aforementioned right but provides joint regulation of two of the measures cited in the roadmap set out by Council Resolution of 30 November 2009, under the heading "Roadmap for strengthening procedural rights of suspected or accused persons in criminal proceedings".[6] This roadmap has modified some legislative techniques of the European Union by foreseeing different measures to protect the procedural rights of the accused in criminal proceedings, in a 'step by step' approach, given the failure of a general proposal initially drafted by the European Commission.

---

[1]OJEU, 14 November 2012, No. L 315, pp. 57–73; error correction in OJEU, 10 December, 2014, No. L 353, pp. 23–24.

[2]BOE [Spain's Official Journal], 28 April, 2015, No. 101, pp. 36569–36598.

[3]See, among others, Magro Servet (2010).

[4]Burgos Ladrón de Guevara (2015).

[5]Directive 2013/48/EU of the European Parliament and of the Council of 22 October 2013 on the right of access to a lawyer in criminal proceedings and in European arrest warrant proceedings, and on the right to have a third party informed upon deprivation of liberty and to communicate with third persons and with consular authorities while deprived of liberty, OJEU, 6 November 2013, No. L 294, pp. 1–12.

[6]OJEU, 4 December 2009, No. C 295, pp. 1–3.

Prior to this Directive, Directives achieving measure A (Translation and interpretation) and measure B (Information on rights and information on charges) were adopted: Directive 2010/64/EU of the European Parliament and of the Council of 20 October 2010 on the right to interpretation and translation in criminal proceedings,[7] and Directive 2012/13/EU of the European Parliament and of the Council of 22 May 2012 on the right to information in criminal proceedings.[8] Two final texts were also recently adopted concerning measure E (Special safeguards for accused persons or suspects that are vulnerable), which is Directive 2016/800/EU of the European Parliament and of the Council of 11 May 2016 on procedural safeguards for children who are suspects or accused persons in criminal proceedings,[9] and part of measure C (the right to legal aid), which is Directive 2016/1919 of the European Parliament and of the Council of 26 October 2016 on legal aid for suspects and accused persons in criminal proceedings and for requested persons in European arrest warrant proceedings.[10] A Directive on measure F (Green Paper on provisional detention) is still to be adopted.

In particular, Directive 2013/48/EU deals with measures C and D concerning legal advice and legal aid (measure C), and communication with relatives, employers and consular authorities (measure D). However, the analysis carried out here will deal only with the first measure, which is sufficient to appreciate the necessary changes in usage and customs that its application causes at the national level.

The legislative history of this Directive will be examined together with its general aspects so as to elucidate the change from the initial proposal of joint regulation of the right of access to a lawyer together with the right to free legal aid; also its scope of application from territorial, temporal, subjective and objective perspectives will be considered, followed by an analysis of its explicit and implicit content, as well as an analysis of the current Spanish framework with some brief final remarks.

2 General Aspects: The Lack of Regulation of the Right to Legal Aid

Directive 2013/48/EU of the European Parliament and of the Council of 22 October 2013, under the extensive and unfortunate title "Directive on the right of access to a lawyer in criminal proceedings and in European arrest warrant proceedings, and on the right to have a third party informed upon deprivation of liberty and to communicate with third persons and with consular authorities while deprived of liberty" does not deal exclusively with the right of access to a lawyer. In fact, as above, the Directive includes, in addition to measure C (legal advice and legal aid), measure D

---

[7]OJEU, 26 October 2010, No. L 280, pp. 1–7.
[8]OJEU, 1 June 2012, No. L 142, pp. 1–10.
[9]OJEU, 21 May 2016, No. L 132, pp. 1–20.
[10]OJEU, 4 November 2016, No. L 297, pp. 1–8.

(communication with relatives, employers and consular authorities), which will not be dealt with in this paper.

However, Directive 2013/48/EU does not provide for the complete regulation of measure C since it excludes any reference to the right to legal aid. The omission is intentional as explained by the European Commission, which understood that the issue "deserves a separate proposal because of its specificity and complexity", according to the report that accompanied the then proposal for a Directive.[11] Indubitably, legal aid was also subject to difficult negotiations in light of past difficulties with adopting Directive 2013/48/EU and during negotiations on the former proposal for a Council Framework Decision on certain procedural rights in criminal proceedings, presented by the Commission in Brussels on 28 April 2004. It is not surprising that the failure of this proposal was essentially due to the lack of agreement between Member States in relation to this procedural right.

Indeed, the greatest criticism of Directive 2013/48/EU concerned the lack of regulation of the right to legal aid, as originally envisaged in the Roadmap on procedural rights proposed by the Council in 2009, as well as in the former proposal for a Framework Decision, drafted by the Commission in 2004. Criticisms with which I do not particularly agree since I had already sustained elsewhere[12] separate regulation of these two guarantees, by understanding that the right to legal aid covers not only legal assistance but, as in Spanish legislation, many other services as well.

Notwithstanding the above, there is evident need to simultaneously regulate both rights, even in different legislative instruments, to give true effectiveness to the right of access to a lawyer; this emerges also from the case-law of the European Court of Human Rights (ECtHR),[13] where the obligation to provide legal aid has been imposed on State authorities when required by the economic situation of the accused in criminal proceedings. The opposite would undoubtedly give rise to discriminatory practices in applying the right of access to a lawyer in the Member States, since its effective application at national level would depend on effectively protecting the right to legal aid in that same country. This would result, in particular, as far as the right of access to a lawyer is concerned, in the *ex-officio* appointment of a lawyer.

Any shortcomings in this area have been compensated for by the praiseworthy work done by various NGOs which pay special attention to protecting procedural rights and guarantees throughout the European Union, as well as the rights to defence and legal assistance in particular. These NGOs include, for example, *Fair Trials International* (FTI), which combines the tireless work of law firms and individual practitioners. They all operate *pro bono* in different Member States of the European Union to provide legal assistance in cross-border cases, both where a

---

[11] Proposal for a Directive of the European Parliament and of the Council on the right of access to a lawyer in criminal proceedings and the right to communicate upon arrest, presented in Brussels on June 8, 2011, document COM (2011) 326 final, p. 1. The Spanish version of the final text has replaced the word "lawyer" with "counsel".

[12] Jimeno-Bulnes (2010), p. 11.

[13] See: *Artico v. Italy*, 13 May 1980, and *Pakelli v. Germany*, 25 April 1983.

foreigner is accused in criminal proceedings, or a person is sought under the European arrest warrant.

The immediate promulgation of a normative text at European level recognising the right to legal aid to ensure the effectiveness of the right of access to a lawyer at national level was thus necessary. A final text was finally adopted,[14] which is the above mentioned Directive 2016/1919/EU on legal aid for suspects and accused persons in criminal proceedings and for requested persons in European arrest warrant proceedings.

3 Scope of Application from a Triple Perspective

In accordance with the above, the purpose of the Directive is to establish "minimum common standards" with regards to the rights of the accused, as explicitly affirmed under Art. 1 and confirmed under Recital 8 of the Preamble. The measure concerns the rights of suspects and accused persons in criminal proceedings "to have access to a lawyer, to have a third party informed of the deprivation of liberty and to communicate with third persons and with consular authorities while deprived of liberty".

However, the scope of application of the Directive is expressly stated in Art. 2 from a threefold perspective: subjective, objective and temporal, the territorial one being dealt with under Recitals 58 and 59 of the Preamble. The Directive provides for the exclusion of the United Kingdom, Ireland and Denmark, which have made use of their particular position in the area of freedom, security and justice using the *opt-in/opt-out* clause.

As far as the subjective perspective of the scope of application is concerned, it refers to suspects or accused persons in criminal proceedings *ex* Art. 2, para. 1, regardless of their nationality, in compliance with Art. 14 European Convention on Human Rights (ECHR), which is an interpretative parameter of this provision. However, and with extensive effect, this provision also applies to those persons other than suspects or accused persons who, in the course of questioning by the police or by another law enforcement authority, become suspects or accused persons, according to Art. 2, para. 3. Still, from the subjective perspective, the Directive applies to persons subject to European arrest warrant proceedings (requested persons) from the time of their arrest in the executing Member State, as provided by Art. 2, para. 2. Therefore, this Directive, as well as all the Directives on minimum procedural rights also applies to proceedings (other than 'criminal proceedings') of judicial cooperation in criminal matters based on the principle of mutual recognition.

The objective scope of application concerns on-going or future criminal proceedings, since the right of access to a lawyer and the right to communication apply from the start of questioning by the police or by another law enforcement authority

---

[14]After the presentation of this paper.

(before formal proceedings have started). As above, it also concerns proceedings that give execution to European arrest warrants. Even in these proceedings, the right of access to a lawyer is guaranteed in accordance with national procedural law, in compliance with Art. 11, para. 2 Framework Decision 2002/584/JHA.[15] By contrast, proceedings before administrative authorities competent to apply administrative sanctions in respect of minor offences are expressly excluded from the scope of application of the Directive. This however applies if such a sanction is appealed or referred to a court with jurisdiction in criminal matters. An exception to this rule is provided where deprivation of liberty can be imposed as a sanction: in this case, the Directive always applies, according to Art. 2, para. 4.

Last, on temporal scope of application, there has been much debate, including within the Council, during the Directive negotiations and especially negotiations of the previous proposal for a Framework Decision on procedural rights. The problem arises with the right of access to a lawyer and its guarantee in the pre-trial stage, given the differences between the criminal procedural laws of Member States. Indeed, there are still countries where the lawyer "does not enter the police station" or "enters late", as opposed to other countries, such as Spain [see Art. 520, paras. 1, c) and 4 Criminal Procedure Act or *Ley de Enjuiciamiento Criminal,* henceforth LECrim] where this is not the case.

However, the Directive addresses this issue insofar as it provides for its application to persons other than suspects or accused persons who, in the course of questioning by the police or by another law enforcement authority, become suspects or accused persons. This is in line with the "*Salduz* doctrine",[16] established by the ECtHR in the interpretation of Art. 6, para. 3, c) ECHR, where the Court has ruled that formal qualification in procedural terms is irrelevant to these effects.[17] Therefore, the rights under this Directive will have their *dies a quo* in the first moment of the accusation, and their *dies ad quem* in the conclusion of the proceedings, which is understood to mean the final determination of the question whether the suspect or accused person has committed the offence, including, where applicable, sentencing and the resolution of any appeal.

---

[15]Council Framework Decision of 13 June 2002 on the European arrest warrant and the surrender procedures between Member States, OJEU of 18 July 2002, No. L 190, pp. 1–18, as amended by Framework Decision 2009/299/JHA of 26 February 2009, OJEU, 27 March 2009, No. L 81, pp. 24–36.

[16]See *Salduz v. Turkey*, 27 November 2008, pp. 52 ff. More recently, see *Yilmaz Demir v. Turkey*, 15 October 2013, and *Navone et others v. Monaco*, 24 October, 2013.

[17]See *Brusco v. France*, 14 October 2010, pp. 44 ff.

4 Content: Rights Recognised in the Directive and Others Missing

Formally, Art. 3 provides for the right of access to a lawyer, regulates its content and is supported by Arts. 4, 9 and 10, which introduce specific regulation concerning the confidentiality of communications between the accused and his lawyer, the possibility of waiving the right to legal assistance, and the right of access to a lawyer in European arrest warrant proceedings. In addition, Art. 11 specifically refers to legal aid, which, far from being regulated, accords with the Charter of Fundamental Rights of the European Union and the ECHR.[18] Last, the general provisions for rights established in this Directive, namely Arts. 8, 12 and 13 (in addition, of course, to the formal ones in Arts. 14 ff.) must also be considered; they concern, respectively, general conditions for applying temporary derogations, effective remedy under national law in the event of a breach of the rights under this Directive, and the particular needs of vulnerable suspects and vulnerable accused persons.[19]

By systematically interpreting all the provisions relating to the right of access to a lawyer, it is possible to affirm that this Directive recognises the indissoluble relationship between the right to defence and the right of access to a lawyer. Undoubtedly, the right of access to a lawyer is essential in criminal proceedings, constituting perhaps the fundamental axis of the right to defence and, therefore, of due process. This is expressly provided for in the Directive, in the understanding that access to a lawyer is what makes it possible, for suspects or accused persons, to "exercise their rights of defence practically and effectively" (Art. 3, para. 1). For this reason, it requires Member States to ensure it "without undue delay" (Art. 3, para. 2) and, in any event, from whichever of the following points in time is the earliest: (a) before suspects or accused persons are questioned by the police or by another law enforcement or judicial authority; (b) upon the carrying out by investigating or other competent authorities of an investigative or other evidence-gathering act, such as identity parades, confrontations, or reconstructions of the scene of a crime; (c) after deprivation of liberty; (d) where suspects or accused persons have been summoned to appear before a court having jurisdiction in criminal matters, in due time before they appear before that court.

Art. 3, para. 3 establishes the obligations imposed on Member States as addressees of the Directive. They shall ensure that suspects or accused persons: (a) have the right to meet in private and communicate with the lawyer representing them, including prior to questioning by the police or by another law enforcement or judicial authority; (b) have the right for their lawyer to be present and participate

---

[18]Arts. 47, para. 3, Charter of Fundamental Rights of the European Union, and 6, para. 3, c) ECHR.

[19]Directive 2016/800/EU of the European Parliament and of the Council of 11 May 2016 on procedural safeguards for children who are suspects or accused persons in criminal proceedings was adopted; however, as its title and Recital 1 of the Preamble show, this Directive concerns only "persons under the age of 18 years".

effectively when questioned; (c) have, as a minimum, the right for their lawyer to attend certain investigative or evidence-gathering acts, i.e. identity parades, confrontations, or reconstructions of the scene of a crime. These provisions, as well as the preamble, have clarified and, where appropriate, established the conditions of such rights with particular attention to provisions of national criminal procedural law of the Member States.

With regard to right to private communications, the special provision concerning confidentiality under Art. 4 must be considered requiring Member States to respect the confidentiality of all forms of communication between a client and his lawyer; this issue may have caused said debate during the process of negotiation of the Directive. Anyway, and in the light of the current provisions, confidentiality will affect any communication between suspects or accused persons and their lawyer which may take place in person (meetings), otherwise (correspondence, telephone conversations), or in any other forms permitted under national law.

Art. 3, para. 4 requires Member States to ensure the effectiveness of this right, in accordance with the relevant rulings of the ECtHR, where the importance of information given to suspects or accused persons is affirmed. In addition, it must be recalled that Art. 3, para. 1, a) of Directive 2012/13/EU of the European Parliament and of the Council of 22 May 2012 on the right to information in criminal proceedings states that information concerning, *inter alia*, the right of access to a lawyer must be given "promptly".

Art. 3, para. 5 and 3, para. 6 provide for derogations from the right of access to a lawyer by Member States. A first derogation from the "undue delay" standard is established in consideration of "geographical remoteness" of a suspect or accused person where deprived of liberty [Art. 3, para. 2, c)]. A second derogation from the general right of access to a lawyer applies only at the pre-trial stage, in exceptional circumstances, i.e.: where there is an urgent need to avert serious adverse consequences for the life, liberty or physical integrity of a person, or where immediate action by the investigating authorities is imperative to prevent substantial jeopardy to criminal proceedings.

By contrast, and as far as the Directive's shortcomings are concerned, the right of the accused person to freely appoint a lawyer is not provided for. However, this right has to be considered as implicit in the Directive, in light of the wording of its preamble and the relevant case-law of the ECtHR,[20] which constitutes an interpretative parameter, as already said above; this reading is also confirmed by other international texts applicable to criminal proceedings. Nevertheless, there is a limitation to this right of free appointment, as in some national legal systems, including, by way of example, the Spanish one by virtue of Art. 527, a) LECrim, in the case of '*detención o prisión incommunicada*', where a lawyer may be appointed *ex-officio*.

---

[20]See: *Pakelli v. Germany*, 25 April 1983, p. 31, and *Croissant v. Germany*, 25 September 1992, p. 29. More recently, see: *Dvorski v. Croatia*, 25 October 2015.

There is no explicit mention of the right to self-defence *(right to proceed pro se)* as such, although Art. 9 expressly provides for a waiver of the right of access to a lawyer under the conditions established thereof, to be interpreted in line with European case-law.[21] This is possible, of course, only where national criminal procedures allow it, which is not always the case; the case of Spain is again an example, where legal assistance is mandatory under Art. 520, para. 8 LECrim, with the only exception concerning crimes against traffic safety under the same conditions established by the Directive, as a result of its implementation (anyway, the waiver can be revoked at any time).

Last, on the list of the Directive's shortcomings, subjective conditions and the professional qualifications of lawyers are not included in the Directive. This is so despite the fact that the initial Green Paper on procedural rights proposed quality control in this regard,[22] a quality control established in other international texts.

To conclude the analysis of the right of access to a lawyer as far as its content is concerned, Art. 10 of Directive 2013/48/EU provides for a special rule with regards to the right of access to a lawyer in European Arrest warrant proceedings. It should be recalled that there is the need to guarantee the presence of a lawyer in judicial cooperation proceedings, in accordance with the law applicable to such proceedings; in particular, Art. 11, para. 2 of Framework Decision 2002/584/JHA provides that a requested person who is arrested for the purpose of the execution of a European arrest warrant shall have a right to be assisted by a legal counsel in accordance with the national law of the executing Member State.[23]

Thus, in spite of the existence of a specific provision concerning such a right in the Framework Decision on the European Arrest Warrant, the Directive reiterates that Member States should ensure that a requested person has the right of access to a lawyer in the executing Member State "upon arrest" (Art. 10, para. 1). In the same way, under Art. 10, the Directive provides for the specific content of this right of access to a lawyer in the execution of a European Arrest Warrant, which is quite similar to that provided for under general provision. This raises the question of whether it would have been better to regulate this right in European Arrest Warrant proceedings together with the right provided for under general provision. In European Arrest Warrant proceedings, also the right to meet and communicate with the lawyer, the right for the lawyer to be present, and the right for the lawyer

---

[21] Among others, see: *Foucher v. France,* 18 March 1997, and *Lagerblom v. Sweden,* 14 January 2003.

[22] See the Commission's Green Paper presented in Brussels on 19 February 2003 under the title "Procedural safeguards for suspects and defendants in criminal proceedings in the European Union", COM (2003) 75 final, pp. 26–27.

[23] In Spain, see Article 51, para. 1 Act 23/2014, of 20 November, on mutual recognition of judicial decisions in criminal matters in the European Union (*Ley de reconocimiento mutuo de resoluciones penales en la Unión Europea,* BOE, 21 November, 2014, No. 282, pp. 95437–95593; english version available at http://www.mjusticia.gob.es/cs/Satellite/Portal/es/servicios-ciudadano/ documentacion-publicaciones/publicaciones/traducciones-derecho-espanol, last visit: 8 April 2018).

to participate during a hearing are equally provided for, *mutatis mutandis* (Art. 10, para. 2).

The most interesting aspect of this specific provision concerning the European Arrest Warrant proceedings stems from the provision concerning the right of access to a lawyer even in the issuing Member State, should this right not be enforceable under the general rule; this is certainly an important novelty, even if the writing of the provision is not entirely successful. Thus, the right of access to a lawyer is guaranteed not only in the executing Member State but also in the issuing one, this resulting in what is called 'dual defence' which implies the sharing of information between the two Member States involved.[24]

Indeed, the competent authority in the executing Member State should inform requested persons that they have the right to appoint a lawyer in the issuing Member State. The role of that lawyer in the issuing Member State is to assist the lawyer in the executing Member State by providing him with information and advice in light of the effective exercise of the rights of the requested persons under Framework Decision 2002/584/JHA (Art. 10, para. 4). The Commission argued that this lawyer could provide legal advice of great importance in relation to the legal system of the issuing Member State, in which the person sought is under proceedings; this lawyer may also provide more information concerning grounds for refusal against the surrender of the requested person in the specific case. However—and this is the critical issue—the wording of the provision seems to imply that the role of this second lawyer is merely 'auxiliary' with respect to the first lawyer; although double defence is certainly praiseworthy, this limitation of the right of assistance in favour of the assistance of this second lawyer is not comprehensible.

To conclude on the right of access to a lawyer in European arrest warrant proceedings, and with specific reference to the right of dual defence, recall the obligation of the executing Member State to provide the requested person with the necessary information to ensure the appointment of the lawyer in the issuing Member State. Information is all the more necessary in cases in which free appointment by the requested person is not foreseen. That is why it could be useful to give the requested person a current list of lawyers, or the name of a lawyer on duty in the issuing Member State, as suggested under Recital 46.

---

[24]In these terms, see Aranguena Fanego (2014), p. 22.

5 Spanish Perspective: Legal Regulation and Forensic Practice

As regards Spain, this Directive was punctually and swiftly implemented at the national level by Law no. 13/2015, of 5 October, amending the Criminal Procedure Act for the strengthening of procedural guarantees and the regulation of technological investigation measures,[25] in force since 1 November 2015. Beforehand there was the enactment of Law no. 5/2015, of 27 April, amending the Criminal Procedure Act and Organic Law no. 6/1985, of 1 July, on the General Council of the Judiciary,[26] aimed at the implementation of Directive 2010/64/EU of the European Parliament and of the Council of 20 October 2010 on the right to interpretation and translation in criminal proceedings, and Directive 2012/13/EU of the European Parliament and of the Council of 22 May 2012 on the right to information in criminal proceedings, cited above. However, this was not the last reform of Spanish criminal procedural legislation in a year of amazing legislative turmoil; later, Law no. 41/2015, of 5 October, was adopted, amending again the Act on Criminal Procedure to simplify criminal justice and strengthen procedural guarantees,[27] which terminated the reform of Spanish criminal procedure.

Thus, Law no. 13/2015, of 5 October, amending the Criminal Procedure Act to strengthen procedural guarantees and the regulation of technological investigation measures entailed the re-wording of Arts. 118, 509, 520 and 527, as well as the *ex novo* adoption of Art. 520 *ter* of LECrim "with the introduction of the provisions required by European Union law, among which those of legal assistance for persons deprived of liberty".[28] Such procedural guarantees are now recognised for the "suspect" or "defendant", according to the new wording of Art. 118 LECrim, in line with other European measures as in the case, for example, of the European investigation order in criminal matters.[29]

Law no. 13/2015, of October 5, makes it clear in its preamble that "any person accused of having committed a criminal offence may exercise the right to defence, with no limitations other than those provided under the law, from the time when the offence under investigation is charged against the suspect until the resolution of the punishment", i.e. from the formal charge of the criminal offence until the serving of the sentence. This time frame is also applied as binding by new Art. 118, para. 2 LECrim, in the implementation of rights provided for in the Directive such as, among others, the right of free appointment of a lawyer and the right to meet in private and communicate with the lawyer. The lawyer "shall attend any questioning,

---

[25]BOE, 6 October 2015, No. 239, pp. 90192–90219.

[26]BOE, 28 April 2015, No. 101, pp. 36559–36567.

[27]BOE, 6 October 2015, No. 239, pp. 90220–90239.

[28]Preamble, section III.

[29]Directive 2014/41/EU of the European Parliament and of the Council of 3 April 2014 on the European investigation order in criminal matters, OJEU, 1 May 2014, No. L 130, pp. 1–36. See Jimeno-Bulnes (2016), pp. 25–56.

as well as any act concerning identity parades, confrontations and reconstructions of the scene of a crime", in compliance with Art. 3, para. 3 of Directive 2013/48/EU; the lawyer, though, does not have the right to actively participate in such acts, while active participation is foreseen by new Art. 520, para. 6, b) LECrim within the regime provided for persons under custody/prisoners; this choice, of course, has been criticised[30] since different case by case treatments are not justifiable.

Of special interest and a novelty is the recognition of the right to meet in private and communicate with the lawyer already from the time when the offence under investigation is charged against the suspect; indeed, this has determined a higher level of protection of the right of access to a lawyer in Spain. In particular, Art. 118, para. 2 LECrim explicitly and clearly provides that client and lawyer shall communicate and meet in private "even before the accused receives a declaration by the police, the prosecutor or the judicial authority, without prejudice to Art. 527". It is not difficult to guess that the special interest and novelty of this provision concern especially the declaration by the police; in fact, this was the first issue raised in the association of Spanish lawyers that called for direct effects of the Directive right after its adoption, which, in principle, could only be invoked once the deadline for implementation had expired, which has not been the case in Spain.

Similarly, Art. 520, para. 6, d) LECrim provides for the new and effective right for detainees to "meet in private" the lawyer, "even before receiving a declaration by the police, the prosecutor or the judicial authority, without prejudice to Art. 527"; a private meeting guaranteed also by current Art. 520, para. 7 LECrim. These are provisions that cannot be fully understood without a systematic interpretation of the whole regulation concerning the protection of the accused and, in particular, as far as the questioning by the police is concerned, the right of the detainee to communicate with his lawyer, including via telephone or video-conference where the geographical distance does not permit personal communication, as a distinct right from the right to personal communication via private meetings, as recognised under the Directive.

Together with the right to meet in private and communicate with the lawyer, "the right to examine proceedings in due time in order to safeguard the right to defence and, in any case, before delivering statements" and "the right to access proceedings that are essential to challenge the legality of detention or imprisonment orders" are provided for under Arts. 118, para. 1, b) and 520, para. 2, d) LECrim.

Indeed, these last articles are the result of the implementation of Directive 2012/13/EU of the European Parliament and of the Council of 22 May 2012 on the right to information in criminal proceedings, mentioned before, and, together with the Directive 2013/48 and all the other relevant measures in this sector, constitute the current legal statute of the defendant in any criminal proceedings carried out at national level. Also, Spanish regulation adds provisions addressed to the bodies that have to guarantee accused persons and detainees effective compliance with the right

---

[30]See Molina García (2015), p. 22.

of access to a lawyer, as well as the right to an *ex-officio* appointed lawyer where free appointment does not apply.

In the end, the enforcement of the provisions of ordinary criminal procedural law as a whole requires these provisions to be applied effectively to fulfil all the procedural rights affirmed in the European Directives in general, and in the one under examination, in particular. This shall undoubtedly and immediately affect daily forensic practice when legal professionals provide their services especially in the difficult relationship with police officers exercising their important mission.

However, only time and good practice of all the actors involved in criminal proceedings will entail effective application of these new provisions implementing the Directive as well as the others.

6 Final Remarks: The Impact of Directive 2013/48/EU

In this work, the inputs and outputs of this European Directive have been presented. For an overall assessment here and now, the initiative taken at European level must be welcomed for providing the rights analysed in this paper, as well as others relevant in the framework of procedural guarantees. This is the only way to maintain the delicate balance between justice and security, resulting in the adoption of criminal procedural measures at the European level which apply the principle of mutual recognition (judicial cooperation in criminal matters) and legislative approximation (minimum standards concerning procedural rights); in this sector, proportionality takes on particular importance as a counterweight between justice and security in the European judicial area.

Despite the drawbacks of the Directive concerning the right of access to a lawyer and the right to communication of the defendant in criminal proceedings, as pointed out in this work, the adoption of this Directive must be welcomed anyway in the framework of procedural rights of accused persons in criminal proceedings. The welcome must be even warmer since the European agenda has paid much attention to the counterpart in criminal proceedings, i.e. the victim, as recalled in the introduction to this paper; this is evident from the recent criminal procedural measures adopted in this scope, as well as from the interest shown by the Commission and, in particular, by the former European Commissioner for Justice, Fundamental Rights and Citizenship, Viviane Reding.[31] It would not be desirable to forget the accused person to protect the victim, even more so where a balance between these two actors (and between their rights) in criminal proceedings is possible.

However, the legislative *iter* undertaken for regulating the procedural rights of the accused person in criminal proceedings has not been completed since further implementation of European legislation on procedural rights at national level is still pending. All this must be considered together with the shortcomings of Directive

---

[31]Reding (2013), pp. 619–622, p. 620.

2013/48/EU which nonetheless affects the still incomplete legal statute of the defendant: this includes principles and guarantees of criminal procedure, such as the principle of *non bis in idem*. The procedural rights of accused persons in criminal proceedings within the European judicial space still have a long way to go in the European Union and in particular in Spain, in the search for the *lex mitior* for the subjects involved.

References

Arangüena Fanego C (2014) El derecho a la asistencia letrada en la Directiva 2013/48/UE. Revista General de Derecho Europeo (32):1–22 http://www.iustel.com

Burgos Ladrón de Guevara J (2015) La tabla de garantías de la víctima en el proyecto de reforma del proceso penal español. Diario La Ley (36):1 http://diariolaley.laley.es

Jimeno-Bulnes M (2010) Towards common standards on rights of suspects and accused persons in criminal proceedings in the EU. Center for European Policy Studies (CEPS) Policy Brief, pp 1–11. Available at ULR http://www.ceps.eu/author/see-jimeno-bulnes

Jimeno-Bulnes M (2016) Orden europea de investigación en materia penal: una perspectiva europea y española. In: Bene T, Lupária L, Marafioti L (eds) L'ordine europeo di indagine: criticità e prospettive. Giappichelli, Torino

Magro Servet V (2010) El nuevo estatuto de la víctima en el proceso penal. Diario La Ley (7495):1

Molina García P (2015) La transposición de la Directiva 2013/48/UE en lo que respecta al derecho a la asistencia de letrado en los procesos penales a la luz del Anteproyecto de Ley Orgánica de modificación de Ley de Enjuiciamiento Criminal. Revista General de Derecho Europeo (36):1–22 http://www.iustel.com

Reding V (2013) L'espace européen de justice: jalons et perspectives. Revue du Droit de l'Union Européenne (4):619–622

"Minimum" Procedural Rights in Judicial Cooperation Procedures

Cristina Mauro

Contents

Abstract To different extents and according to various formulations, traditional laws relative to judicial cooperation in criminal matters usually provide for a clause which conditions assistance on fundamental principles in criminal matters. In tune with and applied according to cultural and national peculiarities, these principles risk being transformed into real obstacles to cooperation.

The process of vertical harmonisation initiated by the case-law of the European Court of Human Rights has highlighted standards of protection which must necessarily be shared by the States which have signed up to the convention. These imposed standards however constitute minimum thresholds of guarantees that national legislators can reinforce and often do not correspond to internal constitutional levels of protection.

On the basis of this common culture of the fundamental principles in criminal matters, Article 82 of the Treaty on the Functioning of the European Union introduces standards of compromise in matters of protection and procedural guarantees common to all the national systems in order to facilitate judicial cooperation. If the objective cannot but be shared, in the absence of a real common procedural culture in which guarantees might be significant, the result risks lowering the levels of procedural guarantees sanctioned today in some countries.

C. Mauro (✉)
Public Prosecutor, Paris, France

Former Professor of Criminal Law and Procedure, University of Poitiers, Poitiers, France

© Springer Nature Switzerland AG 2019
T. Rafaraci, R. Belfiore (eds.), *EU Criminal Justice*,
https://doi.org/10.1007/978-3-319-97319-7_5

1 Foreword

Procedural rights in judicial cooperation procedures are a rather difficult issue to deal with in today's European context of terrorist bombings, which requires the cooperation of police and judicial administrations.

Particularly difficult issue for the French expert who, after the November 2015 killings in Paris, saw the government suspend the articles 5, 6, 7 and 8 of the European Convention of Human Rights and, since then, the proliferation of bills on the *state of emergency* that bestow on administrative authorities certain powers of investigation and guarantees that are normally peculiar to judicial authorities.

Especially complicated for the French expert, moreover, even outside of today's context: the French procedural law, in fact, is still presently an inquisitive-based system which gives judicial authorities great investigation powers to shed light on the historic truth and ensure justice and defense rights. Despite many reforms and the influence of ECHR case-law, French trials still nowadays are not equal-party trials, but are based on the idea of authority. This theoretical approach of criminal procedure has several consequences. Namely, as regards the object of this paper, on the one side, procedural rights have not the same impact they have in other European countries, on the other side and as a consequence, many problems arisen during negotiations regarding the directives on "minimum" rights, derive right from the French Napoleonic tradition. In particular, French negotiators are fairly known for being reticent with relation to provisions of the 2012/13/EU Directive of May 22nd 2012 on the right to information in criminal proceedings. When negotiations were on, the Code of Criminal Procedure did not acknowledge the right to assistance (read presence) of a lawyer during the questioning of a detainee or in case of voluntary statements: in conclusion, in 2014, the Directive led to the introduction of a vague, weak cross-examination in the investigation phase and, according to some observers, to a total distortion of the preliminary stage.

Finally and above all, procedural rights are quite a hard issue to deal with by anyone in the few lines of an article, for two main reasons. Firstly, the analysis of rights necessarily implies, as shown above, that of the trial system where these rights are encompassed. However, as shall be seen, this is the main question that "minimum" rights of European Directives arouse: is it possible to determine and define "minimum" rights outside the system where they will have to be pledged? Secondly, European-guaranteed rights for suspects or accused—translation and interpretation, information, legal aid or presumption of innocence—differ and entail, by consequence, difficulties and observations of different nature. In order not to reprise previous papers related to specific instruments of harmonisation, at risk of being perfunctory, this analysis is a general reflection on questions deriving from logic and methods of intervention of EU sources in this field, considering the more or less traditional instruments of judicial cooperation. Taking a look at present times and future developments will then permit to consider risks and ambiguities of the "minimum nature" of harmonisation in matters of procedural rights.

2 One Step Behind

Let us think back to the 1959 European judicial assistance Convention or the 1957 European extradition Convention. These treaties, specifically and restrictively, always included and still include grounds for refusal based on the observance of some fundamental principles of criminal law: refusal or conditional surrender in case of capital punishment, *ne bis in idem* principle, refusal in case of prescription for extradition, control clause of respect of sovereignty, public order and national interest security for legal assistance. These grounds for refusal, drawn up more or less correctly, have allowed national authorities for years, and still do, to control procedures carried out abroad as well as substantial rules applied, for instance, in case of *in absentia* proceedings, to reject or not, the execution of extradition.

Besides, the 1959 Convention allows the requesting authorities to specify some modalities of carrying out legal assistance which are believed necessary to ensure the possibility to use the elements acquired abroad, although there is no way of pretending that these modalities be complied with if any objection is made by the law of the executing country.

These precautions are motivated by two kinds of reason. On the one hand, the disregard of formalities that are thought to be essential in the European law culture may cause doubts about the equity of cooperation measures. In the case of extradition, for instance, the fact that the person involved cannot realise what is happening and take part in the procedure because he/she does not understand or speak the language of the executing authorities, may raise the doubt that defense rights have not been effectively ensured and exercised. Several systems, however, traditionally admit, in normal practice and for reasons of quickness, the intervention of an interpreter in a language close to that understood, or a non-professional translator in case of uncommon languages, or even a distance intervention, by telephone for example, in most urgent cases. These are, however, practices acceptable when judicial cooperation is an isolated event. They become instead more critical in a European integrated system where cooperation is thought to be obvious and becomes *routine*. It is not surprising then if the 2010/64/EU Directive on the right to interpretation and translation in criminal proceedings introduces specific provisions regarding the right to translation and interpretation in the scenario of European Arrest Warrant, which are made necessary by this procedure's success over the years. Retrospectively, it seems rather surprising that the same provisions had not already been provided for in the 2002 Framework Decision. But it is true that at that time the main concern was the introduction of an automatic surrender procedure and did not regard the guarantees of procedural rights. Presently, however, ECHR obliges to respect those guarantees linked to a fair trial also in the scenario of extradition and expulsion procedures.[1]

---

[1]For instance, for the right to appeal, see ECHR, 23 February 2012, Hirsi Jamaa v. Italy, n° 27765/09.

On the other hand, the disregard of fundamental principles and the consequent doubts on the procedural equity may reveal themselves as an impediment to the effectiveness and efficacy of judicial cooperation, as two well-known examples show.

The first example regards mainly the role and powers of the crime victim in cases showing one or more foreign elements: as a matter of fact, the victim may find it hard to accept, sometimes without being heard first, the jurisdiction of a foreign authority pronouncing itself within a procedure based on foreign law and carried out in a foreign language. French investigating magistrates well know such problem as a source of several positive conflicts of jurisdiction: the victim, who does not acknowledge the legitimacy of a foreign judge, since he/she cannot actively participate in the procedure, will tend to sue for damages before his/her domestic magistrate, even though investigations or inquests are already in progress abroad, which can be done in France or Belgium, where the prosecutor has no monopoly over the legal action. Therefore, just in order to avoid this kind of conflict, and consequently, to ensure recognition of measures carried out abroad, it has been necessary to harmonise the procedural rights of crime victims. The first, essential objective of the 2001/220/JHA Framework Decision of March 15th 2001 on the standing of victims in criminal proceedings beforehand and of the 2012/29/EU Directive of October 25th 2012 establishing minimum standards on the rights, support and protection of victims of crime afterwards, was to prevent victims from being an impediment to cooperation by multiplying procedures in front of authorities which do not present sufficient connection elements with regard to the crime. The harmonisation of victims' rights was the necessary means to reach this end.

A second example regards the role and powers of a judge: can a national judge take into account the elements acquired violating defense rights and the cross-examination principle that are considered as fundamental in his/her law culture? The question was dealt with in the past for the questioning of a suspect. An Italian example is perhaps known, quoted by a lawyer at a congress some years ago: the case of an Italian request for international judicial assistance sent to Dutch authorities. They had been asked to question a suspect and obviously, before a defense lawyer. The Dutch law, however, like the French one at the time, did not provide for the presence of a lawyer throughout the whole enquiring phase while investigating a simply suspected person: Dutch authorities had then asked the lawyer to hide behind the curtains! As shall be seen, thanks to 2012/13/EU of May 22nd 2012 and to 2013/48/EU of October 22nd 2013 Directives on the right to information in criminal proceedings and the right of access to a lawyer in criminal proceedings, respectively, this case is merely anecdotal material.

The question is raised today, however, as regards the investigation acts based on new technologies like GPS detection. Whereas the Italian *Corte di Cassazione* does not require specific guarantees and compares this technique to a tailing, German and French laws, basing on article 8 of ECHR, subordinate GPS detection to the authorisation from judicial authority: will the foreign judge be able to admit the validity of the Italian measure, which is not subordinate to any authorisation? In a recent ruling, the French *Cour de Cassation* had a chance to clarify that, without authorisation from foreign authorities in the context of an international rogatory, the French authorities cannot acknowledge the validity of satellite detection operations carried out abroad, even if they have legally started in France, without getting from the foreign authorities, also *a posteriori*, the permission to use the outcome of these operations.[2]

These difficulties, linked to the execution of legal assistance, triggered the adoption of the May 29th 2000 Convention on mutual assistance in criminal matters, come into force in 2005, which provides, in line of principle, for the implementation of legal assistance in accordance with the formalities and procedures the requesting State law provides for. Obviously, this is to ensure the usefulness of acquired elements. However, art. 4, §1 of this convention contains also a clause called "fundamental principles" bound up to the hypothesis wherein these formalities and procedures are in conflict with the fundamental principles of the requested State. The problem that had been avoided by introducing a sort of presumption of compliance, has arisen again. And it is logical that it be so: in the traditional legal cooperation, requested State authorities must abide with their domestic law and in particular they are strongly subordinate to respect their own national basic principles. Despite the 2000 convention, it had become necessary to harmonise in matter of basic principles.

Theoretically, all these problems should have been solved by simply endorsing, within Tampere Council framework, the mutual trust and recognition principles. They should have been cancelled, almost miraculously, since these two principles were based on the idea, quite common in the academic and law fields, of a strong harmonisation of the European repressive systems by means of the European Convention on human rights' common standards and of the Court of Strasbourg's case-law. Adopted and confirmed by ECHR itself,[3] this issue is well known: in Europe, all national authorities are bound to observe the European convention and at present also the Charter of Nice, and all then respect the same basic principles in the context of a common culture, although the different criminal and procedural codes sometimes provide for different technical settlements. Indeed, this approach has made it easy to rapidly adopt the European Arrest Warrant without the European negotiations being interested in complying with the principles of a fair trial. This subject itself still nowadays justifies the often mild decisions made by the EU Court of Justice on questions of basic principles and European Arrest Warrant.[4] Being influenced by common trends and basic principles, national legislations guarantee and are sufficient to guarantee defense and fair trial rights even in the scenario of judicial cooperation.

National implementing bills and early applications of the Framework Decision have however shown that reality was quite different. For brevity's sake and considering one example only, without taking into account better known and commented

---

[2]Cass. crim., 9 February 2016, n° 15-85070.

[3]ECHR, 4 May 2010, Stapleton v. Ireland, n° 56588/07.

[4]For instance, § 33 ECJ, 1 June 2016, Bob-Dogi, C-241-15 and § 77 ECJ, 5 April 2016, Aranyosi and Caldararu, C-404/15 and C-659/15.

decisions by Constitutional Courts in Poland, Germany, Cyprus and Czeck Republic, regarding a citizen's arrest, one can mention the Italian law which provides for the compulsory refusal if there is a mother with child aged under 3. This ground for refusal, unforeseen by the Framework Decision, has been ironically criticised as an instance of some national legislators' reluctance against EAW. Was it not, instead, the sign of a particular attention to traditions, social structures and a legal culture based on the importance of affective, familiar links, especially in the early years of life? It has to be acknowledged, anyway, that after some hesitation and even if the implementing bill does not provide for any provision similar to the Italian one, the French *Court de cassation* maintains that, basing on article 8 ECHR, a parent's arrest—mother or father—must be turned down if it affects disproportionately the right to a private, family life of a minor.[5] In such case, then, the harmonisation, which did not exist when the Framework Decision was enacted, has occurred subsequently.

The EU Court of Justice case-law itself, then, showed that the guarantees provided for by the Framework Decision, also after the modification in 2009,[6] were probably not completely sufficient or fully in line with ECHR case-law, or with the constitutional needs of the Member States. The Melloni case, in February 2013,[7] with regard to *in absentia* proceedings, is probably the one that, to date, most clearly clarifies the hypothesis of a double horizontal/vertical conflict between EU basic principles, as understood by the Court of Justice, and the constitutional tradition of some Member States as well as the diverse national concepts. It is not a coincidence that the European Commission have deemed it necessary to re-examine the guarantees regarding *in absentia* proceedings in the context of the package related to the principle of presumption of innocence which brought to the adoption of the 2016/343/EU Directive of March 9th 2016 on the strengthening of certain aspects of the presumption of innocence and of the right to be present at the trial in criminal proceedings.

Like many others, these examples clearly indicate that the European Arrest Warrant has not been the outcome of an already implemented harmonisation, but rather the driving force that quickened the harmonisation and adjustment of national legislations to the case-law of the European Court of human rights or of the EU Court of justice.[8]

---

[5]Cass. crim., 12 May 2010, n° 10-82.746; Cass. crim., 22 September 2010, n° 10-86.237; Cass. crim., 10 November 2010, n° 10-87.282.

[6]Framework Decision 2009/299/JHA, 28 March 2009 More Effective Extradition Procedures: European Arrest Warrant.

[7]ECJ, 26 February 2013, Stefano Melloni v. Ministerio Fiscal, C-399/11.

[8]Literature in this sense is significant. For some reference, House of Lords, EU Committee (2006); House of Lords, EU Committee (2013), pp. 56–67; Flore (2014); Albers et al. (2013); Vernimmen-Van Tiggelen et al. (2009); Mitsilegas (2012), pp. 21–142; European Criminal Policy Initiative (2013), p. 430; Smith (2013); Malabat (2010); Koering-Joulin (2009); Masset (2011); Carbone and Chiavario (2008); Schünemann (2006); Fletcher et al. (2008), p. 116.

The inadequacy of guarantees provided for by the Framework Decision and the harmonisation of the national systems had already been perceived by those Member States and by the EU Commission who proposed in 2004 the adoption of another Framework Decision regarding procedural guarantees of defendants and suspects. Two ideas supported this initiative: establishing a minimum level of equivalent protection, not only in the framework of judicial cooperation but for all suspects and accused in all Member States. It was then necessary to harmonise the procedural systems themselves with reference to procedural guarantees. It was quite an ambitious proposal, as it did not insist on the need to provide for a single assistance or cooperation procedure like the EAW, and consequently the same guarantees in the context of the judicial cooperation, but on a joint approach: cooperation fits inside a wider context and procedure, and it is then necessary to intervene and harmonise more extensively.

This change of perspective was and is twice radical, not only because it is a matter of harmonising basic principles that depend on the local criminal and court culture, but also of using EU sources to ensure the effectiveness of the principles ratified by the Human Rights' Convention in the Member States.

From opposite viewpoints, this modification is to be blamed or welcomed. Blamed because while EU sources are basically written texts, adopted once for all and, mainly for Framework Decisions, hardly modifiable, ECHR case-law is by definition evolving and allows for the adjustment of basic principles to the social and more appropriately European judicial changes. Moreover, if European sources, Framework Decisions and Directives, are the result of time-consuming, exhausting negotiations which lead to compromises between cultures where civil rights are more or less defended, the rulings of the Court of Strasbourg have not, at least until recently,[9] suffered from political influences. Finally, the risk cannot be ruled out that, owing to compromises resulting from negotiations, or to needs for effectiveness and quickness of the judicial cooperation, the guarantees themselves be understood and applied differently in the EU context and that of the Council of Europe.

This modification is instead welcomed by the French criminal law specialist. Two examples will suffice to confirm this statement, which anticipates Directives adopted under the Lisbon Treaty. The former is connected with the Directive on the right to translation and interpretation that has led the French legislator to introduce in the preliminary article of the criminal code a new fundamental right, only partially acknowledged by the previous law. The latter, more complex, is connected with the Directive on the right to information, which obliged the legislator to modify thoroughly the detention rules in 2011, to introduce the presence of a counsel during the questioning or in case of spontaneous statements in 2014, and to ensure the defense rights following the arrest according to a European Arrest Warrant.

It is not to be overlooked, however, that if the European Directives have led to sometimes substantial adjustments of member States' systems, the 2004 Framework

---

[9]For instance, ECHR, 15 December 2011, AL Khawaja and Tahery v. UK, n° 26766/05 and 22228/06.

Decision proposal has never been enacted for lack of agreement! It has been used, at
any rate, as starting point for Stockholm Programme and for drawing article
82 TFEU which represents the legal ground onto which directives of the so-called
minimum procedural rights have been adopted.

3   A Glimpse Ahead

As is well known, article 82 TFEU is contained in Chapter 4, titled "Judicial
Cooperation in criminal matters" and provides for a juxtaposition of member States'
law systems as regards a few rights. It is therefore helpful to specify that, *verbatim*, it
is not rights that are "minimum", but their harmonisation. Besides, such juxtaposition or "minimum" harmonisation, provided by art. 82, is understood as a device
connected with judicial cooperation: in other words, harmonisation is serviceable for
the goal of mutual recognition.

Such "instrumental" idea of harmonisation regarding basic guarantees raises
several general questions and has various more or less acceptable consequences.
As a matter of fact, on the one hand, it ensures the respect of national law systems as
it prevents the imposition of a single procedural pattern to member States that have
different traditions or differing models. On the other hand, however, it contributes to
giving a "minimum nature" to the rights on which directives are enacted, and at least
three reasons explain why.

The first regards the relationships between internal procedures and cooperation
and the impact of harmonisation on the former. What the TFEU authors had in mind
is clear: allow national legislators to introduce or maintain stronger or more definite
guarantees in the context of merely domestic proceedings. For instance, in matters of
information about the investigated person, the Italian system provides for the access
to all evidence while being questioned, which is instead not provided as such in the
information Directive. The French system on this point did not provide any access to
files during the preliminary questioning and, as said before, a three-phase reform, in
2011, 2014 and June 2016 was required to encompass access to the whole file.

What had to be done before June 2016 in the context of a request for judicial
assistance? Could an Italian magistrate require that the suspect received communication of the evidence against him/her? It is legitimate to doubt. Since the Directive
only needs limited information, the questioning minutes could be used before the
Italian magistrate even though the suspect did not have any access to evidence
against him/her. The claim by which Member States can push themselves beyond
the directive in order to better ensure procedural rights is certainly well-grounded for
mainly internal procedures; it is not, however, for judicial cooperation. The provisions of art. 82 in this field have mainly the consequence of bringing guarantees
down to a lowest common denominator.

Moreover, the step from judicial cooperation to mainly internal procedures is very
short and brings with it the risk for legislators to trivialise and reduce national
requirements to standards provided by the European Directives. In this context,

European Directives regarding "minimum" harmonisation would become an instrument for interpreting and applying the ECHR case-law, bearing so the risk of conveying a minimal, historically determined interpretation of the criminal code basic principles, as has already been said.

It is not just a theoretical risk. In fact, with regard to the relationships between Constitutional and European sources—ECHR and EU—, art. 82, respectful of national traditions, provides that directives should take into due account the differences between judicial traditions and legal systems of Member States. However, the EU Court of Justice has already had the opportunity to ratify the priority of EU basic principles over the national constitutional ones in the Melki and Abdeli[10] judgment and the principle of consistent interpretation.[11] While interpreting Directives, also in merely domestic cases, the Court will probably be inclined to adopt a restrictive reading of procedural rights, which shall remain as the only possible interpretation of basic principles concerning the rights established by the European Directives. In this regard, one cannot avoid thinking of the evolution of the Court case-law as regards the *ne bis in idem* principle in the context of the European Arrest Warrant, having the case-law, in its latest interventions, seemed to put on a same level, in an uninterrupted balancing, the grounds for refusal of surrender on one side, and the effectiveness of the fight against crime on the other.[12] Once again, the risk is that, owing to the priority given to rulings on interpretation as well as validity of EU sources, from a minimum level of harmonisation one may fall down to a minimum level of rights as understood and applied by the European magistrate.

As a minimisation of these doubts, however, one should recognise that in the first judgment regarding the Directive on the right to translation and interpretation,[13] the Court of Justice seems to leave national authorities fairly free and care about the effectiveness of the rights sanctioned by the Directive in matters of law in particular.

4 Conclusive Remarks

To sum up, it is appropriate to go once again to article 82 TFEU formulation, which provides for the adoption of "minimum provisions" regarding procedural "rights". It is then not a matter of harmonising the national systems with regard to criminal procedure or criminal justice basic principles, but with regard to the individual's rights, either suspect or victim. This formulation raises several issues, theoretical and not. The first issue regards why the formulation has been done so: have perhaps only the rights directly pleaded before the magistrate been sanctioned, so as to ensure their effectiveness? However, can a basic principle not be pleaded by the parties? The

---

[10]ECJ, 22 June 2010, C-188/10 and C-189/10.

[11]ECJ, 16 June 2005, Maria Pupino, C-105/03.

[12]For instance, ECJ, 27 May 2014, Zoran Spasic, C-129/14.

[13]ECJ, 15 October 2015, Gavril Covaci, C-216-14.

latter issue, linked to the former, concerns the nature of regulations susceptible of harmonising: article 82 wording seems in fact to rule out those provisions that, although inspired to basic principles of the discipline, do not ensure real subjective rights like those relating to criminal law. The third issue is about the identification of these rights, the method and the reference text: ECHR, Charter of Nice, or just Directives? Consequently, the fourth issue regards the, limited or not, nature of the list provided by article 82: what became of all the guarantees of art. 5, 7, 8 etc. of the European Convention? It is not just rhetorical asking: disputes on adopting the recent Directive about the principle of presumption of innocence, the EU Court of Justice sentences in Radu[14] and Covaci cases demonstrate that the right to appeal has been totally neglected in art. 82. Luckily, point d) of art. 82 enables the Council to detect "any other specific aspects of criminal procedure which the Council has identified in advance by a decision; for the adoption of such a decision, the Council shall act unanimously after obtaining the consent of the European Parliament". Other relevant issues might be, as suggested in the European Parliament Ludford Report regarding the European Arrest Warrant, the right to appeal, the definition of judicial authority and the principle of proportionality.

But then, it would no longer be a matter of rights and "minimum" harmonisation. Within this approach, the phrase "other specific aspects of criminal procedure" would refer to the basic principles of criminal justice as a whole. Not surprisingly, the Commission deals with detention and incarceration conditions which are a huge obstacle to mutual recognition, namely after Torreggiani's decision by the Strasbourg Court.[15] The harmonisation should then be implemented in all the procedural and essential aspects connected with the issuing and application of the sanction. This statement, which tends to characterise more widely the list of article 82 TFEU, raises a final general issue: within this interpretation, the direct intervention of EU sources, presented as a technical one, made to ensure an effective cooperation, would lead to political and structural choices which would not be "minimum" at all from many points of view. From an institutional and legislative standpoint, one would get, from a restrictive list of rights to harmonise, to a general EU competence to harmonise the procedural systems altogether. From a political, economic and structural viewpoint, from a minimal approach due to judicial cooperation, the European Union would claim to itself the chance of imposing on Member States, by provisions regarding procedural rights, a certain procedural, substantial pattern, being this a possibility unforeseen by the Member States.

The experience of the translation and interpretation Directive is in this case revealing and illustrates the ambiguity of the approach described in article 82 TFEU. We know that this Directive has, ambitiously and courageously, imposed the principle of gratuitousness aimed at ensuring the effectiveness of the interpreting work, being this a principle that brings about financial and organisational problems in the various Member State systems and that, in the end, will necessarily impact on

---

[14]ECJ, 29 January 2013, Ciprian Vasile Radu, C-396/11.
[15]ECHR, 8 January 2013, Torreggiani and Others v. Italy, n° 43517/09, 46882/09 and 55400/09.

the reasonable duration of the proceedings. It is not certain that these consequences have been sufficiently assessed by the European legislator, who has paid more attention to how effectively the right must be interpreted when adopting the directive. At a minimal reading, European Directives risk not to be ambitious enough and reduce the fundamental guarantees. Reading more extensively, on the contrary, the approach of fundamental rights ought to be integrated into a wider harmonisation process that could allow to reflect upon the context wherein these rights are guaranteed.

To date, although these Directives undoubtedly represent a great step ahead, based as they are on known difficulties of judicial cooperation, they do not seem to mirror a general idea, a coherent architecture of the criminal procedure. As French people would say: *elles manquent de souffle...* they lack that spirit which would permit an extensive reading of article 82 TFEU.

References

Albers P, Beauvais P, Bohnert JF, Böse M, Langbroek PH, Renier A, Wahl T (2013) Towards a common evaluation framework to assess mutual trust in the field of EU judicial cooperation in criminal matters, Final report

Carbone SM, Chiavario M (eds) (2008) Cooperazione giudiziaria civile e penale nel diritto dell'Unione europea. Giappichelli, Torino

European Criminal Policy Initiative (2013) A manifesto on European criminal procedure law. ZIS (11):430

Fletcher M, Lööf R, Gilmore B (2008) EU criminal law and justice. Edward Elgar Publishing, Cheltenham

Flore D (2014) Droit pénal européen: les enjeux d'une justice pénale européenne. Larcier, Bruxelles

House of Lords, EU Committee (2006) European arrest warrant - recent developments. 30th Report of Session 2005–2006

House of Lords, EU Committee (2013) EU police and criminal justice measures: the UK's 2014 opt-out. 13th Report of Session 2012–2013

Koering-Joulin R (2009) Mandat d'arrêt européen et contrôle du droit de l'Etat d'émission. D'un "degré de confiance élevé" à une confiance mesurée. In: Études à la mémoire du professeur Bruno Oppetit. Litec-Lexis Nexis, Paris

Malabat V (2010) Confiance mutuelle et mise en œuvre du mandat d'arrêt européen. In: Justice et droit du procès. Du légalisme procédural à l'humanisme, Mélanges en l'honneur de Serge Guinchard. Dalloz, Paris

Masset A (ed) (2011) Pratique du droit pénal européen devant les juridictions nationales. Anthemis, Limal

Mitsilegas V (2012) The area of freedom, security and justice from Amsterdam to Lisbon. Challenges of implementation, constitutionality and fundamental rights, general report. In: Laffranque J (ed) The area of freedom, security and justice, including information society issues. Reports of the XXV FIDE Congress. Tallinn (3):12

Schünemann B (ed) (2006) A program for European criminal justice. Carl Heymanns Verlag GmbH, Köln

Smith E (2013) Running before we can walk? Mutual recognition at the expense of fair trials in Europe's area of freedom, justice and security. New J Eur Crim Law 4(1–2):82

Vernimmen-Van Tiggelen C, Surano L, Weyembergh A (eds) (2009) The future of mutual recognition in criminal matters in the European Union. Editions de l'Université de Bruxelles, Bruxelles

Part II
Transnational Criminal Investigations and Proceedings: Instruments of Judicial Cooperation in Criminal Matters

The European Investigation Order for Evidence Gathering Abroad

Fabrizio Siracusano

Contents

Abstract In the context of the European Union, the structural differences between the various models of evidence-gathering has often been hindering the transnational circulation of evidence. The coming into force of the Lisbon Treaty has created the preconditions for a qualitative leap in European legal integration by establishing 'minimum rules' on the mutual admissibility of evidence between Member States. Even though the 2014/41/EU Directive on the EIO is the most advanced legislative act with reference to the *ultra fines* evidence-gathering in the European "regional" context, there has been no harmonising effect of the procedures aimed at making evidence mutually admissible wherever it is collected. Following a process characterised by an instance of simplified models and hybridism, the Directive has created a system of "blank procedural rules" which require being applied in compliance with fundamental human rights and fundamental principles of national systems, fully consistent with the principle of proportionality. However, entrusted

F. Siracusano (✉)
University of Catania, Department of Law, Catania, Italy
e-mail: fsiracusano@lex.unict.it

© Springer Nature Switzerland AG 2019
T. Rafaraci, R. Belfiore (eds.), *EU Criminal Justice*,
https://doi.org/10.1007/978-3-319-97319-7_6

to the wise evaluation of the judge in the specific case, these rules may create the danger to reduce the level of guarantees and to stop any future harmonisation of national systems.

1 Introduction

Gathering evidence from abroad is certainly not easy because it tends to affect two different entities: on one hand the individual whose personal sphere may be violated by the search for judicial evidence; on the other the foreign State required to cooperate, whose sovereignty may be breached by the *latu sensu* evidentiary request by the requesting State. Both need protection by the predispositions of a suitable mechanism of guarantee: the individual by defined procedural models suited to combining evidence gathering and respect for fundamental rights; the State through a procedural itinerary, aimed at respecting certain requisites which favour judicial cooperation without damaging any intrinsic national principles or values. This requirement should be met whatever the cooperative dialogue: as much centred on mutual assistance as on mutual recognition.

In the context of the 'small Europe' in which judicial cooperation ought to be running the rails of mutual recognition, the difficult balance between the interests of the mechanisms of evidence research and gathering has caused States to adopt a quite timid and fragmentary approach: under the framework of inter-governmental cooperation, with the Convention on Mutual Assistance in Criminal Matters (CMACM) of 2000; in the circuit of mutual recognition from the itinerary launched in 2003 with a Commission Proposal, later shelved, after Framework Decision 2003/577/JHA on orders freezing property or evidence was adopted, to the (disappointing) Framework Decision of 2008/978/GAI on the European Evidence Warrant (EEW).[1]

However, the Lisbon Treaty did promise a 'new era' in transnational evidence gathering. According to Art. 82, para.2 of the Treaty on the Functioning of the European Union (TFEU) it would be possible to establish, by means of directives adopted in accordance with the ordinary legislative procedure, 'minimum rules' on mutual admissibility of evidence between member States. These would be rules regarding research methods such as to make the results admissible and allow their 'free circulation' throughout the EU. It would seem evident that it deals with a choice driven by an awareness of how impossible mutual recognition is—without tentative harmonisation, even sensitive in certain categories—to support alone the weight of the evermore heterogeneous widened EU (including probatory rules).

---

[1]The limited scope of application of Framework Decision 2008/978/JHA—much more restricted than the one under traditional rogatory—and its substantial inadequacy gave rise to its abrogation by Regulation 2016/95/EU of the European Parliament and of the Council of 20th January, 2016.

The intent of Art. 82, para. 2 of TFEU is very clear: mutual recognition postulates (limitedly in certain categories) a concept of cooperation which cannot be realised without minimal integration of norms. Such a policy of harmonisation is adopted to make mutual recognition more functional. Although what the TFEU has introduced is without doubt attributable to harmonisation,[2] it aims to "facilitate mutual recognition of judgments and judicial decisions". The Lisbon Treaty does not intend harmonisation as an instrument to identify identical rules which govern evidence gathering in all the member States, but rather a functional approach to mutual recognition. Harmonisation is possible even with different rules if they are interconnected by a provision which allows a certain uniformity, functional enough to make evidence admissible beyond national boundaries.[3]

Besides, by means of a non-regression clause, there is nothing to stop member States 'maintaining or introducing a higher level of protection for individuals'.[4] Whoever has more rigid standards of admissibility (think of the Italian system and the importance given to the cross-examination principle in its objective and subjective dimension) may maintain them. If it is true that harmonisation is diverging towards a common *law of evidence* in all States, then it is not possible at the same time that this move could be transformed into a forced unification towards more backward standards. In welcoming a transnational probatory element, legal systems which adopt more 'sophisticated' rules would encounter difficulties in adapting to extraneous models which, even though conforming to the minimum requisites, do not respect irrefutably those of the receiving State.

2 A Slow Progression Towards a Minimal "Harmonisation"

The Lisbon Treaty has thus introduced the legal basis for the minimal harmonisation necessary for effective mutual recognition of evidence gathered *ultra fines*: a harmonisation launched to reacquire its status as a regulatory technique; no longer an effect induced by the mutual recognition of judgments and judicial decisions, but a preventative activity necessary to prepare the terrain for the circulation of evidence.

---

[2]In these terms Allegrezza (2008), p. 3886.

[3]Tadic (2002), p. 4, emphasises in general terms how harmony is not synonymous with uniformity: uniformity has been associated with the idea of doing everything in the same way leaving no space for differences or peculiarities. Harmonisation (instead) is a mechanism by which things can function more efficiently and without conflict, leaving any differences or individual choices intact." See also Amodio (2001), p. 553, who claims that there exist values which must be protected: that of the *beauty of diversity*. This teaches us that it is mistaken to believe in one European criminal procedure across all member States.

[4]In reality, Directive 2014/41/EU on the European Investigation Order does not include a non-regression clause as opposed to the Directive on the rights of accused persons in criminal proceedings.

Once mutual recognition is accepted, the transnational gathering of evidence using a minimalist approach can only polarise the identification of obstacles to free circulation so as to remove them. From a similar perspective, the main interest is not to intercept the prevalent orientation, or either to work on a common strategy to promote those most appropriate judicial rules to balance the needs of justice and protection of the individual, but rather to obtain a result—the recognition of evidence originating from one foreign State—by developing a shared ideology.

In the wake of Art. 82, para. 2, TFEU, the European Council intervened and the Stockholm Programme (2009) was created which invited the Commission to propose a general system of evidence gathering in transnational cases, based on the principal of mutual recognition.[5] At the same time, the European Council promoted the Green Paper of 11th November 2009,[6] and formulated a double objective: reform the probatory system 'horizontally' (on the level of judicial cooperation) favouring rapid collaboration between States through mutual recognition; reform the probatory system 'vertically' with a *soft* approach to harmonisation according to minimum standards (using the model in Art. 82, para.2, TFEU).

These proclamations of intent, on the level of legislative programming, were not translated into concrete regulations to harmonise systems and probatory regulations. Compared to the perspective promoted by the Commission, the initiative by seven member States[7] in 2010 for the adoption of the European Investigation Order (EIO) represented an unexpected departure in advance on a political level: the abandonment of a 'binary' strategy in favour of a horizontal one to simplify and make uniform the models of judicial cooperation setting aside the most ambitious project to construct common—or at least harmonised—rules on the admissibility of evidence. A clear symptom of the resistance of single States to give way on sovereignty in the sector of evidence gathering which expresses values and judicial and cultural traditions which characterise each State.[8]

---

[5]See the Stockholm Programme, 10–11th December 2009, in OJ 4th May 2010, C 115/1.

[6]The reference is to the consultation initiated by the Commission within the EU member States by way of 'Green Paper on obtaining evidence in criminal matters from one Member State to another and securing its admissibility', COM(2009)624 def.

[7]The initiative came from Belgium, Bulgaria, Estonia, Spain, Austria, Slovenia and Sweden. On this, see Belfiore (2014), p. 207.

[8]In these terms Spencer (2010), pp. 604f. It is understandable why some States are reluctant to abdicate their sovereignty, foregoing their own rules and evidentiary guarantees. See: Rafaraci (2014b), p. 38.

3 The European Investigation Order (EIO): The Most Advanced Discipline Regarding the Transnational Evidence Gathering and Information Exchange in Europe

For about 3 years, the EU has been equipped with a new legal instrument to be the 'evolved' cornerstone of judicial cooperation in matters concerning evidence gathering and information exchange. According to the intentions of the European legislator, Directive 2014/41/EU regarding the EIO would be the most advanced law on transnational evidence gathering in the European 'regional' circuit.[9] Indeed, this law seems more the result of a compromise: it does not contain anything revolutionary and above all is not endowed with any unifying effect nor even does it harmonise procedures to render mutually admissible or usable any evidence wherever it is gathered.[10] Notwithstanding it is formally founded on Art. 82, para. 2 (TFEU), the Directive is substantially applied beyond the realm of minimum rules, this making it a highly complex instrument which can only weaken guarantees and sterilise future capacity to harmonise national laws.[11]

According to the definition in Art. 1 of the Directive 2014/41/EU, EIO is a judicial decision issued by a competent Authority of a member State (defined issuing),[12] so that one or more specific investigative measures are carried out in another member State (defined as 'executing') to obtain evidence, even when already in the possession of the competent authority of the executing State. Any dialogue between the issuing and executing Authorities, according to the cliché which characterises EU judicial cooperation, is not filtered by any political mediation: the EIO operates using a direct channel of communication between judicial Authorities; this does not exclude, however, designing a central Authority which provides support to the judiciary as outlined in Art. 7, para. 3 and Art. 16, para. 1.

With this type of trigger and its ample scope of application, the EIO should substitute all the instruments hitherto used in gathering and circulating evidence in the EU.[13] The legislator intends to introduce within the European order a "comprehensive system for

---

[9]Daniele (2015), p. 87.

[10]This approach is criticised in general terms by Bargis (2012), p. 920, and by Camaldo (2014), pp. 1ff.

[11]Marafioti (2016), p. 22. More in general on the sterilising effect of harmonisation by mutual recognition, Mazza (2014), pp. 1401ff.

[12]The EIO can be issued not only by a judge or a public prosecutor, but also by any other authority competent in carrying out investigations based on the national laws of the issuing State. In the case of police authority, however, the EIO must be validated by a judicial authority (Art. 2c) so as not to entirely entrust activities which might influence fundamental liberties into the hands of public security agencies.

[13]Expressly stated in Art. 34 of Directive 2014/41/EU.

obtaining evidence in cases with a cross-border dimension" so as to "replace all the existing instruments in this area" (Recital 6 of the Preamble).[14]

Therefore, from 22nd May 2017 according to a process of simplifying models and hybridisation,[15] transnational evidence gathering between member States should be carried out as per this instrument: by coalescing "open-ended legal regulations"[16]—aimed at referring to either the *lex fori* or the *lex loci*—and embryonic forms of harmonisation retraceable to certain specific evidence; however, in compliance with fundamental rights and the fundamental principles of national legal orders,[17] and in accordance to the principal of proportionality.

4   An Effective Simplification of Procedures?

The first requirement of Directive 2014/41/EU is to 'simplify' procedures: a requirement worthy of respect compared to an overall picture of excessive entanglement and foreboding interpretative uncertainties.[18] Recital 5 of the Preamble cites the need to remedy any fragmentation in the legislative panorama concerning the forms and instruments of research and evidence gathering by an operation aimed to *reductio ad unum* of the existing models.

In reality, this objective does not seem to have been pursued: there are areas in which the simplification translates into effective swapping of models, and sectors where the EIO should coexist with the current instruments. There ought to be a complete overhaul of the existing system in a dual strategy: on one hand, through the removal of certain expressly listed instruments (Art. 34)[19] and their substitution (from 22nd May 2017) by the EIO subject to their remaining active to a limited extent in relations between EU States and third States; on the other hand, in relation to evidence research and gathering models agreed to in the Conventions within the

---

[14]This is an undoubted merit of the Directive, according to Allegrezza (2014), p. 54.

[15]See Belfiore (2014), pp. 147f; Caianiello (2015), p. 3, which speaks of the 'syncretism' of the Directive on the EIO since it seems to align with the development of mutual recognition although within it there are flexible solutions under the auspices of a rogatory regime.

[16]The expression is Daniele's (2016), p. 64.

[17]Art. 1, para. 4, states that "This Directive shall not have the effect of modifying the obligation to respect the fundamental rights and legal principles as enshrined in Article 6 of the TEU, including the rights of defence of persons subject to criminal proceedings, and any obligations incumbent on judicial authorities in this respect shall remain unaffected".

[18]On the point see Marchetti (2015), p. 222.

[19]The reference is to The European Convention on Mutual Assistance in criminal matters of the 1959 by the Council of Europe, to the related additional protocols and bilateral agreements concluded as per Art.26; to the Convention on the application of the Schengen Agreement (C.A. A.S.); to the Convention of Mutual Assistance in criminal matters between EU member States (Brussels, 2000); to the Framework Decisions 2008/978/JHA on the European Evidence Warrant and Framework decision 2003/577/JHA on orders freezing property or evidence. The substitution applies both to mutual assistance and mutual recognition instruments.

Council of Europe and not surrogated from the newly born European Order, Recital 35 of the Preamble establishes a sort of 'pre-eminence' principle for the 'new' model compared to those in existence through an intervention which could be described as partially 'substitutive'.[20]

Simplifying procedures—removing and substituting previous ones more or less entirely—gave rise to the inevitable omni-comprehensive character of the EIO. It can be used for whatever evidence needs to be gathered or researched *ultra fines:* whether already existent (material evidence or documents), whether to be constituted (i.e. declarations irrefutably excluded from the EEW scope of application).[21] The EIO can be furthermore employed to obtain real time and continuing data (e.g. phone tapping) or to carry out undercover operations. There remain however areas neglected by the EIO: according to Recital 9 of the Preamble, the Directive should not apply to cross-border surveillance as referred to in the Convention implementing the Schengen Agreement[22]; it shall not cover the setting up of a joint investigation team and the gathering of evidence within such a team as provided under Framework Decision 2002/465/JHA recently implemented in Italy by Legislative Decree no. 34/2016.

5 A "Hybrid" Model of Research and Evidence Gathering

This ample fusion of instruments for research and gathering of transnational evidence can be activated, according to Directive 2014/41/EU, by a protocol of solutions notable for their hybridisation: one part is similar to traditional rogatory; another recalls the EEW; and another includes significant innovation.

So, the EIO expresses an unusual convergence of the typical components of mutual recognition and salient features of mutual assistance; these latest as found in the most evolved version of the European Convention on Mutual Assistance (2000)[23] (which has been recently implemented in Italy by Legislative Decree

---

[20]Consider specific forms of interception of telecommunication as set out by the Convention on cybercrime of the Council of Europe signed in Budapest, 23rd November 2001 and in force on 1st July 2004 once the minimum five ratifications were approved. Among the co-signatories not parties of the Council of Europe were the USA, Canada and Japan.

[21]On the scope of application of the EIO, both *ratione materiae* and *ratione personae,* see Rafaraci (2014b), p. 39.

[22]Notwithstanding Art. 34, b) of Directive 2014/41/EU expressly indicating the Convention implementing the Schengen Agreement among the "legal instruments, agreements and arrangements" which are subject to 'substitution'.

[23]According to Fiorelli (2013), p. 709, the 2000 Convention, as opposed to Directive 2014/41/EU, has not substituted the existing models. Even from Art. 1, the Brussels Convention aims to facilitate the 1959 European Convention of Mutual Assistance, its additional protocol of 1978, and all the other relevant conventional sources between member States, in particular the Convention implementing the Schengen Agreement (C.A.A.S.).

n. 52 of 2017).[24] Because of a multiplicity of models, it is sometimes difficult to identify the distinctive features of EIO compared to the traditional rogatory: although formally ascribable to the 'orders' category (depending on the iteration imposed by mutual recognition), it substantially assumes the connotations of a request (in line with the mutual assistance model) which does not automatically restrain the 'receiving' authority either in order of the '*an*' ('if'), or as regards the '*quomodo*' ('how') of its execution.

By the same admission of the EU legislator—and according to the approach anticipated in § 3.1.1. of the Stockholm Programme—the EIO Directive, while inspired by mutual recognition, does not embrace it thoroughly, preferring to take into account the 'flexibility' of traditional mutual assistance requests (Recital 6 of the Preamble).

In hindsight, it is not a completely new *modus operandi*. Without a precautionary harmonisation strategy, analogous weighty exceptions to the logic of mutual recognition had been introduced by the Framework Decision on the EEW. Beyond its declared objectives, the substituted model of research and evidence gathering had devised various compromise solutions which were not dissimilar to the rogatory system, even in the more modern version defined by the Convention on Mutual Assistance (2000).[25]

Combining the two theoretical models, the setup of the EIO is extremely balanced: on one hand, it considers the *lex loci* crisis—an expression of having surmounted the concept of 'national space' and the consequent transfer of sovereignty to the EU by member States, imposed by the EU Treaties—and reduces its operational sphere; on the other, it does not give in to the temptation of wholly committing to *lex fori*, protecting itself from the risk of suffering the deleterious effects of mutual recognition when not accompanied by significant procedural harmonisation.

Thus, the references between one and the other methodology become evident, modulated according to the degree of invasiveness of the 'ordered' investigative measure. The intersecting of these two models helps identify the area of mutual recognition—where already existing evidence and non-coercive measures are gathered (including oral evidence)—and others in which coercion is necessary thus distancing mutual recognition in favour of mutual assistance.

---

[24]For a first comment on the law authorising the ratification of the 2000 Convention see La Rocca (2016), pp. 1ff; Triggiani (2016), pp. 1ff.

[25]In these terms Daniele (2017), pp. 417f.

6 Between Mutual Legal Assistance and Mutual Recognition

It is certainly due to the dynamics of mutual legal assistance—according to the most up-to-date *cliché* promoted by the 2000 Brussels Convention—that evidence is 'gift-wrapped' abroad according to the formal and procedural 'rules' required by the issuing Authority; these are the forms and procedures necessary to guarantee the probatory result gathered *ultra fines*. As per Art. 9, para.2 of the Directive, the executing Authority must abide by the formalities and procedures expressly indicated in the EIO by the issuing Authority.[26] Relying on *lex fori*, however, leads to an insurmountable limit in possible conflicts between the imported model and 'fundamental principles' of law of the executing State.

The sense of such a provision is clear: to reconcile the need to guarantee the admissibility of evidence in the 'requesting' State with the need to safeguard the law in the 'requested' State, so that invoking *lex fori* should be exploited *cum grano salis* only as strictly indispensable to guarantee the evidence is provided.[27]

This itinerary is certainly derogatory compared to the typical set-up which respects the principle of mutual recognition, but has been put into practise—without particular success, considering its rapid decline—in the sphere of the fleeting experience of EEW (ex Art.12 of the Framework Decision 2008/978/JHA) and provided by Art. 5, para. 1, of the Framework Decision 2003/577/JHA on orders freezing property or evidence; an instrument borrowed from Art.4, para.1, of the 2000 CMACM and taken into account in Art. 725, para.2 and 727, para.5-*bis*, of the Italian Code of criminal procedure.

Drawing on the experience of the rogatory system, there could be participatory research and evidence gathering (as per Art. 9, para. 4 and 5). The 'requesting' State could propose that its own representative participates in evidence activities, as long as there is no conflict with the founding principles of the executing State and such participation does not endanger national security.[28] This participation can also be 'active' and not mere passive assistance commissioned by the executing authority.[29] In this case, to the traditional limits on any incompatibility with fundamental principles, must be added that regarding 'conflicting' activities. Any operations of

---

[26] According to Rafaraci (2014b), pp. 40f, Art. 9, para.2, does not reduce the margin of choice of the issuing authority about the scope of application of the *lex fori* in the carrying out of the requested investigative measure.

[27] According to Caianiello (2015), p. 10, it should be avoided that the authorities applying the EIO face too many difficulties in borrowing from the *lex fori,* thereby limiting any risks of error.

[28] Critical of this formulation, Marchetti (2015), p. 224, who explains that it would have been preferable to oblige the participation of both the issuing judicial authority and the defence.

[29] Fiorelli (2013), p. 712, note 36, highlights how this form of assistance is relevant for the criminal responsibilities of the issuing State's officials, that, according to Art.17 of the Directive, "when present in the territory of the executing State . . . shall be regarded as officials of the executing State with respect to offences committed against them or by them during their stay in the foreign State of execution".

a repressive kind, therefore, remain the total prerogative of the executing Authority and must not tolerate any interference on the part of the issuing State.

The catalogue of situations which allow the executing Authority to refuse an EIO is ample and similar to that which applies to the rogatory system. Among the grounds for refusal there is one reminiscent of models of mutual legal assistance—in conflict with the essence of mutual recognition—which recalls the principle of 'territoriality' as per Art. 11, para *e*, of the Directive 2014/41/EU: the EIO may be refused when it relates to a criminal offence which is alleged to have been committed outside the territory of the issuing State and wholly or partially on the territory of the executing State. As already highlighted, this is a condition which contradicts the idea of a 'European judicial space', to mean territorial unity where EU law applies, seeming to negate the ever increasing phenomenon of transnational crime.[30]

However, other solutions on the recognition of the EIO and forms and procedures to be followed, respond to typical traits of mutual recognition and are inspired by the need to maximise simplification of the procedure, so much so as to exclude any limits of discretion by the executing authority. Following this logic, double criminality is excluded (as per Art. 11, para. g) as to the list of thirty-two crimes already identified in the Framework Decision 2002/584/JHA, as well as the obligation to execute the order 'without any further formality being required'—compared to that prescribed in Art.5 on the content and form of EIO—as if it were dealing with investigation measures authorised by the executing State (Art. 9, para.1) to be carried out rapidly and in any case within the maximum limit of ninety days (as per Art.12).

To this prescription, there is an associated drastic reduction in the grounds for refusal (provided by Art. 11), in fact reduced to zero when dealing with already existing evidence—and some to be gathered—or non-coercive measures, according to the law of the executing State. There is express reference—as per Art. 10, para. 2—to obtaining evidence already in possession of the executing Authority; to the obtaining of information contained in databases held by police or judicial authorities; to the hearing of a witness, expert, victim, suspected or accused person or third party; to the identification of persons holding a subscription of a specified phone number or IP address; to the evidence which, depending on the national law of the executing State, do not "violate the right to private life or property rights" (according to the definition of coercive measures as provided by Recital 16 of the Preamble).[31] In these hypotheses, access to information should always be considered 'free' with 'full' availability for the ordered evidence, even where lacking double criminality or

---

[30]See Caianiello (2015), p. 8, who says that such a ground for refusal might have been opposed where lis pendens occurs. However, he also observes that the best solution would be to identify "clear rules of attributing jurisdiction" so as to ensure the accused is not subjected to a number of procedures for the same 'crime'. Only in this way would every reason be excluded for allowing a State not to cooperate just because the 'crime' took place wholly or in part in its territory. Similar perplexities are voiced by Fiorelli (2013), p. 714.

[31]Belfiore (2015), pp. 3292f, observes that referring to the non-coercive nature of the measure compared to lex loci may create a disparity of treatment since a measure qualifying as such in one State may not qualify as such in another.

the crime concerned does not allow recourse to the evidence required by the EIO (Art. 11, para. 2).

7 'European Models' of Investigation for a 'Reinforced' Protection of the Fundamental Rights of the Person

This product of the hybridisation between the 'rigidity' of mutual recognition and the 'flexibility' of mutual legal assistance is enriched by a series of provisions to regulate investigative measures to offer 'reinforced' protection to certain rights: to personal liberty, to discretion and privacy and to defence. In fact, wherever interference with the fundamental rights of the person risks becoming invasive, the European legislator has aimed at creating real and proper 'European models' of investigation; through "additional rules" or by "practical arrangements" which must "be agreed between the issuing State and the executing State", and which must "accommodate the differences existing in the national laws of those States" (Recital 24 of the Preamble). This means hazy warning signs of the homologation of certain evidence gathering procedures; rules meant to reinforce the rights and guarantees of the parties concerned; the best solutions for the procedural journey to harmonistaion.[32] Nevertheless, we are at some distance from any models which can "guarantee mutual admissibility of evidence, and, above all, a unitary and shared system of sanctions which guarantee effective multilevel protection of the guarantees themselves".[33]

As the Report says, the Council's and European Parliament's choice derives from the need "to provide greater detail compared to the general regime" providing for certain "additional grounds for refusal" which correlate to the specific requested activities. So, Chapters IV and V of the Directive 2014/41/EU define a whole catalogue of common procedures that, given the sufficiently precise instructions which govern them and the absence of conditions for their application, will be applied—in the absence of a transposition within 22nd May 2017—according to the *acquis communautaire*.[34] They include: the temporary transfer of persons held in custody for the purpose of carrying out an investigative measure; hearing by

---

[32]According to Daniele (2016), p. 64, we are facing "only an embryonic form of harmonisation".

[33]See Del Coco (2015), p. 8. What is interesting is that whereas the EU legislator is put to the test in codifying a 'European model' of investigation, he is worried about providing for an explicit probatory prohibition. The reference is Art. 31, para. 3, about interception of telecommunication where no technical assistance is needed: the competent authority of the notified Member States may, in case where the interception would not be authorised in a similar domestic case, notify the competent authority of the intercepting Member State that any material already intercepted while the subject of the interception was on its territory may not be used or may only be used under conditions which it shall specify.

[34]As recalled by Caianiello (2015), p. 1, note 1, this would be fulfilled according to the Court of Justice's method, 19th November 1991, Francovich, joined cases C-6/90 and C-9/90.

videoconference or by telephone conference; information on bank and other financial accounts; interception of telecommunications; investigative measures implying the gathering of evidence in real time, continuously and over a certain period of time; covert investigations.

Even here, none of the models outlined by the Directive introduces anything innovative. Some solutions in Chapter IV and V of Directive 2014/41/EU aim at partial approximation and harmonisation of national legislations in the form of 'recycling' portions of provisions 'substituted' by the EIO: on acquiring bank and financial details—borrowed from Art. 1–3 of the 2001 Protocol of the 2000 CMACM; on videoconferencing or teleconferencing—extrapolated from Art. 10 and 11 of the 2000 CMACM.

8 A Double Check of Proportionality

Having discarded harmonisation of the rules governing the mutual admissibility of evidence between member States—according to the 'minimum rules' itinerary outlined in Art. 82, para.2, TFEU—the EU legislator has decided on a model based on double verification[35]: one entrusted to the authority of the issuing State; the other entrusted to the authority of the executing State. Both are conducted in the wake of the proportionality principle[36]; to be adopted well beyond the mere comparison between the means and the ends. The suitability, necessity and proportionality of the evidence are checked so as to guarantee the lowest possible infringement of fundamental rights on the basis of a reasoned balance between the latter and the need to ascertain the facts.

As per Art. 6 of the Directive, the issuing authority must respect a double condition: the order issued must concern a measure which appears 'necessary' (i.e. functional to the on going proceedings) as well as respect the national rules applicable in a similar domestic case (so as to avoid research for evidence abroad risking becoming a ploy to elude the corresponding national law).[37]

Such a verification is also required by the executing authority: once ascertained that the investigative measure requested by the order is provided for in the national legislation (Art. 10, para. 1, a) and that it is "available" in a "similar domestic case"

---

[35]From the point of view of Daniele (2016), p. 65, such a duplication of checks represents the 'ideal of dual legality'.

[36]Caianiello (2015), p. 5, underlines how such a reference constitutes an evident legal assertion of the case-law in EAW matters. According to Daniele (2016), p. 76, the principle of proportionality derives from the general provision in Art. 52, para.1, of the Charter of Nice.

[37]Daniele (2016), p. 65, defines the first check—on the relevance of evidence—as of 'logical' nature, whereas the second check—concerning the condition of a "similar domestic case"—as of judicial nature.

(Art. 10, para. 1, b)[38] as per Art. 10, para.3, it must be evaluated whether the evidence requested by the issuing State may be gathered through measures which are minimally invasive to individual rights (compared to those solicited)[39]; as per Art. 6, para.2, should there be any doubts about effectively respecting the principle of proportionality on the part of the issuing authority, the executing State can demand clarification and if necessary alternative solutions.

The verification entrusted to the executing State authority has one evident objective: it tempers any excessive encroachment by *lex fori*, thereby guaranteeing the salient sections of the *lex loci* and guaranteeing respect for "the essential connotations of the sovereignty of the State in which the evidence is gathered".[40]

9 Omissions and Aporias of the EIO's Discipline

This ample fusion of provisions within Directive 2014/41/EU—which includes many 'Recitals' which, as often happens in EU law, are paradoxically more numerous than the relative articles—provides a comprehensive instrument which, while animated by an intention to simplify, is full of omissions to ease judicial cooperation. Some are textual; others are substantial.

From a first point of view—reflected by the above-mentioned choice, all but recessionary, compared to any proposal of unification or even harmonisation—no mention is made in the European Directive to a regime which excludes gathered evidence; in line with the European legislator to pay no particular attention to procedural invalidity.[41]

On the subject of substantial 'omissions', and notwithstanding repeated calls to respect defence rights[42] and the innovative possibility for the defence lawyer to take the initiative for the gathering of evidence *ultra fines*,[43] solutions for bridging the

---

[38]Fiorelli (2013), p. 711, as far as these two requisites are concerned, the check which must be carried out should always lead to the identification of a different measure compared to that solicited, so as to allow an "obligatory flexibility"; in the same terms see Del Coco (2015), p. 13.

[39]This may happen within the limits imposed by the hypothesis in Art. 10, para. 2, according to which there must be full 'accessibility' and absolute 'availability' of investigative measures.

[40]The words are from Daniele (2016), p. 66.

[41]Save the mentioned hypothesis in Art. 31, para. 3, on interception of telecommunication.

[42]Defence rights are expressly provided in Art. 1, para. 4, of the 2014/41/EU Directive since they are included within fundamental rights and the legal principles sanctioned by Art. 6 TUE; the Directive must comply with these rights and principles.

[43]The reference is to Art. 1, para. 3, which provides that "The issuing of an EIO may be requested by a suspected or accused person, or by a lawyer on his behalf, within the framework of applicable defence rights in conformity with national criminal procedure". This means being more open compared to the traditional mechanisms of judicial assistance in which the defence played a totally marginal role: the defence could only urge the Public prosecutor for help, 'channelling' through the prosecution for any investigative expectation (in these terms see Mangiaracina (2014), pp. 123f. On the defence promoting investigations abroad via the EIO, see Grifantini (2016), pp. 1ff.

effectiveness of defence interventions in the circuit of evidential judicial cooperation seem to disappear: both under the profile of access to evidence requested by the EIO; and in relation to being able to participate in the carrying out of investigative measures.[44] Thus, today's structure would be profoundly misbalanced in favour of the investigating authority.

The deficiencies associated with accessing the procedural acts of the proceedings in the issuing member State to contest the results of evidence gathering in a foreign State, jeopardise any aspiration to concretise the protection of defence rights. By contrast, as per Art.14, para.2, of the Directive, the reasons for issuing an EIO are contestable "only in an action brought in the issuing State". As has been effectively underlined, "remaining in the dark about such an important section of the investigation makes it clear that with great difficulty would it be possible to effectively oppose a repressive action, as far as conditions inherent to admissibility of evidence are concerned".[45]

In reality, the reference expressed—in Recital 15 of the Preamble—that the implementation of the Directive on the EIO should take into account the rights of the accused in criminal proceedings as set out by the European Parliament and Council in the Stockholm Roadmap might make such omissions surmountable. The right to access the procedural acts (see Art. 7 of Directive 2012/13/EU), as well as the right to a double defence—in the issuing and executing State—(prescribed in the transnational procedure relative to the EAW, by Art. 10 of Directive 2013/48/EU), ought to become salient components of the implementation work given to national legislators. Although the duty of full disclosure, as is the right to dual defence assistance, was not coined expressly to draw on transnational procedures of research and evidence gathering, they should apply extensively; therefore, they should refer to every instrument of judicial cooperation between EU member States.[46]

10   Final Considerations

In a comprehensive plot that, aspiring to simplify, combines features of mutual assistance with those of mutual recognition, constant reference to proportionality so as to respect fundamental rights, and recourse to *lex fori* are the major innovations of Directive 2014/41/EU.

In the absence of the harmonisation of legal models, the use of forms and procedures imported by the issuing State linked to ever-wider and incisive procedures of participation in investigative operations requested by the EIO could produce in the long run a kind of reflex harmonisation. Under the influence of

---

[44]This omission, referring to the Directive Proposal, was stigmatised by Ruggeri (2014), pp. 14f; analogous critical evaluations by De Amicis (2011), pp. 37f.

[45]Thus Caianiello (2015), p. 8; in the same terms Daniele (2016), p. 69.

[46]See Selvaggi (2016), pp. 73f.

ultra fines solicitations and formal and procedural connections invoked by the EIO, the rigidity of national models could in time work alongside other extremely flexible connotations—the fruit of reciprocal hybridisation shaped by the wise use of the rules of proportionality and equivalence.

Directive 2014/41/EU is pushing towards constructing a European evidence model based on case-law[47]: in line with a strategy—from the post-Lisbon era—to create a progressive attenuation of the competences of national legislators, it is taking over a real and proper metamorphosis of national judges who should deal with 'open-ended provisions'.[48] So, the judge would have to build a model of the actual case, examining whether restricting a fundamental right is absolutely necessary and favouring less intrusive measures provided they are equally suitable for the investigative end-result. He should negotiate between national and 'imported' provisions, disentangling EU, conventional and national principles.

The approach is certainly fascinating but at the same time insidious. The proportionality principle—evoked as a guide line for both the issuing and executing authorities—carries a high level of discretion. In this new perspective, the judge may be induced into preferring expedient evidence gathering to the detriment of punctually affirming the fundamental rights of the person. Although protection of fundamental rights is a constant *leit motif* of Directive 2014/41/EU, the reliance on a judge to make calibrated evaluations of proportionality may not always guarantee a solid result. Having recourse to jurisprudence in a sector in which national legal orders are required to yield a portion of their sovereignty,[49] puts at risk a 'drift' guided by a strong instance of efficiency. A 'drift' which might not be adequately checked not even by the Court of Justice, inclined, as we have already seen,[50] to evaluate the balance between the values at play from the point of view of the strong prevalence of the EU's interests.[51]

References

Allegrezza S (2008) L'armonizzazione della prova europea alla luce del Trattato di Lisbona. Cassazione penale 10:3882–3893

Allegrezza S (2014) Collecting criminal evidence across the European Union: the European investigation order between flexibility and proportionality. In: Ruggeri S (ed) Transnational evidence and multicultural inquiries in Europe. Developments in EU legislation and new

---

[47]As effectively highlighted, the EIO "transforms the precise national legislative rules on evidence into flexible principles which are fashioned on a case by case basis by the judiciary": Daniele (2015), p. 87. See also Balsamo (2015), p. 239.

[48]See Daniele (2015), p. 91; in the same terms Del Coco (2015), p. 10.

[49]See Spangher (2016), p. 3053.

[50]ECJ, 26th February 2013, C-399/11, Melloni; ECJ, 26th February 2013, C-617/10, Åkerberg Fransson.

[51]On this point see Rafaraci (2014a), pp. 3f.

challenges for human rights-oriented criminal investigations in cross-border cases. Springer, Cham, pp 51–67

Amodio E (2001) Diritto di difesa e diritto alla prova nello spazio giudiziario europeo. Il Foro ambrosiano 3(4):549–553

Balsamo A (2015) Verso un modello di prova dichiarativa europea: il nesso tra acquisizione e impiego della prova. In: I nuovi orizzonti della giustizia penale europea. Giuffré, Milano, pp 227–239

Bargis M (2012) La cooperazione giudiziaria penale nell'Unione Europea tra mutuo riconoscimento e armonizzazione: analisi e prospettive. Rivista di diritto processuale 4:914–928

Belfiore R (2014) La prova penale "raccolta" all'estero. Aracne Editrice, Roma

Belfiore R (2015) Riflessioni a margine della direttiva sull'ordine europeo di indagine penale. Cassazione penale 9:3288–3296

Caianiello M (2015) La nuova direttiva UE sull'ordine europeo d'indagine penale tra mutuo riconoscimento e ammissione reciproca delle prove. Processo penale e giustizia 3:1–3

Camaldo L (2014) La Direttiva sull'ordine europeo di indagine penale (OEI): un congegno di acquisizione della prova dotato di molteplici potenzialità, ma di non facile attuazione. http://www.penalecontemporaneo.it. Accessed 27 May 2014

Daniele M (2015) La metamorfosi del diritto delle prove nella Direttiva sull'Ordine europeo di indagine penale. Diritto penale contemporaneo 4:86–99

Daniele M (2016) L'impatto dell'ordine europeo di indagine penale sulle regole probatorie nazionali. Diritto penale contemporaneo 3:63–78

Daniele M (2017) Ricerca e formazione della prova. In: Kostoris RE (ed) Manuale di procedura penale europea. Giuffré, Milano, pp 405–455

De Amicis G (2011) Limiti e prospettive del mandato europeo di ricerca della prova. http://www.penalecontemporaneo.it. Accessed 5 Apr 2011

Del Coco R (2015) Ordine europeo di indagine e poteri sanzionatori del giudice. http://www.penalecontemporaneo.it. Accessed 21 Dec 2015

Fiorelli G (2013) Nuovi orizzonti investigativi: l'ordine europeo di indagine. Diritto penale e processo 6:705–716

Grifantini FM (2016) Ordine europeo di indagine penale e investigazioni difensive. Processo penale e giustizia 6:1–9

La Rocca EN (2016) La legge di ratifica ed esecuzione della Convenzione di assistenza giudiziaria in materia penale tra gli Stati membri UE. http://www.archiviopenale.it. Accessed 20 Dec 2016

Mangiaracina A (2014) A new and controversial scenario in the gathering of evidence at the European level: the proposal for a directive on the European investigation order. Utrecht Law Rev 10(1):113–133

Marafioti L (2016) Orizzonti investigativi europei, assistenza giudiziaria e mutuo riconoscimento. In: Bene T, Luparia L, Marafioti L (eds) L'ordine europeo di indagine. Criticità e prospettive. Giappichelli, Torino, pp 9–23

Marchetti MR (2015) Oltre le rogatorie. I nuovi strumenti per la circolazione degli atti investigativi e delle prove penali. In: I nuovi orizzonti della giustizia penale europea. Giuffré, Milano, pp 207–225

Mazza O (2014) Presunzione d'innocenza e diritto di difesa. Diritto penale e processo 12:1401–1410

Rafaraci T (2014a) Diritti fondamentali, giusto processo e primato del diritto UE. Processo penale e giustizia 3:1–5

Rafaraci T (2014b) General consideration on the European investigation order. In: Ruggeri S (ed) Transnational evidence and multicultural inquiries in Europe. Developments in EU legislation and new challenges for human rights-oriented criminal investigations in cross-border cases. Springer, Cham, pp 37–44

Ruggeri S (2014) Introduction to the proposal of a European investigation order: due process concerns and open issues. In: Ruggeri S (ed) Transnational evidence and multicultural inquiries in Europe. Developments in EU legislation and new challenges for human rights-oriented criminal investigations in cross-border cases. Springer, Cham, pp 3–25

Selvaggi E (2016) Soddisfatte anche tutte le garanzie in tema d'informazione. Guida al diritto 43:73–76

Spangher G (2016) Processo criminale italiano e processo sovranazionale. Cassazione penale 7 (8):3052–3054

Spencer JR (2010) The Green Paper on obtaining evidence from one Member State to another even securing its admissibility: the Reaction of one British Lawyer. Zeitschrift für die internationale Strafrechtsdogmatik 9:602–606

Tadic FM (2002) How harmoninious can harmonisation be? A theoretical approach towards harmonisation of (criminal) law. In: Klip A, Van Der Wilt H (eds) Harmonisation and harmoning measures in criminal law. Royal Netherland Academy of Arts and Sciences, Amsterdam, pp 1–23

Triggiani N (2016) In divenire la disciplina dei rapporti giurisdizionali con autorità straniere: appunti sulla l. 21 luglio 2016, n. 149. http://www.penalecontemporaneo.it. Accessed 5 Oct 2016

Freezing Evidence and Property: Already in Force Mutual Recognition Among EU Member States

Gabriella Di Paolo

Contents

Abstract After a general picture of European legal instruments which, on the basis of mutual recognition, are concerned with the execution abroad, within the EU judicial space, of freezing orders for purposes of securing evidence and confiscation of property, the Author examines the Italian implementing legislation (Legislative Decree no. 35/2016) of Framework decision 2003/577/JHA.

1 Premise

The title of this work ("Freezing evidence and property: already in force mutual recognition among EU Member States") requires to deal with so-called 'cross-border freezing orders/seizures', which commonly allude to provisional orders aimed at limiting the availability of property abroad for evidence or confiscation purposes. It is a complex subject even because multiple regulatory sources overlap. So, in dealing with this subject, firstly we will try to reconstruct the regulatory framework; this will be followed by an analysis of Framework Decision 2003/577/JHA and the recent Italian implementing law (Legislative Decree no. 35, 15 February 2016,

G. Di Paolo (✉)
University of Trento, Faculty of Law, Trento, Italy
e-mail: gabriella.dipaolo@unitn.it

© Springer Nature Switzerland AG 2019
T. Rafaraci, R. Belfiore (eds.), *EU Criminal Justice*,
https://doi.org/10.1007/978-3-319-97319-7_7

hereafter d. lgs. no. 35/2016), to verify how and in what measure the obligations stemming from the EU law have been applied. After all, although belatedly, d. lgs. no. 35/2016 has made available to the judicial authorities an undoubtedly limited instrument of cooperation but of immediate access, while the more flexible European investigation order (EIO) needs to be implemented in national systems.[1]

2   Reference Legal Sources: General Panorama

As already noted, speaking of cross-border freezing orders/seizures in the EU requires focussing the legislative measures adopted by the EU (prior to and after adopting the Lisbon Treaty) to facilitate recognition and execution in a Member State of freezing orders issued by another Member State for the purpose of securing evidence and confiscation of property. These are provisional freezing orders typical of the investigative phase with a precautionary function in the broadest sense. These orders are very distinct to those which permanently deprive property following the conviction of an individual, as in the case of confiscation orders.

In this respect, it is worth remembering that, since the Conclusions of the Tampere Council in 1999, the EU has tried to extend the principle of mutual recognition both to orders freezing property or evidence and confiscation orders. But that was based on quite different *rationes* and legal sources.

To ensure recognition and execution of provisional freezing orders,[2] Framework Decision 2003/577/JHA was taken in 2003 on the execution in the European Union of orders freezing property or evidence. A few years later, Framework Decision 2008/979/JHA on the European Evidence Warrant (EEW) was adopted on the subject. Finally, after the Lisbon Treaty came into force, recognition and execution of provisional freezing orders was regulated by two Directives destined to replace, once implemented at domestic level, those in force under the former EU Third Pillar. This refers to Directive 2014/41/EU on the EIO, relating to the seizure of evidence, and to Directive 2014/42/EU on the freezing and confiscation of instrumentalities and proceeds of crime, regarding the precautionary freezing of property with a view to possible subsequent confiscation.

As for recognising and executing permanent orders on property (i.e. confiscation orders),[3] the EU has intervened with various legal sources in answer to diverse objectives: on one hand, there has been an attempt at approximating national laws mostly concerning types of practicable confiscation; on the other, the objective has

---

[1] After the presentation of this paper, Italy implemented Directive 2014/41/EU on the European investigation order, with Legislative Decree no. 108/2017, and Directive 2014/42/EU on the freezing and confiscation of instrumentalities and proceeds of crime, with Legislative Decree no. 202/206.

[2] See: Calvanese (2003), pp. 3895 ff.; Calvanese (2014a), pp. 364 f.; Marchetti (2011), pp. 135 f.

[3] See: Calvanese (2014b), pp. 381 f.; Mangiaracina (2013), p. 369; Marandola (2016), pp. 79 ff.; Maugeri (2015), pp. 300 f.; Vergine (2017), pp. 504 f.

been to strengthen judicial cooperation by applying the principle of mutual recognition to confiscation orders. So, by this reasoning, the EU adopted the Framework Decision 2005/212/JHA on the confiscation of crime-related proceeds, instrumentalities and property, and the subsequent Framework Decision 2006/783/JHA, on the application of the principle of mutual recognition to confiscation orders, as well as, among the 'latest generation' regulatory instruments, the previously mentioned Directive 2014/42/EU on confiscation. Finally, in December 2016, the European Commission presented—as a part of its action plan to strengthen the fight against terrorist financing—a proposal of regulation on the recognition of freezing and confiscation orders across borders. According to the Commission, legislating freezing and confiscation through a single regulation, which is directly applicable in the Member States, could resolve the issues linked to the implementation of the existing instruments, which have led to insufficient mutual recognition. In December 2017, the Council agreed a general approach on the said draft regulation and negotiations with the European Parliament are still ongoing.

Another seemingly indispensable preliminary observation is that the application of mutual recognition to freezing orders implies the circulation within the EU judicial space not only of judicial orders as such but also of goods, so therefore, when freezing orders for the purpose of securing evidence are at stake, it implies the circulation of goods which could potentially be evidence. Thus, the subject of cross-border freezing orders/seizures could lead to a new frontier of enhanced judicial cooperation in the EU, i.e. the movement of criminal evidence in the Area of Freedom, Security and Justice.

3 Framework Decision 2003/577/JHA on the Execution of Orders Freezing Property or Evidence and Framework Decision 2008/978/JHA on the European Evidence Warrant

Already from these brief outlines, it emerges that judicial cooperation between EU Member States concerning the execution of orders freezing property or evidence has been characterised by a tortuous route, aimed at the adoption of a simplified procedure based on the principle of mutual recognition, with all the main features which are typical of measures founded on that principle: (1) compression of the principle of double criminality; (2) standardisation of the cooperation request (by way of a unique form); (3) imposing an obligation of recognition and execution of the foreign order on the judicial authority, except when there are grounds for refusal as expressly provided for at the EU level; (4) promptness of the procedure (with deadlines for recognising and executing the request, and provisions for direct contact between judicial authorities).

The results obtained over a long period are not satisfactory. Above all, this is due to intrinsic limitations in the EU legislation which has set up instruments with reduced operational capabilities. Furthermore, Member States have been rather reluctant to abandon the classical instruments of judicial assistance (letters rogatory) so much so that they have not implemented (or have implemented very late) EU legislation adopted under the former Third Pillar. To remediate this, and therefore impose more stringent obligations on Member States, post-Lisbon the EU adopted Directive 2014/41/EU on the EIO and Directive 2014/42/EU on confiscation which, once implemented at domestic level, should permanently overcome the problem of the ineffectiveness of the previous measures of cooperation.

Now, let's quickly analyse the reasoning and content of EU laws on freezing orders for evidence and confiscation purposes, to verify how they have been applied by d. lgs. no. 35/2016.

As earlier cited, the first step towards the 'free movement' within the EU judicial space of evidence and provisional freezing orders on property is represented by Framework Decision 577/2003/JHA on the execution of orders freezing property or evidence (hereafter Framework Decision 577/2003). Formerly, the subject of international seizure was governed only by conventions issued by the Council of Europe (COE), such as the European Convention on Mutual Assistance in Criminal Matters of 1959 (relating to evidence seizure) and the Convention on Laundering, Search, Seizure and Confiscation of the Proceeds from Crime of 1990; thus this subject was essentially handled through letters rogatory, which were notoriously dubious in time and results.

So, Framework Decision 577/2003 introduces a procedure of recognition and execution of foreign freezing orders which tends to be constrained in the "an" (if) and is more flexible: in relations between Member States, the recognition (and subsequent execution) of a coercive order by any Member State becomes obligatory, except in those cases of refusal peremptorily detailed in the Framework Decision; the new model of cooperation is moreover based exclusively on direct contact between the judicial authorities involved. This makes available a procedure which allows the cross-border taking of goods in urgent cases and in all those situations when it is not possible to wait for the 'classical' procedure of mutual legal assistance. As regards the scope of application of the new cooperation instrument, it would seem to be particularly wide as far as purposes, objects and crimes are concerned.

The combined provisions of Articles 2 and 3 show clearly that "orders freezing property or evidence"—defined as '*any measure taken by a judicial authority. . ..to provisionally prevent the destruction, transformation, removal, transfer, or disposal of an item that may be subject to confiscation or used as evidence*'—may be issued for evidence or confiscation purposes, and may concern any goods (corporeal or incorporeal, movable or immovable) which a judicial authority believes to be the proceeds of an offence, or equivalent to either the full value or part of the value of such proceeds, or constitutes the instrumentalities or the objects of such an offence (Art. 2, let. d) or which could be produced as evidence.

About the offences concerned by the new procedure, in line with the European Arrest Warrant (EAW), it has been stated that for 32 offences recognition is given independently of double criminality, on condition that they are punishable in the issuing State by a custodial sentence of a maximum period of at least 3 years.[4] For

---

[4]In the list under Article 3, there are, *inter alia*: terrorism, trafficking in human beings, illicit trafficking in narcotic drugs and psychotropic substances, illicit trafficking in weapons, munitions

unlisted offences, the Framework Decision provides only that the executing State can subordinate recognition and execution of the foreign order on condition that the acts for which the order was issued constitute an offence under its own law, 'whatever the constituent elements or however described under the law of the issuing State'.

Regarding procedural aspects, the Framework Decision details a model of cooperation with a binding outcome.

Once the foreign order has been received, the judicial authority of the issuing State must first of all recognise it without any particular formality unless it is felt that there is one of the grounds for refusal specified in the EU law (Art. 5, para. 1). Among these, some are merely formal and related to the lack or incompleteness of the 'certificate' (drawn up on the basis of the form attached to the Framework Decision) which must accompany the freezing order (Art. 7, para. 1, let. a); other more significant ones reproduce grounds for refusal which are well known in the field of international judicial assistance and relate to immunity, the prohibition of *ne bis in idem*, violation of the principle of double criminality (naturally when the freezing order regards a crime not listed in the catalogue of Art. 3).

As regards the executive phase, if the judicial authority of the issuing State does not deem there is an impediment to recognition, it must without delay take the necessary measures for its 'immediate execution' in the same way as for a freezing order made by an authority of its own (Art. 5, para. 1).

Still relating to the Framework Decision, two more points are indispensable.

First of all, since the order freezing property or evidence is coercive and impinges on the accused's or third parties' right to own property, the Framework Decision requires the national implementing laws to put into place the necessary arrangements to ensure that any interested parties have legal remedies (without suspensive effect) against a freezing order. It is also clarified that this action can be brought before a court in either the issuing State or the executing State, and that the legitimacy of the remedy must also be assured to *bona fide* third parties. To limit the power of contestation, it is furthermore highlighted that the substantive reasons for issuing the freezing order can only be challenged in an action brought before a court in the issuing State.

A further explanation seems indispensable: according to the Framework Decision, the principle of mutual recognition is limited only to the 'precautionary phase'—i.e. the moment when the freezing of the goods is ordered. EU law fails to consider the subsequent phase, that of transferring the goods to the State which has issued the international order (and that of custody of the goods prior to transfer). Certainly, the EU legislator has provided that the freezing order must be accompanied by a transfer request and/or custody instructions prior to the transfer request (Art. 10, para. 1). But then the legislator hastened to clarify that such a transfer

---

and explosives, corruption, computer-related crime, environmental crime, murder, kidnapping, illegal restraint and hostage-taking, racketeering and extortion, counterfeiting and piracy of products, illicit trafficking in nuclear or radioactive materials, trafficking in stolen vehicles.

request would be processed by the executing State according to the rules applicable to judicial assistance in criminal matters (Art. 10, para. 2), in other words with the rogatory system. This brings to light one of the most critical aspects of Framework Decision 577/2003: its congenital incompleteness. The risk is that the objective of the swift freezing of the goods object of an order may be thwarted by the denial of judicial assistance (or late assistance).[5]

As anticipated, Framework Decision 577/2003 was followed by Framework Decision 978/2008 on the EEW. This instrument was conceived to substitute the rogatory system whenever it dealt with gathering "objects, documents and data" to be used as evidence in criminal proceedings in the issuing State, when they were already in possession of the executing State, according to the 'evidence transfer' paradigm and in accordance with the principle of mutual recognition.

Framework Decision 978/2008 also covered the recognition and execution of seizure. It faithfully followed the model of Framework Decision 577/2003 but with significant integrations to raise efficiency. The most significant novelty consisted in the fact that the Framework Decision on the EEW did not only include the precautionary phase (i.e. the decision to recognise seizure with the consequent application of the freezing) but also the subsequent phase of transferring abroad the seized goods thereby much simplifying the procedure. By applying mutual recognition it was provided that, once the EEW was executed, the executing judicial authority was obliged to transfer "without delay" the objects, documents and data gathered by the issuing State.

Notwithstanding this progress, due to its limited scope of application, even this instrument has proved to be a failure. In many States, among which Italy, Framework Decision 978/2008 has never been implemented and since destined to be replaced by the EIO, it has been officially revoked by Regulation 2016/95/EU, of 20 January 2016.

4 Implementation in the Domestic Legal Order: Legislative Decree No. 35/2016

As we know, Italy implemented Framework Decision 577/2003/JHA only in February 2016 with Legislative Decree no. 3, 15th February 2016, in force from 26th March 2016.[6] There was certainly some fear of risking an infringement procedure. Nevertheless, the timing of the implementing legislation caused much perplexity: due to the huge delay, the implementing legislation is destined to have a

---

[5]According to this framework, the risk is that frozen goods cannot be transferred to the issuing Member State. The risk is not so remote if one considers that under traditional legal assistance double criminality is a general condition.

[6]Adopted following the so called legge di delegazione europea 2014 (European Law of Delegation 2014) (Law of 9 July 2015, no. 114). See, in particular, article 18, para. 1, let. b).

very short life since it is being replaced by the 'new generation' instruments, recalled above (Directive 2014/41/EU on the EIO and 2014/42/EU on confiscation, which also contain dispositions on provisional orders freezing evidence or property with a view to confiscation). Furthermore, and above all, this implementing legislation was born obsolete: when it was adopted, the Official Journal of the EU had already published Directives on OIE and confiscation, but they were not taken into account by d. lgs. no. 35/2016.[7]

As regards the structure of d. lgs. no. 35/2016, it has 13 articles subdivided into three titles. The first relates to general dispositions (arts. 1–2) and aims at the implementation of the definitions provided for in the Framework Decision and at the identification of the purposes of the provisional freezing order. The second and third titles are devoted to procedural aspects, the 'active procedures' (arts. 3–10) and the 'passive procedures' (arts. 3–12).

Addressing the definitional issues, Article 2 should identify the type of decision likely to be executed by the requested authority so as to clarify the scope of application and the purposes of the order subject to recognition. In reality, the definition of 'orders freezing property or evidence'—meaning "whatever order by the judicial authority to provisionally prevent any attempt to destroy, transform, move, transfer or alienate goods seen as bodies of the crime or pertinent to a crime which could be subject to confiscation in cases defined by Article 240 of the Criminal code"—has generated doubts about what type of seizure is feasible.

In particular, given the clarity of the Framework Decision, which was explicitly dedicated to freezing orders for purposes of securing evidence or subsequent confiscation of property, the reference in d. lgs. no. 35/2016 to "goods seen as bodies of the crime or pertinent to a crime which could be subject to confiscation in cases defined by Article 240 of the Criminal code" is debatable and imprecise. Apart from generating conceptual confusion between the spheres of evidence and that of precautionary orders on property, the reference to confiscation as per Art. 240 of the Criminal code would seem to ignore cases of orders freezing evidence as per Article 253 of the Code of criminal procedure[8] and every hypothesis of freezing orders for the purpose of some forms of confiscation (starting with value-based confiscation) not covered by Article 240 of the Criminal code: with a paradoxical limitation unrelated to the Framework Decision (whose range is wide and surely

---

[7]Scholars believe that, in the implementation of European laws concerning orders freezing evidence and property with a view to confiscation, the Italian legislator should have adopted one single, comprehensive legislative act, rather than three different Legislative Decrees (d. lgs. no. 35/2016, d. lgs. no. 202/2016 and d. lgs. no. 108/2017). Stratification of three different implementing legislation in a little more than one year contributed to create confusion on applicable law. See: Daraio (2016), pp. 1133 ff., and 1142; Valentini (2017), pp. 39 ff.

[8]Reference to bodies of the crime or goods pertinent to a crime recalls orders freezing evidence, since Article 253 of the Code of criminal procedure provides the freezing of "body of the crime or goods pertinent to a crime which are necessary for the finding of facts"; but the subsequent clarification seems to reduce the scope of application only to the body of the crime and goods pertinent to a crime which may be subject to confiscation, according to Article 240 of the Criminal code.

includes the value-based confiscation)[9] unseen in the mutual recognition of confiscation orders.[10] The incongruity could be resolved by interpretation: after all, the reference to *corpus delicti* and to goods pertinent to the crime is also suitable for orders freezing evidence; furthermore, the report on d. lgs. no. 35/2016 made reference—as an alternative—to the "goods provided for in Article 253, paras. 1 and 2 of the Code of criminal procedure *or* which could be subject to confiscation". So, it is clear that the legislator intended including both types of freezing orders, and that the cited text of Article 2 is the result of mere oversight.

Again regarding the scope of application of d. lgs. no. 35/2016, the definitions of 'goods' and 'evidence' under Article 2, as well as the catalogue of crimes subject to mutual recognition independently of dual criminality, are in conformity with the Framework Decision. Aside from this catalogue, the requisite of dual criminality is needed, i.e. the freezing order must be issued for facts punishable as crimes by Italian law, independently of constituent elements or legal qualification identified by the law of the issuing State (Art. 3).

Regarding procedural aspects, as noted previously, the legislative decree distinguishes between 'active procedure'—the request for recognition abroad of a freezing order issued by the Italian judicial authority—and 'passive procedure'—the request for recognition and execution in Italy of a freezing order issued abroad.

On the 'active' side (Arts. 11–12), the Italian judicial authority which issued the order freezing evidence or property[11] may address directly the competent authority in the executing State, transmitting the order accompanied by the certificate (written according to the standardised form annexed to the decree and Framework Decision)[12] and by the request of the transfer of evidence or the request for confiscation.

Naturally, the operations presuppose the exact location of the targeted 'goods'. To facilitate the acquisition of this type of information, the issuing authority may use, if necessary, contact points within the European judicial network (EJN) "even to identify the competent authority for execution". This highlights one of the limitations of this cooperation system: it cannot be used as long as the goods need verifying, especially if their existence or location is questionable. In such a case, the traditional mechanisms of judicial assistance are applied (in particular the special procedure under Article 15, para. 4 of the European Convention on Mutual Assistance in Criminal Matters of 1959, which provides for direct contact between judicial authorities) or the Schengen Information System (SIS), commonly used even to find goods whose location is unknown.[13]

---

[9]Art. 2, para. 2, let. c) of Framework decision 577/2003 includes in the notion of good both the proceeds of crime and the equivalent to the value of such proceeds.

[10]Daraio (2016), p. 1142; Valentini (2017), pp. 41 f.

[11]Reference to the judicial authority that, in the course of criminal proceedings, issued a freezing order undoubtedly excludes that legitimated to act are also administrative or police authorities.

[12]The certificate has the function to certify correctness of both information in the order concerning the proceedings, and the goods subject to the order.

[13]Valentini (2017), p. 44.

On the 'passive' side, which sees the Italian judicial authorities as recipients of a corresponding request for recognition and execution of a foreign order, the Public Prosecutor in the tribunal situated wherever the goods or the evidence concerning the provisional order are plays a pivotal role.

This prosecutor is, first of all, authorised to 'receive directly' the requests for recognition and execution originating from the foreign authority as well as their possible re-directing to other offices. The Prosecutor is responsible for transmitting without delay the request to the National Antimafia and Antiterrorism Prosecutor should it refer to any crimes listed in Article 51, paras. 3- *bis* and 3 *quater* of the Code of criminal procedure.[14] He is also responsible for immediately transmitting the request to another office in cases where the freezing order must be executed by another Public Prosecutor on the grounds of territorial competence, or because the request concerns goods or evidence located in more than one court district and therefore requires appointing the office located wherever is the majority of goods or evidence (or for equal amounts, the office which first received the freezing order).

Once the foreign freezing order is received, the Public Prosecutor proceeds directly with its recognition and execution by motivated decree in cases of orders freezing evidence ("sequestro probatorio"). In cases of order freezing property with a view to confiscation ("sequestro preventivo"), the Public Prosecutor must present his request (not necessarily favourable) to the judge of the preliminary investigation (Art. 5) who can decide (by motivated decree) to authorise the immediate execution of the order.

In both cases, not only has the Ministerial screening been eliminated, but so has the *exequatur* of the Court of Appeal, whereas typical of the rogatory system. Therefore the decision on recognition and execution of the foreign order implies very circumscribed supervision. After a formal screening concerning the lack or incompleteness of the certificate which accompanies the freezing order (shortcomings remediable by a request to integrate the missing information, according to Art. 6, para. 5), the request for recognition can only be rejected for the lack of the requirements for recognition and execution, without even being able to check the validity of the foreign order. So, it is provided that the request for recognition may be rejected not only for the mentioned formal reasons (the certificate has not been provided, it is incomplete or the information it contains does not correspond to the freezing order), but even if the subject of the freezing order enjoys immunity recognised by the Italian State which limits the initiation or continuation of criminal proceedings, if any violation of the principle of *ne bis in idem* is evident as per Article 649 of the Code of criminal procedure, and finally for crimes not listed by Article 3 where the requisite of dual criminality is not satisfied (Art. 6).

With positive decisions, there is an obligation to proceed to immediate execution according to the *lex loci*, in other words according to domestic laws (Art. 6, paras. 1 and 3). It should also be noted that the criteria of *lex loci* can be derogated in cases

---

[14]And to the General Prosecutor of the Court of Appeal if it refers to proceedings for crimes listed under Article 407, para. 2, let. a) of the Code of criminal procedure.

of orders freezing evidence, should the issuing authority request specific formalities and procedures to validate the evidence; in the case of orders freezing property for the purpose of confiscation, all the dispositions in the Code of criminal procedure must be adhered to (Art. 6, para. 2).

Article 7 provides for cases where execution of the foreign order can be postponed, when in the requesting State a criminal investigation may be prejudiced by the freezing of goods or goods have already been frozen because of on-going investigation. Scholars argue that the catalogue of possible grounds for refusal ought to be widened to include the hypothesis in which the requested order has form or content in conflict with fundamental principles of the State's legal system, given this check must be carried out anyway.[15]

Since the orders subject to recognition and execution are provisional, d. lgs. no. 35/2016 deals with the duration of the freezing (Art. 8). Things remain frozen until such time a definitive decision is made on the requested transfer or confiscation, which should accompany the recognition request. Should the issuing of the transfer request exceed the deadline, the authorities involved initiate dialogue: the Public Prosecutor may invite the authority of the issuing State to formulate such a request within 30 days, under penalty of revoking the freezing. The Italian judicial authorities can also invite the issuing State to formulate any observations on the persisting need for evidence underpinning the freezing order, with the power to revoke the freezing measure wherever there are no longer such needs.

Finally, as per the Framework Decision, Article 9 of d. lgs. no. 35/2016 deals with remedies, i.e. the means to challenge a freezing order, in particular the decision of recognition and execution of the foreign order taken by the Public Prosecutor or by the judge of preliminary investigations.

By analogy with precautionary orders on property, the accused, his defence and interested third parties (those whose goods have been frozen and would have the right to restitution) can file an appeal (called "re-examination") as per Article 324 of the Code of criminal procedure. Proposing an appeal is likewise doable as per Article 322-bis of the Code of criminal procedure against orders freezing property with a view to confiscation (e.g. should the judge of preliminary investigations reject the request of recognition and execution of the freezing order). Finally, Article 325 of the Code of criminal procedure concerning Supreme Court of Cassation appeals can also be applied, including direct appeal to the Supreme Court or appeal against a decision issued after "re-examination".

In all these cases, the power of the appeal judge is significantly limited,[16] since it is expressly precluded to challenge, before the judicial authority of the executing State, the substantive reasons for issuing the freezing order (Article 9, para. 2). Conforming with the Framework Decision, similar complaints could be made only

---

[15]Valentini (2017), pp. 49–50.

[16]According to Valentini (2017), p. 50, because of this limitation, the re-examination is deprived of its typical feature, since *ex* article 8, para. 2 the check on the merit (i.e. on the substantive reasons for issuing the freezing order), reserved for the foreign judicial authority, is precluded.

by bringing an action before the judicial authority of the issuing State. It would take little to conclude that this system really sacrifices the right to defence and even more drastically reduces the category of reasons behind an appeal: the defence may challenge the decision of recognition and execution only to complain about the existence of any grounds for refusal (violating *ne bis in idem*, immunity, etc.), or even lamenting the violation of the provisions concerning execution (provisions on the modality of executing the freezing order) or the violation of the fundamental principles of the State.

5 Conclusions

In light of all of the above, it is clear that the weak points of d. lgs. no. 35/2016 are due to the limitations of the supranational source as well as to shortcomings and incongruities stemming from poor quality in the formulation of the national implementing law. Framework Decision 577/2003 had been conceived as an instrument of reduced operational potential, since it does not cover the phase of transfer abroad of the 'sanctioned' goods. It is hoped that, from the implementation of Directive 41/2014 on the EIO and Directive 42/2016 on confiscation, or from the adoption of the proposal of Regulation on the recognition of freezing and confiscation orders across borders, a legislation which is organic and complete may eventually result.

References

Calvanese E (2003) La cooperazione giudiziaria in materia di sequestro. Cassazione penale (12):3894–3900

Calvanese E (2014a) Perquisizioni e sequestri. In: Kostoris RE (ed) Manuale di procedura penale europea. Cedam, Padova

Calvanese E (2014b) L'esecuzione delle decisioni di confisca. In: Kostoris RE (ed) Manuale di procedura penale europea. Cedam, Padova

Daraio G (2016) L'attuazione della d.q. 577/2003 sul reciproco riconoscimento dei provvedimenti di sequestro a fini di prova o di confisca. Diritto penale e processo (9):1133–1147

Mangiaracina A (2013) Cooperazione giudiziaria e forme di confisca. Diritto penale e processo (3):368–377

Marandola A (2016) Congelamento e confisca dei beni strumentali e dei proventi da reato nell'Unione europea: la "nuova" direttiva 2014/42/UE. Archivio penale (1):79–98

Marchetti MR (2011) Dalla convenzione di assistenza giudiziaria in materia penale al mandato europeo di ricerca delle prove e all'ordine europeo di indagine penale. In: Rarafarci T (ed) La cooperazione di polizia e giudiziaria in materia penale nell'Unione europea dopo il Trattato di Lisbona. Giuffrè, Milano

Maugeri AM (2015) La direttiva 2014/42/UE relativa alla confisca degli strumenti proventi da reato nell'Unione europea tra garanzie ed efficienza: un "work in progress". Diritto penale contemporaneo (1):300–336

Valentini C (2017) I provvedimenti ablativi. In: Ruggieri F (ed) Processo penale e regole europee: atti, diritti, soggetti e decisioni. Giappichelli, Torino

Vergine F (2017) Il d. lgs. 29 ottobre 2016, n. 202: un ulteriore ampliamento della confisca di estrazione europea, tra le "solite" novità e i mancati adeguamenti. Processo penale e giustizia (3):504–513

Conflicts of Jurisdiction in Criminal Proceedings in Europe: Between *Bis In Idem* and *Lis Pendens*

Lucia Parlato

Contents

Abstract The purpose of this paper is to highlight the main issues concerning conflicts of jurisdiction within the EU, also from an italian perspective. The reason of conflicts of jurisdiction's increase lies in the non-full application of the territoriality criterion, but especially in the transformation of criminality: the opening of borders and free movement of people, as well as the using of IT tools, can cause a fragmentation, among different countries, in the commission of crimes. The discussion on the overlap of proceedings for the same facts involving the same person revolves around various sources of law. Because of interpretative difficulties, many questions regarding conflicts of jurisdiction are still under debate, also in the national and supranational case-law.

L. Parlato (✉)
University of Palermo, Department of Law, Palermo, Italy
e-mail: lucia.parlato@unipa.it

© Springer Nature Switzerland AG 2019
T. Rafaraci, R. Belfiore (eds.), *EU Criminal Justice*,
https://doi.org/10.1007/978-3-319-97319-7_8

1 Conflicts of Jurisdiction and Reasons of Their Increase

We can refer to conflicts of jurisdiction any time two or more States claim simultaneously the right of exercising punitive authority for the same fact and towards the same person. Accordingly, we can differentiate potential conflicts of jurisdiction from real ones. The first hypothesis occurs when involved States all abstractly have a specific case jurisdiction and could all claim the power of exercising it, while, the second hypothesis occurs when two or more States effectively prosecute the same fact involving the same person. What comes out is a double requirement. On one side, it is required to act preventively by setting specific criteria in order to orient these States towards a spontaneous composition of potential conflicts. On the other side, it is necessary to assign to a representative body the task of taking action bindingly any time these preventive criteria do not work, generating a real conflict.

In respect to what just mentioned, according to a sort of inverted sequence, the issue may be described in two different ways. In a way, the problem deals with the *ne bis in idem* principle, to which the first part of this paper is dedicated. As is well known, this principle considers those situations in which, after proceedings are definitively closed, there are still pending proceedings for the same fact against the same person. In another way, the issue is considered within the *lis pendens* phenomenon, which will be discussed in the second part of the paper and which occur when, although proceedings are not finally closed, there is an overlap of more ongoing proceedings involving the same facts and persons. According to this twofold perspective, it is easy to understand how the *ne bis in idem* principle is considered a sort of *extrema ratio* in respect to any kind of mechanism aimed at preventing or resolving *lis pendens* phenomena.[1]

Before starting to consider this principle and its related existing normative sources, it is important to determine the reasons why conflicts of jurisdiction have increased in the last years.

Recently, a series of different reasons contributed to doubling, or either multiplying, the number of proceedings starting in different States, making urgent the need of assuring the respect of human basic rights for all those individuals who are undergoing a plurality of criminal proceedings. In this regards, first it is necessary to consider a couple of general trends that could both have importance.

Each single State tends to be unaffected by repressive methods adopted in other countries, whereas is keen on expanding its own jurisdiction up to covering also unknown territorial scopes by invading them.

Given the above, the situation concerning a multiplicity of punitive authorities can depend on various factors.

In the first place, in order to determine judicial competence, many countries apply specific criteria, not necessarily linked to the territoriality principle.

---

[1]Paulesu (2017), pp. 480 f.; Procaccino (2016), p. 268; Luparia (2012) *passim*; Galantini (2011), pp. 3 f. In this regard, the main reference point in Italian case-law is: Cass., Sez. un, 28.06.2005, Donati, in *Cass. pen.* 2006, 28 ff.

This specific principle, for instance, is not totally accepted by the Italian Criminal Code (c.p.), as it is contaminated by other criteria, such as those related to universality or absolute extra-territoriality *ex* art. 7 c.p., as well as to the nationality of the "guilty", or to the protection and defense criteria, *ex* art. 9 and art. 10 c.p. In particular, the value given to the principle of universality, stemming from the need for the State to guarantee effective protection, is considered crucial; more specifically, that kind of effective protection such to assure punishment of the "criminal", no matter where the violation of the law comes from and who is effectively responsible for it. If all the States would agree on applying the same territoriality criteria, the only way of avoiding risk of conflicts would be to strictly apply this criterion. However, from a different standpoint, this strict application would bring to the risk of leaving a guilty unpunished any time the constituent elements of the crime are not precisely locatable in a particular State.[2]

Secondly, the notion of crime committed within the State tends to expand: for instance, in the Italian system, according to art. 6 c.p., in order to establish if a crime is committed (or attempted) in a specific State, it is enough that a single "fragment" of the criminal conduct, combined with other acts committed abroad, is present in that specific State.[3] In this way, where a number of people is involved in the same crime, the participation of one person to whatever activity within the Italian territory, no matter if highly or poorly related to the crime, brings to consider the crime as committed in Italy, making punishable also the other involved subjects who acted abroad.[4]

Furthermore, beside this jurisdiction's expanding trend, followed by national legislator on the basis of solidarity in a supranational perspective, another trend has been progressively consolidated towards promoting "criminalization" of violations of common interests. Prosecuting and preventing these kinds of violations requires cooperation and joint efforts. In this regard, to compensate for incomplete national jurisdictions, many conventions,[5] joint actions and framework decisions,[6] especially in the EU, followed one another.

---

[2]Amalfitano (2009), pp. 1293 ff.

[3]Among others, see: Cass., sez. VI, 24.11.1995, Sara, *Cass. pen.* 1997, 66; Cass., sez. I, 7.12.1995, D'Agostino, *Giust. pen.* 1997, II, 98; Cass., sez. VI, 7.1.2008, n. 1180, *CED Cass.* n. 238228.

[4]Cass., sez. V, 14.10.1996, Colecchia, *Cass. pen.* 1998, 114; Cass., sez. VI, 15.11.1999, Moceri, *Cass. pen.* 2001, 3056; Cass., sez. VI, 7.1.2008, n. 1180, *C.E.D. Cass.*, n. 238228.

[5]For instance, Convention on the protection of the European Communities' financial interests, 26.07.1995; Convention drawn up on the basis of Article K.3 (2) (c) of the Treaty on European Union on the fight against corruption involving officials of the European Communities or officials of Member States of the European Union, 26.05.1997.

[6]In particular, Joint action of 21.12.1998 adopted by the Council on the basis of Article K.3 of the Treaty on European Union, on making it a criminal offence to participate in a criminal organisation in the Member States of the European Union; Council Framework Decision of 13.06.2002 on combating terrorism (2002/475/JHA); Council Framework decision of 24.02.2005 on attacks against information systems (2005/222/JHA).

Nevertheless, the main reason for the increase in jurisdictions' overlap is the progressive transformation of criminality itself, which has a more and more markedly transnational dimension as national economies and borders gradually open, giving criminality the opportunity of acting within a context territorially and economically expanding. Several factors contributed to this situation, among these: free movement of people, increasing migration flow, but also changing labor market and globalization. Moreover, several types of crime, because of their proper configuration, are not suitable for remaining restricted into national territorial borders.

For their strong tendency to transnationality, organised crime, together with terrorism, money laundering, fraud, corruption, organ and people trafficking, make it difficult to detect the *locus commissi delicti* as they are normally committed in several countries.

Above all, fragmentation in the commission of crimes—with consequent increase in conflicts and multiple jurisdiction—depends on the increase of specific types of criminality which, like the one concerning IT, strongly tend to be committed in more countries.[7] Beyond these types of criminality, this trend may involve also other crimes, like those committed with IT tools.

2 The Cornerstone: The *Ne Bis In Idem* Principle and Its Complex Normative Basis

The *ne bis in idem* principle, recognised with various meanings in each national legislation,[8] is the object of several normative sources and of an articulated interpretative elaboration. This contributes to create a complex net of specifications and distinctions.

This principle is considered as the negative effect of a final court decision, that is to say, the "barring effect on further prosecution" after a court decision becomes final, preventing the opening of new proceedings for the same fact against the same person. It plays an important role both in substantive criminal law and in criminal procedure: indeed, it protects the individual not only from second punishment, but also from second criminal proceedings.

The main issue (related to the plurality of criminal proceedings involving the same person and the same facts) concerns two different situations: when new proceedings start, despite a final judgment, and when parallel criminal proceedings take place, determining the *lis pendens* phenomenon.[9]

These situations may occur also within a single State, nevertheless particularly important issues refer to the case where different proceedings start in different States.

---

[7]Paulesu (2017), p. 458.

[8]Mancuso (2012), pp. 403 ff.; Normando (2015), pp. 521 ff.

[9]Paulesu (2017), p. 457.

In this regards, we can talk about "parallel jurisdiction", with the consequent overlap of punitive authorities on the same fact.

Focusing on supranational sources, we first need to consider that we are talking about Art. 4 of Protocol n. 7 of the European Convention of Human Rights (ECHR) and Art. 14, para. 7 of the International Agreement on Political and Civil Rights, as well as Art. 50 of the EU Charter of Fundamental Rights (CFREU) and Art. 54 ff. of the Convention Implementing the Schengen Agreement (CISA).[10]

It is important to start by saying that, on one hand, provisions contained in the mentioned Art. 4 play a role in an internal dimension[11]: it is true that they are supranational, but they concern *bis in idem* occurring in the context of a single State. On the other hand, the mentioned European Union provisions concern the transnational dimension: they refer to *bis in idem* involving different countries.

As for the internal dimension, it is relevant to point out that ECHR's original text had a gap, determined by the lack of a provision on *ne bis in idem*. This gap was filled in 1984, by a specific provision in the context of Art. 4 of Protocol n. 7 (ratified by Italy with Law 9.4.1990, n. 98, that came into force on February, 1st 1992). This provision intends to be a compromise between two different traditions, the "British" and the "continental" one. The first, through the double jeopardy prohibition, tends to protect the single individual, by avoiding double persecution. The second, relying on the certainty of law, tends to prefer an impersonal approach.

The mentioned ECHR Protocol considers *ne bis in idem* as an individual, *ad personam* guarantee: it is a guarantee that originates in the moment the punitive right is exercised by a judicial authority, "exhausting" prosecution powers in the entire system. The outcome is a subjective situation consisting of the right for the individual of not being involved, any longer, in proceedings on the same facts.[12]

In several respects, the impact of the principle as defined by Art. 4 results being minimalist and not fully satisfying. Mainly because of the previously mentioned sphere of internal dimension, corresponding to the provision which does not prevent a signatory State, or a third State, to prosecute the same person for the same facts.

As for the transnational dimension, and therefore the European Union normative sources of the principle, the attention needs to be focused first on the "Schengen acquis" (CISA),[13] which extends the prohibition of *bis in idem* to criminal jurisdictions in the Member States of the Union, by giving the principle a European dimension.

Also, the Lisbon Treaty gave the CFREU legal value. Art. 50 provides for the right of a person not to be judged or punished twice for a crime for which this same

---

[10]Paulesu (2017), p. 463; Nascimbene (2018), pp. 3 ff.

[11]On this provision, see in particular: Allegrezza (2012), pp. 894 ff.

[12]Procaccino (2016), p. 269.

[13]Convention implementing the Schengen Agreement of 14 June 1985 between the Governments of the States of the Benelux Economic Union, the Federal Republic of Germany and the French Republic on the gradual abolition of checks at their common borders Applicative Convention of Schengen Treaty.

person has already been finally acquitted or convicted in one of the EU Member State. It is a provision that puts together both internal and "communitarian" *ne bis in idem*.

Internally, the Italian Constitution (Cost.) does not prohibit double jeopardy, although the Constitutional Court considers it a constitutionally protected value deriving both from the right to judicial protection, *ex* Art. 24 Cost., and the principle of reasonable duration of the proceedings, *ex* Art. 111 Cost.[14] Basic contents of the principle can be found under Art. 649 and Art. 669 of the Code of Criminal Procedure (c.p.p.). This last one, which refers to the executive phase (following a court final judgment), provides that, among many final judgments on the same facts against the same person, the choice should be done on the basis of the principle of *favor rei*.

2.1 Most Controversial Aspects: The Concept of "Criminal Matters"

In relation to the principle under examination, many doubts have been raised before the European Court of Human Rights, but also before the Court of Justice of the EU.[15]

The first controversial aspect relates to the notion of "criminal matters".[16] The *ne bis in idem* principle is, indeed, relevant, independently of the fact that the second proceedings are structured and defined by a national legislation as "nominally" criminal, that is to say, independently of their qualification by the national legislator. This occurs when, although not formally "criminal", proceedings have anyway "punitive" repercussions on the subjective sphere of the involved individual, making them substantially "criminal".

In this regard, we have to admit the possibility of a "heterogeneous" *bis in idem*, that is to say, concerning criminal and non-criminal proceedings,[17] in addition to a "homogeneous" *bis in idem*, that is to say, concerning proceedings all considered formally criminal. To this purpose, Art. 4 of Protocol n. 7 of the ECHR only refers to criminal proceedings. However, it is crucial to determine what we mean by "criminal matters". For the European Court of Human Rights, criminal or civil "qualification" assigned to proceedings on the basis of national legislation cannot be considered as an exclusive criterion, otherwise, it would end up entrusting the operational nature of the principle to States discretional decision.

It is also crucial to control the cumulative use of those sanctions that, although mystified by different names, have a strong para-criminalistic vocational nature,[18] in

---

[14]In this regards, among others, see Corte Cost., 30.04.2008, n. 129.

[15]For an interesting overview, see Galantini (2011), pp. 1 ff.

[16]In particular, see Mazzacuva (2013), pp. 1899 ff.

[17]Procaccino (2016), p. 275.

[18]Dova (2016), p. 2.

order to avoid an excess of punitive effect.[19] Therefore, it is not only internal qualification to play an important role, but also the nature of the infraction, its severity, as well as the proceedings. A sort of "presumption of criminal nature" applies when the imposed penalty turns into deprivation of personal freedom.

As far as the concept of "criminal matters" is concerned, it has been widely interpreted. In a first phase of the jurisprudential elaboration, the European Court of Human Rights established some fundamental criteria based, first, on the legal qualification of the violation according to national legislation, then, on the effective nature of the violation and, lastly, on the level of severity of the "penalty". It is the punitive repressive goal to represent the discriminating factor. As to these criteria, the reference point is the ruling in the "Engel Case".[20]

A second interpretative phase developed around a very popular case, that is to say, the case of "Grande Stevens", which involved Italy. The European Court of Human Rights found a violation of Art. 6 ECHR and Art. 4 Protocol n. 7 of the ECHR because the appellant was convicted, despite formally administrative proceedings had already been carried out in our country. Indeed, although the appellant had already been convicted in formally administrative proceedings for market abuse, new formally criminal proceedings were started anyway. The decision, based also on the recalled Engel's criteria, highlighted the particular criminal nature of sanctions and their preventive repressive aim, with not only restorative purposes.[21]

In this case, the European Court of Human Right's decision was based on internal legislation's "structural" features, with regard to market abuse. This brought the italian Court of Cassation to challenge the constitutional legitimacy—in relation to Art. 117, para. 1 Cost., and Protocol n. 7 of the ECHR—of the internal provisions regarding the administrative sanction for insider trading (Art. 187-bis of the Consolidated Finance Act—"Testo Unico della Finanza"—TUF)[22] and, subsequently, the administrative sanction for market abuse (Art. 187-ter TUF). All that came along with the introduction of the EU Regulation 596/2014 and Directive 2014/57/EU, that required national legislators to respect the *ne bis in idem* principle.[23]

According to the marked criminal value that the Italian legislation gives to this subject—in light of Legislative Decree (D.lgs.) March 10, 2000, n. 74—the issue originated from market abuse came back in relation to fiscal matters. Preliminary rulings were asked to the Court of Justice (that however declared itself incompetent) on Art. 50 CFREU and Art. 4 Protocol n. 7 of the ECHR.[24] Other issues concerning

---

[19]CJEU, 26.02.2013, Åkerberg Fransson (C-617/10).

[20]ECHR, Gr. Ch., 9.06.1976, Engel and others v. The Netherlands; Gr. Ch., 1.02. 1984, Oetzuerk v. Germany.

[21]ECHR, 4.03.2014, Grande Stevens v. Italy; later, among others, see ECHR, 20.05.2014, Nykanen v. Finland.

[22]Legislative Decree (D.lgs.) 24.02. 1998, n. 58.

[23]Procaccino (2016), p. 288; Paulesu (2017), p. 465; De Amicis (2014), pp. 201 ff.

[24]CJEU, 15.04.2015, Burzio (C-497/14).

constitutional legitimacy were raised in Italy in relation to Art. 117 Cost. (specifically concerning Art. 649 c.p.p., in the part where it does not allow the application of the *ne bis in idem* principle to formally administrative decision, even though substantially criminal), whereas some courts decided to directly apply the principle established under the "Grande Stevens" ruling, declaring that—*ex* Art. 529 c.p.p.— they could no longer proceed, however in contrast with the case-law of the Grand Chamber ("Sezioni Unite") of the Court of Cassation.[25]

Similar interpretative difficulties arose in social security matters, in respect to which there was an attempt to call upon the Constitutional Court, then halted by the Court of Cassation.[26] Clearly, this issue could be extended to other fields, such as the one concerning "measures of prevention" ("misure di prevenzione")—despite resistances shown by internal and supranational case-law[27]—or disciplinary actions, especially within the penitentiary system.[28]

An additional hermeneutic phase, that still does not seem having exhausted, comprehends a sort of metabolising moment of the final conclusions adopted in the case of "Grande Stevens", as well as an occasion to highlight some specific points and make some steps backwards. This new phase essentially concerns fiscal crimes.

Following the "Grande Stevens" case, a judgment was issued by the European Court of Human Rights according to which also those proceedings that apply an economic sanction must be considered as "criminal" to the purpose of the application of Art. 4 Protocol n. 7 of the ECHR. In relation to this aspect, though, we need to point out that carrying out two parallel proceedings ("mere duplication") can result compatible with this provision: in particular "when, in a situation of two parallel sets of proceedings, the second set of proceedings is discontinued after the first set of proceedings has become final".[29]

Nevertheless, the Grand Chamber of the European Court of Human Rights excluded the violation of *ne bis in idem* when, in the event of criminal proceedings, the charged individual was already sanctioned by the fiscal administration (through the payment of a sanction equal to 30% of evaded taxes), as long as there is "a sufficiently close connection between [the different sanctions], in substance and in time".[30]

Following this development in the European Court of Human Rights's case-law, the Italian Constitutional Court, called upon to assess the legitimacy of Art.

---

[25]Cass., sez. un., 28.3.2013, n. 37424, in *www.penalecontemporaneo.it*.

[26]Cass., sez. III, 14.1.2015, n. 31378, in *www.penalecontemporaneo.it*.

[27]Procaccino (2016), pp. 295 ff.

[28]Among others, see: ECHR, 8.11.2007, Stitic v. Croatia; 9.5. 1977, X v. Switzerland.

[29]ECHR, 20.5.2014, Nykanen v. Finland §§ 47, 49; 10.2.2015, Kiiveri v. Finland; 27.11.2014, Lucky Dev v. Sweden.

[30]ECHR., 15.11.2016, A and B v. Norway; on the same criteria, for a different outcome, see later 18.05.2017, Jóhannesson and others v. Island; Viganò (2016), pp. 1 ff.

649 c.p.p., decided to send back the case to the judge of the proceedings, suggesting to take into consideration the more recent supranational interpretation.[31]

More recently, the Grand Chamber of the Court of Justice, according to Art. 50 CFRUE, in relation to fiscal crimes as well as information and market abuse,[32] addressed three different issues by emphasising the principle of proportionality.

In this regard, it cannot be overlooked how the Italian case-law on fiscal matters justified the non-application of *ne bis in idem* mainly on the basis of the asserted "non-severity" of the corresponding sanction,[33] although this position is in contrast with supranational case-law.[34] According to the internal standpoint, this solution is further supported by the fact that national provisions on *ne bis in idem* exclusively refer to criminal proceedings.

2.2 Continued: Notions Related to "Bis", "Idem", "Final Judgment" and "Execution of the Decision"

In addition to the problem regarding the identification of "criminal matters", there are several further controversial aspects that we will briefly summarise hereunder.

A particularly interesting aspect in the case-law concerns the notion of "bis", that is new proceedings from which violation of the prohibition stems. In respect to this, the outcome of the proceedings is irrelevant. Indeed, it is not crucial whether the second proceedings end with conviction or acquittal. Violation of the principle may occur even when proceedings close with a final decision that does not affect the merits of the case. This is in line with art. 50 CFREU.

Nevertheless, confirming the Italian case-law, the European Court of Human Rights gives specific relevance to the hypothesis that the opening of "new" proceedings on the same fact against the same person occurred "unintentionally", that is to say, without judicial authority being aware of previous decision. Consequently, it is deemed that the prohibition needs to be considered violated for the sole reason of the intentional "new" opening of the proceedings. In this respect, the European Court of Human Rights states that, whenever a judicial authority recognises the incorrectness of the reopening of proceedings and provides a restorative measure, the appellant must not be regarded as a victim, as he has no prejudice to complain for.[35] In this scenario, one could argue that this position would end up by introducing

---

[31]Corte cost., 24.01.2018, n. 43; Galluccio (2018), pp. 234 ff.

[32]CJEU, GC, 20.03.2018, C-524/15, Menci; C-537/16, Garlsson Real Estate and others.; C-597/16, Di Puma, Zecca; see Nascimbene (2018), pp. 2 ff.

[33]Dova (2016), pp. 2 ff.

[34]ECHR, 20.05.2014, Nykänen v. Finland.

[35]ECHR, 3.10.2002, Zigarella v. Italy; see later ECHR, GC, 10.02.2009, Zolotukhin v. Russia; see Mancuso and Viganò (2016), p. 379.

an additional criterion, which is not present in Art. 4 of Protocol n. 7 of the ECHR, concerning the operational nature of the principle.[36]

Another largely debated issue concerns the notion of "idem" or "the same fact". In this respect, the issue concerning whether considering *idem factum* or legal *idem* is crucial. Sometimes, what is given value are the "material elements" of the conduct or the real circumstances of the fact, sometimes, is the legal qualification of the fact. What is certain, anyway, is that the subjective identity is necessary, that is to say the violation of the principle must be excluded when an offense comes from a different person, in particular from a legal person.

In this regard, the European Court of Human Right's case-law has shown, in time, a variation among different orientations. Up to 2009, the interpretative strand tended towards valorisation of the fact's legal qualification,[37] more than towards the identity of a subject's conduct, in a naturalistic and historical sense. Another strand tended to focus on the identity of the material conduct: sometimes by paying particular attention to the fact that from the same conduct more different crimes may derive.[38]

In 2009, the European Court of Human Rights adopted a more favorable approach towards the individual, the type of approach that focuses on the identity of material facts, that means on the sameness of events: therefore *idem factum* and not legal *idem*.[39] The outcome was the exclusion of any kind of formalistic interpretation based on the legal qualification of the fact. In this way, the issue crosses over with the one related to "criminal matters": indeed, the European Court of Human Rights's decision of 2009 concerned both concepts by referring to "heterogeneous" *bis in idem*. This orientation was followed by other decisions.[40] Also the Court of Luxembourg had already supported this orientation, especially in relation to a "homogeneous" *bis in idem* for crimes concerning drug trafficking.[41]

In Italy, the issue was dealt with via a challenge of constitutional legitimacy of Art. 649 c.p.p. for violation of Art. 117 Cost. in relation to Art. 4 Protocol n. 7 of the ECHR. In this regard, the Court of Cassation's case-law was unambiguous in limiting the prohibition of *bis in idem* to same "legal facts", that is to say, regarding a specific circumstance, typified by the criminal norm and not by the "historical fact". This brings to inoperativeness of the prohibition in case of "concorso formale di reati", that is the simultaneous violation of more criminal norms through the same conduct. However, in contrast with this interpretation, the Constitutional Court found a conflict between the internal norm and the supranational one, on the basis

---

[36]Allegrezza (2012), pp. 899 f.

[37]ECHR, 30.07.1998, Oliveira v. Switzerland ; per una soluzione compromissoria, ECHR, 29.05.2001, Fischer v. Austria; 30.05.2002, W. F. c, Austria; 6.6.2002, Sailer v. Austria.

[38]The case-law in this area is varied: in particular, possible differences as to the historical fact may lie in the criminal intention or the aim pursued (ECHR, 14.09.2004, Rosenquist v. Sweden), or on an aggravating circumstance (ECHR, 2.9.2004, Bachmaier v. Austria).

[39]ECHR, GC, 10.02.2009, Zolotukhin v. Russia, cit.

[40]ECHR, 23.6.2015, Butnaru er Bejan, Piser v. Romania; see also ECHR, 4.3.2014, Grande Stevens v. Italia; 20.5.2014, Nykanen v. Finland.

[41]CJEU, 09.03.2006, Van Esbroeck (C-436/04).

of Art. 117 Cost., in relation to Art. 4 Protocol n. 7. Indeed, the Constitutional Court recognised the applicability of the *ne bis in idem* principle—also in the case of "concorso formale di reati", where more crimes are committed by a single action—if elements of the first offence (already object of a final judgment) coincide with those of the other (object of new proceedings), in an empirical dimension.[42]

Another aspect concerns the evolution of the concept of "final decision", from which prohibition of *bis in idem* comes from. An important contribution on that comes from the Court of Justice's case-law that refers to Art. 54 CISA and Art. 50 CFREU.

A very popular decisions of the Court of Luxemburg was issued on the opportunity to recognise "barring effect" to a "transaction" between the prosecutor and the suspected, without the judge's intervention. The positive answer provided in the "Gözütok and Brügge" case, essentially based on "mutual trust" between Member States, is a point of reference in the application of the *ne bis in idem* principle.[43]

What remained an open question, in order to establish when the principle applies, was the matter regarding the need of assessing the accused's responsibility. This matter, addressed by the Court of Justice in the "Miraglia" case in relation to procedural decisions based on the existence of obstacles to a determination as to the merits of the case, was solved by excluding that these decisions may be considered as barring further proceedings.[44]

In this case-law, we can also include those rulings concerning convictions *in absentia*, in respect to which each national legislation must protect the unaware accused's right to obtain a new decision.[45]

Further issues addressed by the Court of Justice concerned the "barring effect" of decisions of acquittal for "lack of evidence",[46] or because of statute–barred crime[47]: both issues were positively decided by specifying, in relation to the second, that the "barring effect" occurs only when a decision is issued following a formal charge. Other preliminary rulings were asked in relation to the effect of a decision of the Police, not considered as a final decision,[48] as well as "the decision not to prosecute", which is considered to bar further prosecution unless there are new elements in the charge of the accused.[49]

---

[42]Corte Cost., 31.5.2016, n. 200; Zirulia (2016), pp. 1 f.; see also Corte Cost., 12.05.2016, n. 102.

[43]CJEU, 11.02.2003, Gözütok (C-187/01) and Brügge (C-385/01).

[44]CJEU, 10.3.2005, Miraglia (C-469/03); more recently, see CJEU, GC, 29/06/2016, Kossowski (C-486/14).

[45]In particular, see ECHR, 18.05.2004, Somogy v. Italia (later, in Italy see L. 28.04.2014, n. 67).

[46]CJEU, 28.9.2006, Van Straten (C-150/05).

[47]CJEU, 28.09.2006, Gasparini (C-467/04). On this topic, see: CJEU, GC, 5.12.2017, Taricco (C-42/17); Paulesu (2017), pp. 475 f.

[48]CJEU., 22.12.2008, Turansky (C-491/07); later see 16.11.2010, Mantello (C-261/09), concerning the European Arrest Warrant.

[49]CJEU, 5.6.2014, M. (C-398/12).

To conclude, among the most relevant issues, also the one regarding the need of effectively imposing the penalty, or effectively stating the impossibility of imposing it, came out. Indeed, a clause that subordinates *ne bis in idem* functioning to this condition is foreseen by Art. 54 CISA. Interpretation of this clause resulted controversial, specifically in the event of a custodial sentence, to which conditional suspension of the penalty was applied. In this regard, the Court of Justice decided that the punishment must be considered as "executed" and, more specifically, "in course of execution" from the moment the conviction becomes effective and during the period of suspension of the sentence, whereas "executed" once the suspension period is due.[50]

This clause is satisfied, allowing *ne bis in idem* functioning, also when a sentence remains unexecuted because of specific procedural reasons. Among these reasons, the Court of Justice takes into account *in absentia* proceedings.[51]

Differently, when excluding the application of the *ne bis in idem* principle, the Court of Justice observed how, when a final decision brings to custodial and financial penalties, the sole execution of the first is not enough to consider the overall punishment as effectively "executed". The ruling on this issue was very important as it clarified the relationship between Art. 54 CISA, that includes the above-mentioned clause, and Art. 50 CFREU that does not foresee it: the first provision, by limiting the *ne bis in idem* guarantee, which is more widely recognised by the second one, does not compromise its foundation.[52]

3 Between *Bis In Idem* and *Lis Pendens*: Initiatives, Normative Sources and Possible Solutions

The need of preventing and settling conflicts of jurisdiction brought to many initiatives, each one in its way different from the others for "strengths" and "weaknesses". Among these initiatives, we have to mention the proposal of a group of academics from the Freiburg Max Planck Institute for Foreign and International Criminal Law, in 2003. The main strength of this initiative consists in having set three different directives: a series of criteria of coordination between the Member States, for jurisdiction attribution; the guarantee *of ne bis in idem* as the last resort in case of "failure" of these criteria; the deduction, from the second sanction to be enforced, of the first sanction, applied in another State. In particular, criteria identified to determine the competent court are: the *locus commissi delicti*, the accused nationality or residency, the victim's nationality, the place where evidence is located. For the rest, the proposal highlights the need for exchange of information to the purpose of a spontaneous composition of possible conflicts. However, the weakness

---

[50]CJEU, 5..07.2002, Kretzinger (C-288/05).

[51]CJEU, 11.12.2008, Bourquain (C-297/07).

[52]CJEU., 27.05.2014, Spasic (C-129/2014).

of the proposal lies in the lack of a hierarchy among those criteria. In addition, there is concern with regard to an "open ended" factor that gives an important role to "basic interest of the State".[53]

It is also crucial to consider the 2005 Green Paper, which highlighted two needs. The first one concerns effective exchange of information between Member States on proceedings, final decisions and other related decisions. The second concerns the recognition of the ability for the prosecuting authorities of a Member State to refrain from initiating a prosecution, or to halt an existing prosecution, on the mere ground that the same case is being prosecuted in another Member State. For those legislations that already foresee it, like the Italian one (*ex* Art. 112 Cost.), this need would require a revision of the mandatory prosecution's principle.

Moreover, particular mention should be made of 2009/948/JHA Framework Decision, on prevention and settlement of conflicts of exercise of jurisdiction in criminal proceedings, tending to prevent *ne bis in idem* violation. First, this source provides that the Member State that has "reasonable grounds" to believe that parallel proceedings in respect of the same facts involving the same person are being conducted in another Member State, shall contact the competent authority of that other Member State. The contacted authority must respond "without undue delay", or "as a matter of urgency", in case the involved person is in custody. Several consultations follow this step, and exchange of information has to be documented. Furthermore, where it has not been possible to reach consensus, referral to Eurojust may apply. Also this Framework Decision shows weaknesses and, specifically: it does not indicate deadlines for consultation activities; it is extremely generic by not suggesting an alternative way to identify the competent court in case consensus is not reached, and by not recognising any role to the defense.

In Italy, this Framework Decision was implemented through Legislative Decree (D.lgs.) n. 29, February 15, 2016, which, relying upon direct contacts with competent judicial authorities, aims at avoiding parallel proceedings from the very beginning of the preliminary investigation phase. Art. 6 of the mentioned D.lgs. lists all the pieces of information that the Italian authority has to attach to a request for information; it also provides for a mechanism of direct consultation, which does not necessarily bring to proceedings' suspension (however for no more than 20 days), but always prevents judgment delivery. If consensus is reached on Italian jurisdiction, the period spent in custody abroad by the involved person is taken into account and, according to Italian legislation, materials gathered abroad can be used according to Italian law. Whereas, if the consensus is reached on another Member State's jurisdiction, the Italian judicial authority will declare absolute bar to proceedings.

In this respect, also the Italian legislation shows lack of predetermined and mandatory criteria, raising doubts on the respect of the principle of the "natural judge", *ex* Art. 25 Cost.

In the context of judicial cooperation, the system based on the transfer of criminal proceedings—foreseen also by 1972 European Convention on the Transfer of

---

[53]Paulesu (2017), p. 48.

Proceedings in Criminal Matters—can play an important role. According to this system, in case of a plurality of States dealing with the same crime, jurisdiction is recognised only to one of them. There are doubts, also in this respect, on the principle of the "natural judge". Other issues regard the admissibility of evidence gathered before the transfer of proceedings: 2009/C/219/3 proposal of Framework Decision tended more to protect already gathered evidentiary materials, in line with 2008/978/JHA Framework Decision on the European evidence warrant.

In any case, whatever system aimed at preventing or settling conflicts of jurisdiction implies effective exchange of information between States, especially in those cases where there is already a final decision: it is therefore necessary having efficient databases. Following the decision of not implementing a European Central Criminal Record Office, 2005/876/JHA Framework Decision provided for the exchange of information extracted from the criminal record. This Framework Decision was repealed by 2009/315/JHA Framework Decision on the organisation and content of the exchange of information extracted from the criminal record between Member States that, together with 2009/316/JHA Framework Decision, is considered the most relevant normative source on informational flow's management between Member States. The first of these two sources implies a tighter commitment of each Member State to quickly communicate, to the other Member States, convictions issued in its territory and to forward, upon request, all related sentences. All that has to be done through a European criminal certification and in the official language of the Member State receiving the request. To this purpose, there are data that have to be necessarily communicated (such as identification of the subject and contents of the conviction) and have to be sent only in case they are entered in the criminal record (such as disqualifications arising from the conviction); others are communicated only if available (such as identification documents or fingerprints). The mentioned Framework Decision 2009/316/JHA established the European Criminal Records Information System for information on criminal records, with the purpose of creating an information technology system based on the criminal records databases in each Member State, with the obligation to regularly update data, without foreseeing a direct access to other Member States' criminal records. This Framework Decision came into force in Italy through the Legislative Decree (D.Lgs.) n. 75, May, 15, 2016.

All these legal sources show how the problem of conflicts of jurisdiction is currently not fully resolved. Uncertainties concern also the functioning of judicial cooperation's instruments, where the violation of the principle of *ne bis in idem* constitutes a ground for refusal (in particular, see Art. 11 of the Directive 2014/41/EU, regarding the European Investigation Order). The path to a solution is still *in fieri* and is affected by the load of the complex matters related to this principle, involving national and supranational courts.

References

Allegrezza S (2012) *Sub* Art. 4, Prot. 7. In: Bartole S, De Sena P, Zagrebelsky V (eds) Commentario breve alla Convenzione europea dei diritti dell'uomo. Cedam, Padova, pp 894–905

Amalfitano C (2009) La risoluzione dei conflitti di giurisdizione in materia penale nell'Unione europea. Dir. pen. proc. 10:1293–1303

De Amicis G (2014) Ne bis in idem e "doppio binario" sanzionatorio: prime riflessioni sugli effetti della sentenza "Grande Stevens" nell'ordinamento italiano. Dir. pen. contemp:201–218

Dova M (2016) Ne bis in idem e reati tributari: a che punto siamo? www.penalecontemporaneo.it. 09.02.2016, pp 1–16

Galantini N (2011) Il ne bis in idem nello spazio giudiziario europeo: traguardi e prospettive. www.penalecontemporaneo.it. 22.02.2011, pp 1–7

Galluccio A (2018) Ne bis in idem e reati tributari: la Consulta restituisce gli atti al giudice a quo perché tenga conto del mutamento giurisprudenziale intervenuto con la sentenza A. e B. c. Norvegia. Dir pen contemp: 13.03.2018, 234–238

Luparia L (2012) La litispendenza internazionale. Tra ne bis in idem europeo e processo penale italiano. Giuffré, Milano

Mancuso EM (2012) Il giudicato nel processo penale. Giuffrè, Milano

Mancuso EM, Viganò F (2016) In: Ubertis G, Viganò F (eds) Diritto a non essere giudicato due volte. Giappichelli, Torino

Mazzacuva F (2013) La materia penale e il "doppio binario" della Corte europea: le garanzie al di là delle apparenze. Riv. it. dir. proc. pen:1899–1940

Nascimbene B (2018) Ne bis in idem, diritto internazionale e diritto europeo. www.penalecontemporaneo.it. pp 1–13

Normando R (2015) Esecuzione penale. In: Kalb L (ed) IV Impugnazioni, Esecuzione penale. Rapporti giurisdizionali con autorità straniere, in Spangher G, Marandola A, Garuti G, Kalb L (dir) Procedura penale. Teoria e pratica del processo. Utet, Torino, pp 504–551

Paulesu PP (2017) Ne bis in idem e conflitti di giurisdizione. In: Kostoris RE (ed) Manuale di procedura penale europea. Giuffrè, Milano, pp 457–494

Procaccino A (2016) Il ne bis in idem dalla "certezza del diritto" alla certezza del "diritto soggettivo". In: Gaito A, Chinnici D (eds) Regole europee e processo penale. Cedam, Padova, pp 267–306

Viganò F (2016) La Grande Camera della Corte di Strasburgo su ne bis in idem e doppio binario sanzionatorio. www.penalecontemporaneo.it. 18.11.2016, pp 1–5

Zirulia S (2016) Ne bis in idem: la Consulta dichiara l'illegittimità dell'art. 649 c.p.-p. nell'interpretazione datane dl diritto vivente italiano (ma il processo Eternit bis prosegue. www.penalecontemporaneo.it. 24.07.2016, pp 1–2

Joint Investigation Teams in the Italian Legislation Implementing Framework Decision 2002/465/JHA

Rosanna Belfiore

Contents

Abstract The Author examines the belated Italian legislation implementing Framework Decision 2002/465/JHA on Joint Investigation Teams. The work focuses in particular on provisions concerning the scope of application of joint investigation teams, their duration and structure, highlighting the missed opportunity to provide for the participation, in the activities of the teams, of representatives of supranational bodies, such as Eurojust and Europol. Also matters regarding investigation measures available to joint teams and exchange of information between their members are examined: overall, the Italian implementing legislation complies with the corresponding EU law. Lastly, attention is paid to the fairly balanced *ad hoc* rules established for the use, in Italian criminal proceedings, of investigation material gathered by joint teams. However, only bare provisions are dedicated to the use of information lawfully obtained by Italian members or seconded members while part of such teams.

1 Preliminary Remarks

The European Union's objective to develop a common Area of Freedom, Security and Justice is to be achieved by preventing and combating crime through closer cooperation between competent authorities of Member States. For this purpose, the instrument of joint investigation team has been adopted, aimed at facilitating shared

R. Belfiore (✉)
University of Catania, Department of Law, Catania, Italy
e-mail: rbelfiore@lex.unict.it

© Springer Nature Switzerland AG 2019   131
T. Rafaraci, R. Belfiore (eds.), *EU Criminal Justice*,
https://doi.org/10.1007/978-3-319-97319-7_9

criminal investigations outside the scope of application of traditional mutual legal assistance, especially to combat trafficking in drugs and human beings, as well as terrorism.[1] Joint investigation teams, therefore, represent an instrument which reveals the new spirit of collaboration which Member States have wished to embed in judicial cooperation, conscious that common action is needed already in the pre-trial investigation stage.

This instrument has been invoked for the very first time by the European Council held in Tampere in 1999, and has been formally ruled first by the European Convention on mutual legal assistance in criminal matters of 2000 (Art. 13) and then by Framework Decision 2002/465/JHA on Joint Investigation Teams (which reproduces verbatim the text of Art. 13). The reason of a twofold legal basis originates from the expectations of the EU legislator to push Member States to implement joint investigation teams thanks to the adoption of a binding Framework Decision, in the face of the slow ratification process of the 2000 EU Convention.

Italy has been the last Member State to implement Framework Decision 2002/465, by Legislative Decree no. 34 of February 2016; a delay which is particularly embarrassing if one considers that the 2000 EU Convention has been ratified only afterwards, in July 2016, by Law no. 149.

2 The Implementation of Joint Investigation Teams in Italy: Scope of Application

According to Framework Decision 2002/465, the competent authorities of two or more Member States may set up a joint investigation team for a specific purpose and a limited period to carry out criminal investigations in one or more of the Member States setting up the team. However, not every type of investigation may lead to the setting up of a joint investigation team. Indeed, a team may be set up only where: (a) *a Member State*'s investigations into criminal offences require difficult and demanding investigations having links with other Member States; or (b) *a number of Member States* are conducting investigations into criminal offences in which the circumstances of the case necessitate coordinated, concerted action in the Member States involved.

In addition to these requirements, the Italian implementing Legislative Decree provides that a team may be set up on Italian initiative also when criminal investigations are conducted into the offences listed under Art. 51, paras. 3-bis, 3-quater and 3-quinquies, and Art. 407, para. 2(a) of the Code of Criminal Procedure,[2] as well as into crimes punishable by life sentence or custodial sentence for a maximum

---

[1]See Recital 6 of the Preamble, Framework Decision 2002/465/JHA on Joint Investigation Teams, OJ L 162, 20 June 2002, 1.

[2]These are very serious crimes, such as organised crime, mafia organised crime, terrorism, child pornography, computer related crimes, etc.

period of at least 5 years. Clearly, the Italian legislator has wished to emphasise the opportunity to set up joint investigation teams when investigations are conducted into very serious criminal offences, on the basis of the presumption that such investigations are difficult and demand coordination at supranational level because of their inherent transnational nature.

Anyway, the most typical feature of this instrument is its case-by-case application, both when the team is set up against difficult investigations that need to be coordinated and when the team is set up against very serious crimes: the investigation pool is set up to face specific investigations, at the end of which it ceases to exist.

As already mentioned, a joint investigation team can be set up for a specific purpose and a limited period, which need to be set out in an Agreement, normally accompanied by an Operational Action Plan: both these preliminary documents are functional to the organization of the investigation team and its ultimate efficiency. The Italian Legislative Decree requires that the Agreement identifies the object and purpose of investigations, in line with the Model Agreement set out by Council Resolution of 26 February 2010,[3] where it is expressly provided that the description of the specific purpose of the team shall include the circumstances of the crime (s) being investigated (date, place and nature). Again in line with the Model Agreement, the Italian implementing legislation also provides that the object and purpose of investigations may be changed when there is a specific investigation need.

As for the duration of joint investigation teams, according to the Framework Decision and the Model Agreement, the Italian Legislative Decree requires that the Member States involved agree on the duration of a joint investigation team, which can be extended in case of specific investigation need.

The Italian authority competent to request the setting up of a joint investigation team and to receive an equivalent request from the authority of another Member State is the "Procuratore della Repubblica" (the head of the Public Prosecution Office), who shall inform of the request (either sent or received) the "Procuratore generale presso la Corte di Appello" (the head of the Public Prosecution Office in the Court of Appeal), and the "Procuratore nazionale antimafia e antiterrorismo" (the head of the national Public Prosecution Office specilising in mafia crimes and terrorism) when crimes fall under his/her competence (according to Art. 51, paras. 3-bis and 3-quarter of the Code of Criminal Procedure). The aim of this information duty in favour of Public prosecutors at highest level is to allow possible coordination with other ongoing investigations in the national territory.

When receiving a request that implies execution of investigation measures which are against the law or contrary to fundamental principles of the Italian legal order, the "Procuratore della Repubblica" shall refuse the request, after consulting the "Procuratore generale presso la Corte di appello", or the "Procuratore nazionale

---

[3]Council Resolution of 26 February 2010 on a Model Agreement for setting up a Joint Investigation Team (JIT), OJ C 70, 19 March 2010, 3.

antimafia e antiterrorismo" where applicable. The refusal must be communicated to the Ministry of Justice. This is the only case where the representative of the Government seems to have a certain margin of appreciation: it is not clear whether the Ministry of Justice may assess the opportunity of refusal—an option which is surely not provided for under the relevant EU legislation. Indeed, Framework Decision 2002/465 represents a break with traditional mutual legal assistance procedures founded on letters rogatory, where the *dominus* is actually the representative of the Government. This is so even if joint investigation teams do not apply the principle of mutual recognition, which 'jurisdictionalisation' of procedures is normally identified with.

The Agreement on the establishment of a joint investigation team shall indicate, together with object, purpose and duration, the participants in the team. Members of the team are 'national members' (from the Member State in which the team operates), who may be either police officers or public prosecutors (replaceable only in exceptional circumstances) according to the Italian Legislative Decree, and 'seconded members' (from Member States other than the Member State in which the team operates), who are identified according to the relevant national legislations.

The Italian implementing Legislative Decree does not allow for the participation in the activities of the team of persons other than representatives of the competent authorities of the Member States setting up the joint investigation team, such as officials of Europol, Eurojust,[4] OLAF, or representatives of authorities of non-Member States, notwithstanding Framework Decision 2002/465 expressly provides for this possibility and European institutions have repeatedly encouraged to make use of it.[5] The reason of this choice at national level must be found in the need to preserve secrecy of criminal investigations according to Art. 329 of the Code of Criminal Procedure. However, this general restriction seems to be too extreme, especially when concerning the participation of representatives of Eurojust and Europol, which are EU bodies expressly devoted to coordinating criminal investigations and facilitating exchange of information.[6] On the other hand, such a restriction risks to increase frictions when establishing a joint investigation team between

---

[4]See the Joint Investigation Teams Manual, prepared in the framework of the joint JITs Project of Eurojust and Europol, Brussels, 4 November 2011, 15790/1/11, REV 1, 13 f.

[5]Under the Stockholm Programme (10–11 December 2009), the European Council has encouraged Member States to use the investigative tool of joint investigation teams as much as possible in appropriate cases, to systematically involve Europol and Eurojust in major cross-border operations, and to inform the European bodies when joint investigation teams are set up (par. 4.3.1). The European Council did the same already during the Tampere Council (15–16 October 1999, para. 43). On the opportunity to involve such bodies, see: Nagy (2009), p. 153 ff., Rijken (2006), p. 104, and Scella (2017), p. 148. On the opportunity to involve Olaf, see De Moor (2009), p. 95 ff.

[6]Eurojust National Members, as well as Europol, may suggest the competent authorities of the Member States concerned the setting up of joint investigation teams in specific cases. See: Decision 2002/187/JHA setting up Eurojust with a view to reinforcing the fight against serious crime (OJ L 63, 6 March 2002, 1), amended by Decision 2009/426/JHA (OJ L 138, 4 June 2009, 14), and Regulation (EU) 2016/794 on the European Union Agency for Law Enforcement Cooperation (Europol) (OJ L 135, 24 May 2016, 53). On this point, see De Amicis (2016), p. 10 f.

Italy and other Member States, every time the latter wish to include in the activities of the team persons other than representatives of the competent authorities of the Member States involved.

As far as the direction of the team is concerned, the leader shall be a representative of the competent authority participating in criminal investigations from the Member State in which the team operates, as provided for under Framework Decision 2002/465. This means that the leader changes every time the Member State in which the team operates changes; after all, the team shall carry out its operations in accordance with the law of the Member State in which it operates, in compliance with the principle of *lex loci*. In line with this rule and with Art. 327 of the Code of Criminal Procedure, the Italian implementing legislation provides that, when the team operates in Italy, the leader shall be always a public prosecutor.

If this fractioned leadership may be seen as frustrating effective coordination of transnational investigations, it must be actually deemed as unavoidable. It would be difficult to allow a leader from one Member State to direct investigations conducted in another Member State, yet in accordance with the law of that Member State: indeed, the leader of the team shall act within the limits of his/her competence under domestic legislation and shall guarantee that the team complies with national law.

2.1 Investigation Measures and Exchange of Information

Provisions concerning investigation measures are emblematic of the new development that the European legislator has wished to promote in mutual legal assistance in criminal matters in the EU. According to Framework Decision 2002/465, seconded members of a joint investigation team shall be entitled to be present when investigation measures are taken in the Member State of operation—save when the leader of the team, for particular reasons, in accordance with the law of the Member State where the team operates, decides otherwise.[7] Moreover, seconded members of a joint investigation team may, in accordance with the law of the Member State where the team operates, be entrusted by the leader of the team with the task of taking certain investigation measures where this has been approved by the competent authorities of the Member State of operation and the seconding Member State.

---

[7]The expression 'particular reasons' has not been defined but it can be taken to include, for example, situations where evidence is being taken in cases involving sexual crimes, especially where the victims have been children. Any decision to exclude a seconded member from being present may not be based on the sole fact that the member is a foreigner. In certain cases operational reasons may form the basis for such decisions. This is the explanation given in the Explanatory Report concerning the relevant provision of the Convention of 29 May 2000 on Mutual Assistance in Criminal Matters between the Member States of the European Union, OJ C 379, 29 December 2000, 18.

The Italian Legislative Decree further contributes to strengthen the innovative impact of these provisions. Besides regarding officials from a Member State other than the Member State of operation as officials of the Member State of operation with respect to offences committed against them or by them—as required by the relevant Framework Decision—, the implementing Legislative Decree affirms that these officials shall be considered as national police officers where entrusted with the task of taking certain investigation measures. This is definitely the most tangible sign of the abolition of frontiers between national jurisdictions, whose borders are traditionally made impassable by the principle of sovereignty, which is the ultimate reason for rules on mutual legal assistance in criminal matters.

However, it is not clear why the Italian Legislative Decree has ignored an important provision, that also marks a departure from traditional mutual legal assistance: indeed, Framework Decision 2002/465 provides that, where the joint investigation team needs investigation measures to be taken in one of the Member States setting up the team, members seconded to the team by that Member State may request their own competent authorities to take those measures (that shall be considered under the conditions which would apply if they were requested in a national investigation). An equally important provision which the Italian Legislative Decree has implemented only implicitly (see *infra*, § 2.2) deals with the possibility that a member of a joint investigation team may, in accordance with his/her national law and within the limits of his/her competence, provide the team with information available in the Member State which has seconded him/her for the purpose of the criminal investigations conducted by the team.

Anyway, what is relevant is that traditional mutual legal assistance procedures are definitively set aside, and criminal investigations conducted by joint investigation teams are entirely considered as criminal investigations having purely national dimension. The only room left to traditional legal assistance concerns the case where the joint investigation team needs assistance from a third State, or from a Member State other than those which have set up the team—should Directive 2014/41/UE on the European Investigation Order in criminal matters not apply.[8]

In fact, joint investigation teams operates even regardless of the most innovative EU legal assistance instruments based on the principle of mutual recognition. This is clearly revealed by Directive 2014/41, where it is provided that the setting up of a joint investigation team and the gathering of evidence within such a team fall outside the scope of application of the European Investigation Order. This equals to say that the sum of the territories of the Member States that participate in a joint investigation team constitutes, for a specific purpose and a limited period, a common space where the team can freely move, without the need to put forward mutual legal assistance requests, whatever the form (either via letters rogatory or via European Investigation Orders), only on the basis of the agreement concluded by the Member States involved.

---

[8]See Art. 3 Directive 2014/41/EU, OJ L 130, 1 May 2014, 1.

However, in such a scenario, it becomes increasingly necessary to make the abolition of frontiers in favour of crime repression useful for defence lawyers too, who have been repeatedly denied by the Italian Supreme Court the capacity to conduct defence investigations outside the Italian borders: material gathered by defence lawyers abroad cannot be presented as evidence in Italian criminal proceedings.[9] This case-law is implicitly confirmed by the ruling delivered by the "Sezioni Unite" (Grand Chamber) of the Italian Supreme Court, according to which defence lawyers carrying out defence investigations exercise a public function of judicial nature[10] (which is therefore possible only within national boundaries).

The only recent sign of change in favour of defence's prerogatives in transnational cases is ascribable to a new provision included in the Code of Criminal Procedure under Art. 234-bis, which states that it is always allowed to enclose to the trial dossier ("fascicolo per il dibattimento"), and therefore use as evidence, documents and IT data stored abroad, even if not available to the public as long as the title holder gives his/her consent. This provision refers to any documents or data stored abroad, regardless of the fact that documents or data have been obtained by judicial authorities via a request of mutual legal assistance; therefore this provision also refers to documents or data stored abroad and gathered by defence lawyers during defence investigations.

2.2   The Use of Investigation Material and Information in National Criminal Proceedings

As already said, a joint investigation team shall carry out its operations in accordance with the law of the Member State in which it operates, in compliance with the principle of *lex loci*. However, investigation material possibly gathered in different Member States, according to different legislations, is destined to be used in national criminal proceedings. Therefore, a crucial issue concerns to what extent the results of shared investigations conducted by the team can be used in national criminal proceedings.

The Model Agreement provides that the leader or a member of the team may be entrusted with the task of giving advice on the obtaining of evidence. His/her role may include providing guidance to members of the team on aspects and procedures to be taken into account in the taking of evidence. Also the Operational Action Plan mentions the possibility to identify, according to the relevant jurisdiction(s), any legislation, guidelines, procedure etc. which must be taken into account. However, the issue of the use of investigation material gathered by joint investigation teams has not been addressed by Framework Decision 2002/465, in consideration of the

---

[9]Court of Cassation, 29 May 2007, Kaneva.

[10]Court of Cassation, 27 June 2006, S.L.

significant differences between national criminal procedures. Such issue has been deferred to national implementing legislations.

The Italian Legislative Decree provides for *ad hoc* rules on the possible use of investigation material gathered by joint investigation teams. After all, this material is not gathered via traditional legal assistance requests and therefore is extraneous to already existing provisions under the Code of Criminal Procedure concerning the use of material obtained via letters rogatory.[11]

First of all, the Italian implementing legislation takes into consideration investigation material gathered by a joint investigation team that is impossible to be gathered again before the trial court ("verbali di atti irripetibili"), whichever the Member State of operation: it shall be disclosed, enclosed to the trial dossier according to Art. 431 of the Code of Criminal Procedure, and then used as evidence. Reference to Art. 431 is significant because it concerns investigation material that is impossible to be gathered again before the trial court regardless of its origin: it does not matter whether this material has been gathered in Italy by the public prosecutor, the police or the defence lawyers, or abroad and obtained by judicial authorities via letters rogatory; it shall be used as evidence in court.

It is clear that the choice made by the Italian legislator has been to give great relevance to the impossibility to gather this material before the trial court for any reason: because it results from investigation activities that have an element of surprise, that are urgent, or that cannot be 'repeated' in court with the same characteristics, once carried out.

Yet, the Code of Criminal Procedure provides that specific material must be gathered at the presence of the suspect's defence lawyer. The problem is how to justify the use of material gathered abroad by the joint investigation team without suspect's defence rights being fully exercised. A solution may lie in good practice: one could imagine that, when investigation material is meant to be used in Italian criminal proceedings, Italian seconded members who are present when investigation measures are carried out in the Member State of operation, encourage the leader of the team to guarantee the suspect with the presence of his/her defence lawyer—who may be an *in loco* Court-appointed counsel in case of urgency—as long as this is compatible with the *lex loci*. Thus, the presence of Italian authorities as seconded members when criminal investigations are conducted by the team *ultra fines* is of utmost importance to give relevance to procedural requirements which are indispensable under national law.

Secondly, the Italian implementing legislation takes into consideration investigation material gathered by a joint investigation team abroad that can be gathered again before the trial court ("atti ripetibili"). This can be used to the same extent that similar investigation material gathered in Italy can be used according to the Code of Criminal Procedure. Thus, material gathered abroad by a joint investigation team is entirely equated with material gathered in Italy by domestic authorities.

---

[11]For more details on rules concerning the use of investigation material gathered by joint investigation teams under the implementing Legislative Decree, see Belfiore (2016), p. 3892 ff.

This choice could raise some concern, especially in consideration of the fact that a joint investigation team shall carry out its operations in accordance with the law of the Member State in which it operates, in compliance with the principle of *lex loci*. However, it must be borne into mind that the team operates in the investigation stage, and the Italian implementing Legislative Decree provides that only material that is impossible to be gathered again before the trial court shall be used as evidence, regardless of the place where it has been collected. All the other material gathered by the joint investigation team shall be used according to Italian law, which normally allows the use of investigation material only within the investigation stage to shape the decision of the public prosecutor whether or not to prosecute[12]—save when this material is used as evidence in special consensual proceedings.

This explains why this type of investigation material is not enclosed to the trial dossier. A coherent choice that marks a difference with the questionable rule, under the Code of Criminal Procedure, concerning the use of investigation material gathered abroad via traditional letters rogatory and apt to be gathered again before the trial court: this material is anyway enclosed to the trial dossier and used as evidence, provided that defence rights were complied with during the investigation activities abroad.

A further sensitive issue concerns the possibility to hear Italian seconded police officers who were present when investigation measures were taken in the Member State of operation. The examination of these persons may be important in order to guarantee oral evidence and the principle of cross examination with regard to activities that have taken place prior to the trial. Although this possibility has not been expressly provided for by the Italian Legislative Decree, it certainly applies, within the limits laid down by the Code of Criminal Procedure, when investigation measures have been carried out abroad by the team. Also the Model Agreement provides that the parties may inform each other about giving testimony by members of the team, and suggests that the issue concerning the identification of the likelihood and procedures in place for each jurisdiction in respect of the requirement for the joint investigation team's members to give evidence must be addressed.

With respect to this, the presence of authorities from all the Member States participating in the team in the Member State of operation is of utmost importance. Within Italian criminal proceedings, it may allow the testimony of Italian seconded members even when investigation measures were carried out abroad. Should Italian seconded members not be present in the Member State of operation, the only possible way to guarantee oral evidence and the principle of cross examination would be to hear members of the Member State of operation, however via instruments of legal assistance, i.e. letters rogatory or EIOs.

Another very delicate issue concerns information lawfully obtained by a member or seconded member while part of a joint investigation team, which is not otherwise available to the competent authorities of the Member State concerned: this

---

[12]This material can be used by judicial authorities also to ground pre-trial detention orders or other restrictive orders, as well as interception of telecommunications' orders.

information can be used only for the purposes expressly listed under Framework Decision 2002/465,[13] which the Italian Legislative Decree has implemented verbatim. Nonetheless, the scenario stemming from these provisions is not very reassuring.[14] Information can circulate freely once exchanged within a team, up to the point where it seems to become independent from both its source and the purpose for which it has been initially shared. Such free circulation is not counterbalanced by sufficient guarantees, not even in the light of the recent Directive 2016/680/EU on the protection of natural persons with regard to the processing of personal data by competent authorities for the purposes of the prevention, investigation, detection or prosecution of criminal offences or the execution of criminal penalties, and on the free movement of such data.[15]

Since the Italian Legislative Decree does not add any further provision on this specific issue, information shared within a team should be dealt with as if it was police information, that in Italian criminal proceedings can be normally used only to continue ongoing investigations or to initiate new investigations where information concerns details on other criminal offences. No evidentiary value could ever be recognised to this information.

The only additional provision in the Italian Legislative Decree is that the "Procuratore della Repubblica" may request the competent authority of another Member State to delay—for a maximum period of 6 months—the use of information for purposes other than those indicated in the agreement, when such use may jeopardise ongoing investigations or criminal proceedings in Italy. To the same extent, the Legislative Decree provides that the "Procuratore della Repubblica" shall comply with a corresponding request made by the competent authority of the Member State that shared the information.

---

[13]The following purposes are listed under Art. 1, para. 10: (a) for the purposes for which the team has been set up; (b) subject to the prior consent of the Member State where the information became available, for detecting, investigating and prosecuting other criminal offences. Such consent may be withheld only in cases where such use would endanger criminal investigations in the Member State concerned or in respect of which that Member State could refuse mutual assistance; (c) for preventing an immediate and serious threat to public security, and without prejudice to subparagraph (b) if subsequently a criminal investigation is opened; (d) for other purposes to the extent that this is agreed between Member States setting up the team.

[14]Scella (2017), p. 150 is critical on this point.

[15]This Directive (OJ L 119, 4 May 2016, p. 89)—which repeals Council Framework Decision 2008/977/JHA—provides that Member States shall "ensure that the exchange of personal data by competent authorities within the Union, where such exchange is required by Union or Member State law, is neither restricted nor prohibited for reasons connected with the protection of natural persons with regard to the processing of personal data" [Art. 1, par. 2(b)]. For the purposes of this Directive, 'personal data' means *any information* relating to an identified or identifiable natural person (Art. 3, no. 1 – emphasis added –).

3   Some Final Considerations

Annual reports delivered by the JITs Network since 2005 show that joint investigation teams are a fully operational instrument available to public prosecution offices in many Member States, mostly concerning investigations on drugs, human trafficking, money laundering, fraud, corruption and organised robbery.[16]

Italy is finally in line with the rest of the EU. We have to wait to see what impact this instrument will have on investigations involving Italian prosecution offices. However, it is already possible to take into account the prognosis made in the technical report which accompanied the domestic implementing legislation: the establishment of up to 25 joint investigation teams per year has been foreseen, each costing 12,400 Euros, for a total annual cost of 310,000 Euros (estimated costs relate to travel and accommodation expenses, reimbursements and allowances,[17] for an average stay of 15 days abroad involving one magistrate and two police officers).

This is not an irrelevant economic burden. However, costs could be partially covered by Eurojust, that provides specific financial support to joint investigation teams' activities, subject to the invitation of concerned Eurojust National Members to participate in such activities.[18] Undoubtedly, this is one (the most tangible) of the many good reasons to hope that Eurojust representatives will be allowed to participate in the activities of joint investigation teams of which Italy should be part.

References

Belfiore R (2016) Le squadre investigative comuni nel decreto legislativo n. 34/2016. Cassazione Penale 10:3886–3897

De Amicis G (2016) I decreti legislativi di attuazione della normativa europea sul reciproco riconoscimento delle decisioni penali. Cassazione Penale (suppl. to no. 5):5–85

De Moor S (2009) The difficulties of joint investigation teams and the possible role of OLAF. Eucrim 3:94–99

Nagy J (2009) About joint investigation teams in a nutshell. Curr Issues Bus Law 4:141–159

Rijken C (2006) Joint investigation teams: principles, practice, and problems. Lessons learnt from the first efforts to establish a JIT. Utrecht Law Rev 2:99–118

Scella A (2017) Squadre investigative comuni. In: Investigazioni e prove transnazionali. Giuffrè, Milano

---

[16]*Communication from the Commission to the European Parliament and the Council. Second Report on the implementation of the EU Internal Security Strategy*, Brussels, 10 April 2013, COM (2013) 179 final, p. 5.

[17]Surprisingly, the technical report does not mention interpretation and translation costs, that are quite relevant in the activities of joint investigation teams, as demonstrated by experience. See Nagy (2009), p. 156. It is significant that the Model Agreement provides for specific arrangements on this issue (Council Resolution of 26 February 2010, p. 6).

[18]See Art. 9 *septies*, Decision 2009/426/JHA on the strengthening of Eurojust, amending Decision 2002/187/JHA. See also the *JITS Funding Guide* (version of 19 February 2016), available on the official website of Eurojust.

Judicial Cooperation System in the Fight Against Transnational Organised Crime

Francesco Testa

Contents

Abstract The Author goes over the origins of the United Nations Convention against Transnational Organised Crime (UNTOC) and deals with the most significant sections of its actual application in national laws, particularly in Italy. The strength of the innovative tools on international cooperation provided for in the Convention is highlighted, as well as the obligation of Member States to appropriately criminalise organised criminal groups, establishing a legal framework consistent with the most varied criminal systems and judicial traditions. The Author also proposes a brief comparison between the system of international cooperation in the Convention and the level of integration achieved within the European Union. Great significance is also given to the importance of adopting a mechanism to review the implementation of the Convention in all State Parties, so as to monitor the effective application of its provisions and identify any challenge and gap that might impede their full application.

F. Testa (✉)
Chief Prosecutor, Court of Chieti, Chieti, Italy

Former Legal Adviser to the Permanent Mission of Italy to the International Organisations, Vienna, Austria
e-mail: francesco.testa@giustizia.it

© Springer Nature Switzerland AG 2019
T. Rafaraci, R. Belfiore (eds.), *EU Criminal Justice*,
https://doi.org/10.1007/978-3-319-97319-7_10

1 United Nations and the Fight Against Organised Crime. Origin and Main Contents of the Palermo Convention and of "Additional" Protocols

The first scenario in which the United Nations examined and discussed matters related to organised crime was the fifth UN Congress on Crime Prevention, held in Geneva in 1975. Indeed, the Congress devoted a session ("Changes in shape and dimension of transnational and national crime") to crime organization seen as both a national and transnational business.

It was later, however, at the seventh Congress on Crime Prevention held in Milan in 1985, that it became clearer and clearer how the increase of organised crime represented a real threat globally. In particular, the Congress realised the fact that organised crime had reached totally new geographical extension, international dimension and diversification of lucrative businesses.

Also the eighth Crime Congress, held in Havana in 1990, dealt with questions regarding organised crime (at the point "national and international actions against organised crime and terrorist activities"). The Congress examined the issue of organised crime in the light of the new historic events. In fact, the quick increase of countries that had reached independence, together with the expansion of criminal activities beyond national borders, triggered the need for new international institutions which might adopt measures to ensure order and increase the effectiveness of crime prevention efforts.

On the basis of the Congress's recommendations, in 1991 the General Assembly made a first step which was to reveal itself as essential to the political process under discussion, that is the creation of the Commission on Crime Prevention and Criminal Justice, as a commission of the Economic and Social Council, composed of members of 40 countries. In this way, the direct involvement of governments was ensured in decision making and supervision of programmed activities.

Since then, the Crime Commission has become the UN policy-making body responsible for defining and adopting universal policies in questions of crime prevention and criminal justice.

The first session of the Crime Commission was held in 1992, and in the same year the Economic and Social Council (res. 1992/22) decided that the Commission would deal with questions related to transnational and organised crime, economic crime, including money laundering, and crimes against the environment.

The question regarding the making of a convention against transnational organised crime came up again after the resolution of the General Assembly 51/120 of December 12th 1996, followed by Poland's initiative to submit to the Assembly the draft of a convention against transnational organised crime.

In the workings of its sixth session (1997), the Crime Commission set up an "in-sessional open-ended working group" aiming at taking into consideration the possibility to work out a convention or conventions against transnational organised crime and detect the elements which might be part of it.

The working group realised it would be advisable to work out an as comprehensive convention as possible. Getting to a generally shared definition of organised crime would be a problem. Several countries believed that such definition was not necessarily a major scope of the Convention and that this instrument could certainly come to life even without first defining what organised crime is. In this direction, also the idea came up that organised crime was evolving so rapidly that a definition would limit the context of the Convention's application, neglecting scenarios where criminal groups might be interested in. Other countries, instead, maintained that the lack of a definition would send a wrong message as to the willingness and political commitment of the international community.

The Convention, besides, had to be a "capacity building" instrument for States and United Nations, handling the collection, analysis and exchange of information, as well as judicial assistance. Furthermore, it was meant to provide for measures against money laundering, include measures that would force countries to confiscate illicit assets, and also regulate banking secrecy.

Finally, the Convention had to ensure adequate defence and protection of human rights and guarantee conformity with the fundamental principles of national laws.

During the seventh session of CCPCJ (1998), a few Member States raised questions of their interest which might deserve being seen also within an international scenario. So, Argentina proposed to work out a new convention against the trafficking in minors (even if the debate went further to embrace first women trafficking and then trafficking in human beings as a whole). Austria presented to the Commission a draft of an international convention against "smuggling of migrants", whereas Italy presented a Protocol draft against the maritime trafficking of migrants. Japan and Canada represented the idea that matters related to the illicit manufacturing of and trafficking in firearms was mature enough to be seen from a regulatory viewpoint.

The political decision obtained envisaged the close interrelation between these proposals and that related to creating a convention against transnational organised crime. On that occasion it was preferred referring to "additional instruments" with regards to the new proposed tools.

The General Assembly (Res. 53/111 of December 9th 1998) finally decided to set up an "open-ended intergovernmental *ad-hoc* Committee" in order to work out an international comprehensive Convention against transnational organised crime and discuss the elaboration of international instruments regarding trafficking in human beings, illicit manufacturing of and trafficking in firearms, their parts and components, and ammunition, as well as illicit trafficking (also by sea) of migrants.

It was this Committee to negotiate the Convention text and Protocols, that, in the year 2000, were finally adopted by the General Assembly with resolutions nos. 55/25 (the Convention and the Smuggling of Migrants and Human Trafficking Protocols) and 55/255 (Firearms Protocol).

2   Relevance of UNTOC for the Italian System. Ratification Law No. 146/2006

One can certainly state that the so called Palermo Convention is the most innovative, balanced and universally flexible cooperation instrument in criminal matters. It counts, to date, 179 States Parties out of 193 UN Member States.

The Convention, however, is a flexible instrument which escapes a traditional "thematic" classification of multilateral treaties and is instead liable to be applied to any form of transnational criminal activity (as specified in para. 6 of Res. 55/25 of the General Assembly, which refers precisely to "all forms of criminal activity"). It then has a potentially boundless application context, suitable to cover the most varied illegal phenomena.

2.1   Definition of Transnational Crime and Aggravating Circumstance ex Art. 4. Definition of "Organised Criminal Group" and Differences with Criminal Conspiracy (Ref. Court of Cassation, Grand Chamber, No. 18374/2013)

The scope of the Convention—well described in Art. 1—is to promote the States Parties' cooperation to prevent and fight transnational organised crime more effectively.

Against the overflowing of cross-border organised crime, the international community has become aware of the dangers of this phenomenon and of the need that special measures, proportionate to the new criminal organisations' methods, have to be taken to better fight against it. In such common perspective, they have attempted to make the Member States' action plan as homogeneous as possible, through the conventional obligation to criminalise certain illegal activities ascribable to international criminal groups (even the sheer participation in them, according to Art. 5) and the assessment of judicial and police cooperation modalities to make investigation tools more effective, within an agreed-upon context of specific measures of judicial assistance, extradition, transfer of criminal proceedings, seizure and confiscation of proceeds of crime.

The need to provide for an obligation to criminalise organised criminal phenomena is to be appreciated if one thinks that no elaboration whatsoever of organised criminal groups, able to substantiate specific crimes, was known in the legal and cultural traditions of some countries. The Italian system, on the contrary, had been dealing with pluri-subjective criminal phenomena since 1930, from the most elementary form of 'involvement of persons in a crime' ("concorso di persone") as from Art. 110 of the Criminal Code, to the more complex criminal conspiracy described in Art. 416 of the same Code. Later, particular criminal aggregations have been step by step identified, such as, among others, organised criminal groups finalised to foreign manufactured tobacco smuggling, whereof in Art. 291-quater of Decree no. 3/1973; Mafia criminal conspiracy, whereof in Art. 416-bis Criminal Code; conspiracy finalized to drug trafficking, whereof in Art. 73 of Decree no. 309/1990; until the group sex assault provided for by Art. 609-octies Criminal Code and race discrimination forms whereof in Art. 3 of Law no. 654/1975, which exploits, alternatively, the notions of organization, association, movement or group.

The Palermo Convention was ratified in Italy with the Law no. 146/2006.

Art. 3 of the Law stipulates: "to the ends of the present Law a transnational crime is a crime punishable, in its maximum, with no less than 4-year imprisonment, in case an organised criminal group is involved, as well as: a) the crime is committed in more than one State; b) or is committed in a single State, although a substantial part of its preparation, planning, direction or control occurs in another State; c) or is committed in a State, but an organised criminal group is involved which operates in criminal activities in more than a State; d) or is committed in a State but has substantial effects in another one".

The text of Art. 3 allows, meantime, to state that transnationality is not to be by itself considered a crime, which adds anything to the already great number of illegal acts of the criminal world. It is instead, a peculiar way of expression or predicate, referable to any type of crime (excluding the fines), on the condition that the same crime, both for objective reasons and its referability to the sphere of action of an organised group acting in more than a State, takes on a cross-border dimension.

In detail, the quoted Art. 3 connects the characterisation of transnationality to the presence of three parameters.

The first parameter is linked to the crime's gravity, determined by the statutory punishment (not inferior, at its maximum, to 4-year imprisonment), thus on the basis of a non-flexible gravity coefficient, in conformity with the idea of "serious crime" acknowledged by the Convention itself that, in Art. 2, qualifies as "serious crime" exactly the conduct punishable "by a maximum deprivation of liberty of at least 4 years or a more serious penalty".

The second parameter provides for the involvement of an organised criminal group. The term takes on a purposely generic significance, which can encapsulate, due to the width of its formulation, different system models of criminalisation of the broadly speaking association phenomenon, the "association de malfaiteurs", peculiar to civil law systems, Mafia criminal conspiracy, mainly Italian, and the conspiracy, traditional instrument of judiciary contrast to organised crime in common law criminal systems, where, as is known, the gap between participation of persons in a crime and cases of association is not so distinct.

The third parameter, instead, features one of the elements provided for, this time, in alternative guise: (a) commission of the crime in more than one State; (b) commission in a State but with a substantial part of its preparation, planning, direction or control in another State; (c) commission in a State, but involvement in it of an organised criminal group which deals in criminal activities in more than a State; (d) commission in a State but with substantial effects in another one.

The formalisation of the transnationality connotation, although it has no specific, preceptive or sanctionary content, however, does not comply with purely defining or descriptive needs, but heralds, instead, significant effects as regards substantial and procedural law. These effects certainly imply that a transnational crime has to be considered more serious compared to its ordinary version, considering the higher danger coefficient assigned to it by national law. We hereby refer: to the provision of the administrative liability of legal persons whereof in Art. 10 of Law no. 146/2006 that, right in those cases foreseen in Art. 3, decrees the applicability of certain administrative penalties; to the mandatory confiscation, even value-based confiscation, provided for by Art. 11 of the same Law exactly for crimes described in the above said Art. 3; to the extension of the public prosecutor's investigation powers "within term and to the ends whereof in Art. 430 of the Code of criminal procedure", with the aim of ensuring an as extensive confiscation as possible of proceeds deriving from illegal activities under Art. 12; to the assignment, to the National Anti-Mafia Prosecutor of the same competences as those given to the Public Prosecutor and Chief of Police in matters of preventive measures (including financial investigations and the application of non-conviction based confiscation), as provided—always for crimes whereof in the quoted Art. 3—by the following Art. 13: to the possibility of transferring criminal proceedings (provided by Art. 21 of the Convention), that has to take place exclusively in the forms and extent provided by international agreements (Art. 7 of ratification Law).

As said before, by introducing a merely definitional norm, Art. 3 provides no penalty.

Instead, Art. 4 of the Law so provides: "1. For crimes foreseen with a penalty no less, at its maximum, to 4-year imprisonment in whose commission an organised criminal group involved in illegal activities in more than a country has contributed, the penalty is increased from one third to half".

It is, obviously, a "special" aggravating circumstance—applicable only to certain crimes, believed to be serious and punished with sentence not inferior, at its maximum, to 4-year imprisonment—and, at the same time, "to special effects" due to the increase of the penalty, superior by a third, under Art. 63, para. 3 of the Criminal Code.

The reading of the rule by word cannot be separated—in the unescapable need for a systematic perspective—from the analysis of the immediately previous one that, defining "transnational crime", is strictly linked to it, and takes on an undoubtedly central role in the complex framework of the discipline under exam.

Art. 4 actually introduces a special aggravating circumstance for "serious" crimes which are committed with the contribution of an organised criminal group, involved in illegal activities in more than a State.

From the confrontation of the two dispositions, it turns out clearly how the provision of this aggravating circumstance has been modelled only on one of the alternative relevant elements in order to define transnationality, whereof at point (c). The circumstance is then "cut off" selectively from the previous definition which, only for one of the hypotheses of transnationality—that is the "implication" of an organised criminal group involved in criminal activities in more than a State—has provided for an increase in penalty.

When only one of the hypotheses provided by Art. 3 has been extrapolated from the transnationality parameters, the term "implicato" (involved) contained in point (c) has been changed into the syntagm "given its contribution" contained in Art. 4. From the non-technical and non-specific formula "implication" an expression has been here adopted which is much more appropriate to the criminal lexicon. As a matter of fact, "give a contribution" is nothing else but lending a causally significant support in terms of material causality, meaning that the commission of whatsoever crime in the State, provided it is punished with an imprisonment non-inferior to 4 years, at its maximum, must have been determined, or even only made easier, in all or partly, by the instrumental contribution of a transnational organised criminal group.

The unequivocal rule formulation, by specifically recalling the causal contribution of an organised criminal group, does not allow for a different interpretative option as to the application of this aggravating circumstance to any condition of transnationality, in the number of conditions foreseen by Art. 3 of Law no. 146/2006, each and every time a crime is ascribable to the sphere of activities of a transnational organised criminal group. Owing to the selective intervention of the legislator, a higher rate of involvement is therefore necessary, in order to increase the penalty, that is, the performance of a causal contribution to committing a crime, since, from what has been said, only this situation, by discretional choice of the legislator, is thought to be of greater gravity and social alert.

The generic regulatory reference to any crime, provided it goes with the above sanctionary provision, brings us to believe that the causal contribution of such a group maybe accounted for with regard to any criminal activity, and then also to the conspiratorial one.

According to regulatory data and to the inspiring lines of the Convention, there seems to be no reason why the specific aggravating circumstance can be applied only to end-crimes and not also to the conspiratorial one which is the means for the related perpetration. There is then no reason—neither textual nor logical-systematic—to consider the special aggravating circumstance incompatible with the latter crime.

Besides, the expressions: "criminal conspiracy and organised criminal group", apart from the inappropriate promiscuous use that can sometimes exist in common language, do not express, from a legal standpoint, similar or ideally overlapping realities.

And indeed, as to the expression "organised criminal group", one cannot refer but to the Convention's definition which, according to the ratification and execution Law no. 146/2006, has been introduced, in its wholeness, into our legal system. Then, under Art. 2, point (a) of the TOC Convention, "organised criminal group" shall mean "a structured group of three or more persons, existing for a period of time and acting in concert with the aim of committing one or more serious crimes or offences established in accordance with this Convention, in order to obtain, directly or indirectly, a financial or other material benefit".

Point (c) of the same Art. 2, then, gives the definition of "structured group", to be intended as a group "that is not randomly formed for the immediate commission of an offence and that does not need to have formally defined roles for its members, continuity of its membership or a developed structure".

It is therefore a composite notion, with clear descriptive traits, well distinguished from those which characterise the 'involvement of persons in a crime' ("concorso di persone") under Art. 110 of the Criminal Code, and criminal conspiracy under Art. 416 of the Criminal Code.

"Organised Group" is, certainly, a bit more compared to a sheer common participation of persons in a crime, but it is,—with the same certainty—a bit less, compared to criminal conspiracy. In order to exist, in fact, only a certain stability of relations is required, as well as minimal organisation with no formal definition of roles, its non-casualness or extemporaneity, its formation in sight of a single crime and the obtaining of a financial or another material benefit; instead, in order for the crime described in Art. 416 of the Criminal Code to exist, an articulate structural organisation, although minimal or elementary, as well as basically stable and permanent is needed, with a definite distribution of roles and the planning of an indeterminate series of crimes. The structural organisation, then, has to serve the commission of an indefinite number of crimes, even without the ultimate financial or material gains of the organisation being required to the ends of the regulatory layout, the final profit deriving from the contribution of the single end-crimes, to whose execution it be properly arranged.

2.2 Brief Considerations on the External Participation in Organised Criminal Groups (see Art. 5, a, ii, b of the Convention)

This is quite a significant issue, especially as regards the *vexata quaestio* of the assumed (in)determinateness of "external" participation in organised criminal groups.

It may appear as a provocation, but pay attention, the issue of a "conscious support activity" to an organised criminal group was clearly at play in the Palermo Convention negotiation tables, and it was certainly among delegates of common law countries, where the difference between participation of persons in a crime and participation in a criminal group is much more shaded.

It may look like another provocation, but if we consider that the Convention has been acknowledged *in toto* in our system by ratification, and if we also consider that the States Parties are required to criminalise offences defined by the Convention through "legislative or other measures", one may be led to conclude that the consolidated tendency of the Court of Cassation about the characterisation of the "external participation" is sufficient to implement the conventional provision and that a new regulatory intervention in our system is not at all necessary in this regard.

According to Art. 5:

1. Each State Party shall adopt such legislative and other measures as may be necessary to establish as criminal offences, when committed intentionally:

(a) Either or both of the following as criminal offences distinct from those involving the attempt or completion of the criminal activity:

(i) Agreeing with one or more other persons to commit a serious crime for a purpose relating directly or indirectly to the obtaining of a financial or other material benefit and, where required by domestic law, involving an act undertaken by one of the participants in furtherance of the agreement or involving an organized criminal group;

(ii) Conduct by a person who, with knowledge of either the aim and general criminal activity of an organized criminal group or its intention to commit the crimes in question, takes an active part in: (a) Criminal activities of the organized criminal group; (b) Other activities of the organized criminal group in the knowledge that his or her participation will contribute to the achievement of the above-described criminal aim.

2.3 Modernity of UNTOC. Other Provisions of the Ratification Law and Correspondent Conventional Provisions. Main Procedural Instruments and Their Correspondence with European Integration Level

(1) Seizure and value-based confiscation (Art. 12 UNTOC) and reversal of the burden of proof (Art. 12 para. 7 UNTOC);

(2) non-conviction based confiscation (prevention measures; UNCAC Art. 54 para. 1., c), regulated today in the EU by Directive 2014/42[1];

(3) extensibility of the national jurisdiction, with a tendential "universalization" of transnational crimes (Art. 15);

(4) joint investigation teams (Legislative decree no. 34/2016, which implements Framework Decision 2002/465/EU—see Art. 19 UNTOC);

(5) special investigative techniques (controlled deliveries, electronic surveillance and undercover operations—Art. 20 UNTOC)—Undercover operations provided in Art. 9 Law 146/2006

(6) transfer of criminal proceedings (Art. 21 UNTOC)

(7) criminalisation of obstruction of Justice *ex* Art. 377 *bis* of the Criminal Code (see Art. 23 UNTOC);

---

[1]At the European level, the new EU Directive (2014/42) on the freezing and confiscation of instrumentalities and proceeds of crime was adopted on 3 April 2014. The Directive establishes minimum rules on the freezing of property with a view to its subsequent confiscation for the serious crimes listed in Article 83(1) of the Treaty on the Functioning of the European Union. It maintains conviction based confiscation as a general rule, but introduces non-conviction based confiscation, even though as a residual hypothesis. Thus, non-conviction based confiscations shall be introduced in the EU Member States' national legislation, but the scope of application of such confiscation is limited in the Directive to the cases in which a final conviction could not be obtained as a result, *inter alia*, of illness or flight of the suspected or accused person. It is also requested that a criminal proceeding have been initiated for a criminal offence which is liable to give rise to economic benefit, and that such proceeding could have led to a criminal conviction.

(8) European investigation order, regulated by Directive 2014/41/UE(Art. 18, points a-c-d UNTOC);
(9) Seizure and freezing orders (Art. 13 UNTOC and Legislative decree no. 35/2016, which implements Framework Decision 2003/577/EU).

3   Other Issues Under Discussion at the United Nations. The Role of the European Union Inside UN Commissions

– Of course, there is a big difference among the various levels of regulatory integration between UN and EU (EU experience is unique worldwide). However, it must be underlined the added value of international decisions and commitments made at UN, the only authority able to ensure the universality of these decisions and the possibility to require their execution by all the countries in the world.
– UNTOC plays an essential role in promoting technical assistance to developing countries, in connections with sustainable development (Art. 30 UNTOC; legislative reforms, capacity building and raising awareness) in the fight against organised crime.
– It has already been said that the UNTOC Convention is a flexible instrument, suitable to "cover" the most varied phenomena of illegality. To this purpose, I would signal the results obtained by Italy, on a negotiation stance, with the resolutions on smuggling of migrants (Res. no. 2014/23 ECOSOC) and trafficking in cultural goods (Res. no. 69/196 GA—International Guidelines) adopted over the last 2 years.

However, the international community has been arguing for quite a while and alternatively whether and how to include the so-called "new and emerging form of crimes" in the UNTOC scope of application, such as environmental crimes (among which trafficking of protected species, poaching and waste trafficking), trafficking in cultural goods, forging, trafficking of precious ores, trafficking of organs, piracy and recently also transnational fiscal and corporate crimes (Italian initiative, still at the beginning of a difficult path).

– Can we make use of the Palermo Convention to fight also the modern jihadist international terrorist movements? The discussion is open to different interpretations, each heralding all but minor political repercussions.

If one takes a look at reality, though, I claim so, since the overlapping of traditional organised crime and modern terrorist groups has in my opinion been totally achieved (elements: structured group composed of more persons; commission of major crimes punished with sanctions superior to 4 years; criminal activities performed by groups active in more countries, indeed with an already dominating international profile; pursuit of profits and evermore shaded or even inconsistent ideological component).

These are diversified and often delicate issues, politically speaking, as they involve different sensibilities, cultures and historic traditions that are quite distant from each other. Besides, they have huge echoes on the economic orders of entire Regions.

4   Reviewing Mechanism (Art. 32 Para. 3, d) of the Convention Compared to UNCAC Reviewing Mechanism. State-of-the-Art of Negotiations for the Adoption of a Reviewing Mechanism of the Convention and of Protocols. Italian Standpoint

According to what provided by Art. 32 of the Convention, the States Parties' Conference needs to adopt, among others, a mechanism for periodically reviewing the implementation of the Convention.

It is about a disposition similar to that contained in other multi-lateral instruments (i.e. UNCAC or the European Council Convention against corruption), but UNTOC has until now been unsuccessful. Negotiations to reach an agreement upon a reviewing mechanism failed twice, in 2010 and 2012, and only in 2014 (thanks to the resolution 7/1, adopted under Italy's initiative) did negotiations start again with the creation of an intergovernmental group of experts delegated to find a practicable and shared solution.

Every existing reviewing mechanism is based on three assumptions: 1. collection of information; 2. analysis of collected information; 3. a work scheduled calendar for a complete check of all the instrument's provisions.

Controversial points for UNTOC:

(a) characteristics and goals of reviewing mechanism (an intergovernmental/political or merely a technical process?)—detection of weaknesses and assessment of technical assistance needs;
(b) participation of civil society to the exercise (an open process or a restricted, reserved exercise?);
(c) financing and costs (ordinary budget or voluntary contributions?);

As said before, Italy strongly supports the adoption of the reviewing mechanism. These are the main reasons:

(1) It gives an assessment of the state of implementation of a legal instrument in all States Parties: it is the only way to identify, if any, lapses in our national legislation. It then enables the States Parties to prepare most suitable (regulatory but also organisational) measures, and can be a stimulus on the basis of their commitment as Parties of a legally binding instrument.

(2) It is the only "scientific" instrument available for identifying technical assistance needs that developing countries may have. Such mechanism will then help both givers and UN agencies direct their efforts in the right way.

(3) It generates a reservoir of reasoned and organised information about all Convention and Protocol regulated aspects, upon which successive initiatives may be grounded, especially the political ones, aimed at improving international cooperation among countries.

Some practical examples (taken from my personal experience, as information is not available in this regard):

– employment of joint investigation teams (which, to be true, have been implemented quite late, here in Italy);
– employment of house searches during the nighttime, as an essential investigative tool, which still are not allowed in many countries, including some EU countries;
– the full and correct criminalisation of smuggling of migrants (missing in a number of countries, particularly in Africa);
– the need to allow judicial authorities an easier access to bank accounts and reports for investigative purposes (in many countries banking investigations can be exploited only when crimes punished with more than 4-year imprisonment are prosecuted—which makes this instrument useless for many crimes through which early investigations are started on complex criminal conduct like organised crime);
– the working of the "double criminality" clause, as to the extradition and transfer of criminal proceedings. These are two essential instruments in matters of judicial assistance, but things can work only when the double criminality requirement is met.

These are factors involving aspects sometimes crucial for the judicial systems of States, sometimes even referable to their sovereignty, although at the same time they play a primary role in the concrete scenario of cooperation instruments. For this reason, the negotiation process might still be long, engaging and tortuous, and maybe final results will not live up to expectations. Maybe we will have to content ourselves with what other Countries are willing to grant, and accept a compromise, as often happens in multilateral processes.

Part III
The Establishment of the European Public Prosecutor's Office: Steps Forward *Versus* National Resistances

Brief Notes on the European Public Prosecutor's Office: Ideas, Project and Fulfilment

Tommaso Rafaraci

Contents

Abstract In this paper the Author introduces an analysis of the Regulation on the establishment of the European Public Prosecutor's Office (EPPO) highlighting the main characteristics of this body and its functional applications. A picture emerges which, on one hand, denotes a strong contrast between EPPO's European judicial nature and the decisive influence of its national components, and, on the other, shows procedures and unprecedented inter-relations which suggest that the aspiration to supranational judicial integration, even if timidly supported, could follow further, yet original, ways to progress.

1 Approval of the EPPO Regulation

Definitive approval on 12th October 2017 of the EU Regulation 2017/1939 by the Council "implementing enhanced cooperation on the establishment of the European Public Prosecutor's Office ('the EPPO')" opens an important new chapter in the move for European integration in criminal justice. Without doubt it is a controversial chapter. On one hand, instituting EPPO has not given rise to any impetuous eruption

T. Rafaraci (✉)
University of Catania, Department of Law, Catania, Italy
e-mail: trafaraci@lex.unict.it

© Springer Nature Switzerland AG 2019
T. Rafaraci, R. Belfiore (eds.), *EU Criminal Justice*,
https://doi.org/10.1007/978-3-319-97319-7_11

of supranationality in a particular sector like criminal law, in which every progress has up until now only been possible within the margins of manoeuvre allowed by 'horizontal' procedures of cooperation; on the other, from now on things cannot be what they were yesterday given that the recently approved Regulation, despite all its limitations (among which the necessary application of cooperation procedures), represents a sound basis for a move towards gradually increasing judicial integration across the European Union.

Notwithstanding, an appropriate realistic attitude should accompany the Regulation's analysis, especially if a concise comparison is carried out between the Commission's Proposal of 17th July 2013 and the text which, after 4 years of negotiations, was recently approved following enhanced cooperation. As we will see, the significant differences truly suggest a further dilution of the (already limited) features of supranationality.

2 Shared Competence

As per Article 86 para. 2 TFEU, the EPPO's material competence covers criminal offences affecting the financial interests of the Union as provided for in EU Directive 2017/1371, VAT frauds included, which involve at least two Member States and exceed fixed levels of damages, as well as participation in a criminal organisation, as per Framework Decision 2008/841/JHA, focussing on crimes against financial interests. However, the EPPO will be likewise competent for any other crime "inextricably linked" to crimes against financial interests (as long as they are less serious than the latter). As can be seen, it already has a certain breadth as well as, by connection, a certain variability, the area in which the EPPO, in compliance with Article 86 para. 2 TFEU, will exercise its competences to carry out investigations, prosecute, and bring a case to judgment before the judicial authorities of participant Member States.

It should nonetheless be noted that—as a result of negotiations in which a very strong meaning of the principle of subsidiarity prevailed—all of this needs to contend with a system of concurrent competences between the EPPO and national authorities in the fight against crimes which harm the financial interests of the EU, based on the mere right of evocation by EPPO (see Recital 12 and 13 of the Preamble, and Art. 27 Reg.).

3 Modifications to EPPO's Structure and National Link

So, what has changed today in EPPO's tasks compared to the Regulation Proposal of 2013? The latter, as we know, was far from envisaging really supranational investigations. To briefly summarise, beyond the formal affirmation of the principle of European territoriality and with some limits directly stemming from the text of the proposal (in particular the obligation to make available a series of measures[1]; the obligation to request authorisation for certain coercive measures, even when it was not provided for by national law), it was established that the investigation carried out by European Delegated Prosecutors was covered directly by national law and, consequently, that in transnational investigations, for the measure to be carried out in another Member State, nothing other than the traditional *lex loci* was to be applied.

From this point of view, the recently approved Regulation is not much different. The substantial absence of European rules on EPPO investigations was and remains the real symbol of the difficulty of creating a system, however sectorial, with a real supranational identity. Nevertheless, in the 2013 proposal, almost compensating for this deficit, a vertical structure of the EPPO was envisaged which would allocate the power to open an investigation, direct it, as well as decide on prosecution before national jurisdictions.

Tangible changes in the recently approved Regulation can be seen, as we know, within EPPO's structure and in the correlated physiognomy of the relationships between central and peripheral levels of the Office with prominent emphasis on the direction and control of the investigation, operationally entrusted to European Delegated Prosecutors.

In this regard, it would be useful to remember that the 'vertical' structure planned by the 2013 Proposal (at central level: one European prosecutor with four deputies directing the investigation; and at decentralised level: European Delegated Prosecutors—at least one per Member State—carrying out the investigation) gave way early on in negotiations and eventually in the Regulation to an Office consisting of a European Chief Prosecutor (with two deputies), a College (consisting of the European Chief Prosecutor and one European Prosecutor per Member State) and Permanent Chambers (chaired by the European Chief Prosecutor—or one of his/her deputies—and consisting of two European Prosecutors). It should be noted that the direction and supervision of, first, the investigation and, then, the prosecution before a national jurisdictional body are essentially entrusted to the European Prosecutor of the same Member State of the European Delegated Prosecutors running the case.

The national link between the decentralised and central levels therefore remains decidedly—and intentionally—prominent, with a significant shift in the decision-making centre of EPPO towards a national one. This seems much more real considering, at the decentralised level, that the European Delegated Prosecutors, despite being an integral part of EPPO—and therefore responsible in EPPO

---

[1]The list was longer than the one under the Regulation (Art. 30), which now however expressly includes interception of telecommunication, under certain conditions, with the possibility for Member States to limit it to specific serious offences. As for measures concerning personal liberty, they may be ordered directly or after authorisation according to national law applicable in similar domestic cases. Also European arrest warrant may be issued, where it is necessary to arrest and surrender a person who is not present in the Member State in which the handling European Delegated Prosecutor is located.

investigations to the central authorities—, remain placed at a national Prosecutor's Office and empowered to continue their relative roles (the 'double hat' system).

It is true that the College and Permanent Chambers (the latter in particular), while primarily engaged in general direction and supervision, also engage in supervising the investigations of single cases and have quite wide-reaching powers therein. The Permanent Chamber can, for example, formally supervise the investigation, as well as decide on prosecution, dismissal or simplified prosecution procedures.[2] It seems evident, however, that exercising this role provides the European Prosecutor of the State of investigation with decisive influence not only because he/she directly supervises the investigation by the European Delegated Prosecutors, but also because he/she normally takes part in the consequent deliberations by the Permanent Chamber. The European Prosecutor therefore remains the essential and decisive reference point in the Permanent Chamber.

And so, if an EPPO investigation is run along the lines of national law and entrusted to bodies (the European Delegated Prosecutors) placed at a national Prosecutor's Office, and is directed and supervised by the European Prosecutor of that same country of investigation, who participates in the decision-making by the Permanent Chamber, the result seems to be a merely formal supranationality, more predicated than practised, where the 'supervised' end up being at the same time the 'supervisors'. After all, an EPPO investigation would never abandon the ground where investigation and especially direction are mainly national, although the signs are those of an EU body.

4 Judicial Controls

The little practical relevance of the European nature of EPPO is also confirmed by the judicial control of its procedural acts. On this issue, according to the rule of law, Article 83 para. 3 TFEU binds the Regulation to imposing specific rules. It would be expected, given EPPO's European nature, that its acts would be subject to judicial review by European bodies of guarantee. However, in reality, judicial control remains mostly entrusted to national law and national judicial authorities rather than European ones (Article 42 para. 1 Reg.). The same EU Court of Justice has in reality a limited role relegated to giving preliminary rulings in only a few cases as per Article 42 paras. 2 ff. Reg.[3]

---

[2]See, *infra*, under § 5.

[3]According to Art. 42, paras. 2 ff., the Court of Justice shall have jurisdiction on: the validity of procedural acts of the EPPO, in so far as such a question of validity is raised before any court or tribunal of a Member State directly on the basis of Union law; the interpretation or the validity of provisions of Union law, including the Regulation; the interpretation of Articles 22 and 25 of the Regulation in relation to any conflict of competence between the EPPO and the competent national authorities; decisions of the EPPO to dismiss a case, in so far as they are contested directly on the basis of Union law; and any dispute concerning compensation for damage caused by the EPPO,

Particularly pinpointed is the absence of European judicial control concerning the decision on which Member State should host the investigation and, subsequently, have jurisdiction. In both cases, the Regulation (Article 26 para. 4, art. 36) establishes the criteria applicable as a rule and the powers entrusted to the Permanent Chamber. Rules, therefore, established at the European level and to be applied by a European body. And yet with regard to this—especially with regard to the decision on which Member State should bring the case to prosecution—no European judicial control has been established, despite dealing with quite sensitive matters both in terms of legality principle and the effectiveness of the right to defence.

5 Decisions on Prosecution

In any case, regarding determinations on prosecution, the Regulation, as anticipated, provides for a decision by the Permanent Chamber. More precisely, once the investigation has been completed, the handling European Delegated Prosecutor should formulate to the Permanent Chamber his/her own proposals by submitting a report containing a summary of the case and a draft decision whether to prosecute or consider a referral of the case, dismissal or simplified prosecution procedures. If a draft decision proposes bringing a case to judgment, a sort of *favor actionis* is applied: the Permanent Chamber cannot decide to dismiss the case (Article 36 para.1).

Concerning dismissal of the case, the Regulation in itself does not seem to leave much room for merely discretionary evaluations. The same formula as in 'the lack of relevant evidence' does evoke objective criteria. However, it is still true that Article 39 para. 1 Reg. indicates, as a parameter to evaluate where prosecution has become impossible, the law of the Member State of the handling European Delegated Prosecutor.[4] The Permanent Chamber, where it does not decide to dismiss the case, has the power to request the European Delegated Prosecutor to re-examine the case. It is even possible, if proposed by the European Delegated Prosecutor, that the Permanent Chamber decides to apply a simplified prosecution procedure, of a

---

arbitration clauses contained in contracts concluded by the EPPO, staff-related matters, and the right of public access to documents.

[4]The grounds for dismissal of the case, as provided under Art. 39, para. 1 Reg., will have to be assessed on the basis of the law of the Member State of the handling European Delegated Prosecutor, although they are not uniformly recognised across the EU. They are: the death of the suspect or accused person (or winding up of a suspect or accused legal person); the insanity of the suspect or accused person; amnesty; immunity (unless it has been lifted); expiry of the national statutory limitation to prosecute; the suspect's or accused person's case has already been finally disposed of in relation to the same acts; and—as already said—the lack of relevant evidence. According to Art. 39, para. 2 Reg., the competent Permanent Chamber may decide to reopen investigations on the basis of new facts which were not known to the EPPO at the time of the decision.

consensual and transactional nature, to the extent this is allowed under the law of the concerned Member State.[5]

Although this all seems to provide for a significant central role of the Permanent Chamber, it would be difficult to imagine the result of a concrete case without a decisive role being played by the national prosecutor of the State of investigation.

6 Procedural Guarantees

Regarding the procedural guarantees, it has been established that EPPO's activities must be carried out in compliance with the rights established under the EU Charter of Fundamental Rights and the five Directives relating to the defence guarantees already adopted by the EU, while respecting the right to the highest level of protection provided under relevant national law.[6] But it should be noted again that, in the first place, in the absence of any European procedural rules in the Regulation, EPPO's actions will be substantially regulated by the applicable national law. Secondly, the reference to the Charter of Fundamental Rights and to the Directives on the procedural rights already adopted, despite being useful, do not constitute in themselves an indicator of the European nature of the Office and its actions, given that the rights established by the Charter of Fundamental Rights and by the Directives on procedural rights already represent a standard to be guaranteed in national criminal proceedings in EU Member States.

In fact, the reference seems to suggest a need, given the lack of real European territoriality, which is relevant in transnational investigations. In Article 31, the Regulation provides that the European Delegated Prosecutors shall act in close cooperation by assisting and regularly consulting each other. More precisely, where a measure needs to be undertaken in a Member State other than the Member State of the handling European Delegated Prosecutor, the latter European Delegated Prosecutor shall decide on the adoption of the necessary measure and assign it to a European Delegated Prosecutor located in the Member State where the measure needs to be carried out. Except for special cases, it is not necessary to employ mechanisms of judicial cooperation based on mutual recognition. Nevertheless, the simplification represented by the direct assignment of the measure—if it is in itself wholly consistent with the formal participation of the European Delegated Prosecutors of every Member State in one single European body—will have to be detailed

---

[5]In this case, the Permanent Chamber will take into consideration the grounds listed under Art. 40, para. 2: the seriousness of the offence, based on in particular the damage caused; the willingness of the suspect offender to repair the damage caused by the illegal conduct; the conformity of the use of the procedure with the general objectives and basic principles of the EPPO; as well as guidelines on the application of these grounds which the College may adopt.

[6]It is expressly provided the possibility to present evidence, to request the appointment of experts or expert examination and hearing of witnesses, and to request the EPPO to obtain such measures on behalf of the defence (art. 41, para. 3 Reg.).

and tried out in practice. And it is to be believed that common minimum standards of guarantee will facilitate the strengthening of such an unprecedented and peculiar relationship, which would no longer be an expression of mere inter-state cooperation, nor even one genuinely based on real European territoriality.

7 Conclusions

Even understanding many limitations and ambiguities, EPPO as defined by the Regulation should be evaluated without prejudice as regards its progress in making the EU more united in combating crimes which damage the financial interests of the EU and, in perspective, terrorism. Indeed, some criticisms might be purely theoretical if EPPO proves in reality to be an effective deterrent on a wider scale. However, it is difficult to be prejudicially optimistic, given how heavily this project is weighed down at a bureaucratic level.

On the other hand, the real profile of EPPO will gradually emerge over time. There are many stages to complete before the beginning of its work, forecast to be 3 years from now. In the meantime, the Office must set itself up and issue the regulations for its internal procedures, as well as other norms and directives on important matters. It should then establish the forms of support and collaboration with OLAF and Eurojust, as well as regulate its relationships through agreements with the non-participant Member States and with third countries.

These phases and the beginning of the activities will have to be observed to understand the future place of EPPO in the judicial panorama of the EU.

The European Public Prosecutor: Controversy Expressed in Structural Form

Marianne L. Wade

Contents

Abstract This article highlights the structural differences between the Regulation for a European Public Prosecutor's Office (EPPO) passed after intense Council negotiation and that initially proposed by the European Commission. It attributes the structural complexity now imposed to concerns about and a significant degree of resistance against the very idea of this revolutionary office. Nevertheless, the EPPO is born. This essay argues that by watering down its potential power structurally, the Member States, however, ultimately failed to recognise that such a revolutionary step—no matter how hampered by inefficient, nationally influenced structures—requires the creation of corresponding accountability structures. It closes highlighting that the failure to ensure political and judicial accountability for such a body raises serious concerns, also likely to feed into some of the broader challenges dogging the EU.

M. L. Wade (✉)
Birmingham Law School, University of Birmingham, Birmingham, UK
e-mail: m.l.wade@bham.ac.uk

© Springer Nature Switzerland AG 2019
T. Rafaraci, R. Belfiore (eds.), *EU Criminal Justice*,
https://doi.org/10.1007/978-3-319-97319-7_12

1   Introduction

A European Public Prosecutor (now a European Public Prosecutor's Office, abbreviated to EPPO) has featured prominently in discussion for some time. It emerged from the Corpus Juris study[1] and faced stringent criticism upon being mooted in a Green Paper by the European Commission in 2001.[2] That paper's central recommendation was the creation of a European Public Prosecutor to ensure effective protection of the Communities's financial interests. Since the Treaty of Lisbon entered into force, this topic has been the subject of intense discussion and activity. Following careful groundwork,[3] the Commission introduced a Regulation proposal in 2013.

The legal basis for this proposal is article 86 of the Treaty of the Functioning of the EU (TFEU) which reads: "*the Council, by means of regulations adopted in accordance with a special legislative procedure, may establish a European Public Prosecutor's Office from Eurojust. The Council shall act unanimously after obtaining the consent of the European Parliament.*" Given that, for example, modest reforms of Eurojust's powers in 2007 were headed off by 14 Member States,[4] the unanimity requirement within the Council was a high bar acknowledging the controversial nature of this potential creation. The prescription of the special legislative procedure requiring only the consent of the European Parliament was further evidence that the Member States wished to retain maximum control over any such development. It is interesting to note that an explicit steer on structure was included in the Treaty.

The creation of a Prosecutor's Office at the EU level is a clear expression of supra-national sovereignty in a core area usually reserved for (and jealously guarded by) the Member States. Full control over the systems which administer criminal justice upon their territory lies at the centre, and close to the heart, of liberal democracies across Europe.[5] The envisaged justice revolution was tabled at a point in time when the winds of Euroscepticism were already blowing strong. Criminal justice measures such as the European Arrest Warrant had become the fodder of anti-EU movements and even the least reticent Member States reacted sensitively to cases such as *Pupino*,[6] the environmental protection[7] and ship-source pollution[8] litigation which saw the CJEU underlining that the EU has an independent right to impact upon domestic criminal justice systems. The unbalanced focus of EU

---

[1]European Commission (2000).

[2]European Commission (2001).

[3]European Commission (2013b).

[4]See eucrim 3-4/2007, p. 84f.

[5]See Wade (in print), Vol. 1, Part III.

[6]C-105/03.

[7]C-176/03—see http://ec.europa.eu/dgs/legal_service/arrets/03c176_en.pdf.

[8]C440/05—see http://ec.europa.eu/dgs/legal_service/arrets/05c440_en.pdf.

measures on improving the punitive efficiency of criminal justice systems had been subject to considerable criticism.[9]

The move towards an EPPO can be viewed as the logical conclusion of deliberations triggered by the famous Greek Maize case.[10] In this cornerstone judgment the European Court of Justice ruled that the Member States are under an obligation to protect the European Communities' interests by equivalent means to those with which they protect their own respective interests.[11] The *raison d'etre* of the EPPO is protection of the financial interests of the EU from crimes such as fraud. There is no argument that this substantive field relates to criminal justice. The EU Anti-Fraud Office: OLAF have long complained that the current reliance upon national prosecution services equates to inadequate protection. National authorities often face enormous challenges when called upon to prosecute frauds against the EU budget[12] because complex cases may require consideration of acts committed or evidence found in one or more other Member States. Furthermore, the financial regulations of the EU are often new to prosecutors, raising further problems. Finally, national prosecution services may be so overloaded[13] in their daily business that the prospect of taking over or pursuing the prosecution of crimes against another sovereign involving the breach of complex "foreign" rules, may be impossible. These are the problems faced even where national authorities share the same vision as OLAF in protecting the financial interest of the EU.

Calls for the establishment of a European Public Prosecutor have thus almost exclusively been the call for a specialist service dedicated to ensuring such cases of complex and large-scale fraud are brought to justice.[14] Logically article 86 (1)TFEU therefore provides: "*In order to combat crimes affecting the financial interests of the Union, the Council, by means of regulations adopted in accordance with a special legislative procedure, may establish a European Public Prosecutor's Office from Eurojust*" and goes on in article 86 (2) TFEU "*The European Public Prosecutor's Office shall be responsible for investigating, prosecuting and bringing to judgment, where appropriate in liaison with Europol, the perpetrators of, and accomplices in, offences against the Union's financial interests, as determined by the regulation provided for in paragraph 1. It shall exercise the functions of prosecutor in the competent courts of the Member States in relation to such offences.*".

---

[9]Even e.g. by former Commission Vice-President Frattini, who expressed his concern that the EU had developed an Area of Security although its mandate was to develop one of Freedom, Security and Justice upon the occasion of a German Presidency conference on the failed Framework Decision of Fundamental Rights in Criminal Proceedings, 20.02.2007, Berlin. See http://www. bmj.bund.de/enid/
68e692448b67b5925478ba1197305426,33d0e45f7472636964092d0933303334/Deutsche_EU-Praesidentschaft_2__7/Verfahrensrechte_im_Strafverfahren_18q.html.

[10]Case 68/88 Commission v Greece [1989] ECR 2965.

[11]Case 68/88 Commission v Greece [1989] ECR 2965, paras. 23–25.

[12]Robledo and Cajani (2009), p. 25.

[13]See Jehle (2006), p. 5ff.

[14]European Commission (2001), p. 12f.; Delmas-Marty (1998) p. 13f.

2   Providing for Protection of the EU's Financial Interests

Given the issues at stake, it is not surprising that the debate surrounding a European Public Prosecutor immediately became embroiled in the bitterest of wrangles with Eurosceptics accusing the Commission of advancing the move to a Federation by stealth, encroaching upon the liberties won in, and of, Member States, to serve its own ends.[15] Given the opposition it knew it was facing, the Commission introduced a very strongly founded proposal for the centralized, European office it regarded as needed in 2013.[16] This legislative move was proceeded by extensive consultations amongst practitioners and accompanied by considerable documentation explaining the Commission's reasoning.[17] A clear argument was presented that a centralised impulse for, and oversight of, investigations and prosecutions was required. Although this is only achievable in partnership with the Member States and their relevant authorities, a clear message was sent that reliance only upon the Member States was a tried and tested path which had repeatedly failed. Thus some handover of sovereign powers was necessary.

There is no question that a European Public Prosecutor dealing with crimes against the financial interest of the EU requires specialist knowledge of the financial laws and regulations within the EU. Nevertheless he or she is required to investigate offences within the Member States and thus naturally tied to the investigative and constitutional standards of the territory upon which he or she is acting (*locus regit actum*). Article 86 makes the dependence upon national law abundantly clear, laying down that the European Public Prosecutor "shall exercise the functions of prosecutor in the competent courts of the Member States in relation to such offences."[18]

2.1   *Structural Issues as Key to the Functioning and Creation of the EPPO*

Clearly the EPPO must encompass detailed knowledge of the national law of the Member States over which he or she is given jurisdiction. While there may be strong arguments for a centralised co-ordinating authority, accountable to EU structures, any European Public Prosecutor requires an arm per Member State to be effective across the Union. Not only must a European Public Prosecutor investigate on Member States' territory, the agency also requires advocacy skills and jurisdiction

---

[15]See https://blogs.ec.europa.eu/ECintheUK/tag/corpus-juris/ and e.g. http://www.silentmajority. co.uk/silentmajority/eurorealist/corpus_juris.html but note also that the British Government tied any participation in an EPPO to an assumedly insurmountable referendum requirement in the European Union Act, 2011, c.11, s.6.

[16]European Commission (2013a).

[17]European Commission (2013b).

[18]Article 86 (2) TFEU, see also Sensburg (2008) 662 et seq.

within the respective courts. The TFEU vision of the EPPO is one of an office strongly entwined, co-operating with and dependent upon the criminal justice systems of the Member States. The reference seen above to an EPPO developing *"from Eurojust"* is a further indication that the drafters of the Treaty were well aware of this and that they intended a tried and tested structural path to be taken.

Eurojust—the EU's judicial cooperation unit[19]—is structured as a College (i.e. is governed by a board consisting of representatives from each of the Member States,) headed by a President but in which decisions are fundamentally subject to discussion and debate amongst this College.[20] This takes the form of a round table in which all Member States' representatives have a place, a vote and an actively used right to speak and be heard. It is fundamentally a co-operative office with members of the College retaining an unbroken link to their Member State jurisdiction.

It is difficult to imagine a working EPPO not operating along the lines the model Eurojust utilises: integrating at least one representative from each Member State and indeed an experienced and seasoned prosecutor (or investigator) who knows the workings of his or her system intimately. Any investigation will require the co-operation and assistance of national systems. All structural iterations of an EPPO logically foresaw a service well integrated into the respective national system despite serving the Union's interests. The structure foreseen for the EPPO could, however, clearly demonstrate its ultimate loyalty to the Union more or less clearly, given this necessity. Whilst any European Public Prosecutor requires a specific remit and standing, independent of the Member States to imaginably serve its *raison d'etre* better than the Member States have in the past, the idea of an exclusively centralised office was always highly unlikely to achieve the desired results. Consequently the potential of a European Public Prosecutor always rested with the willingness of the Member States to hand over some power or at least to guarantee a high degree of cooperation.

As we shall see, with the advent of the proposed Regulation for the EPPO, debate as to *whether* a European public prosecutor's office should be created turned to the *how*. This latter discussion then in many ways became a surrogate for the former with structural discussion allowing the Member States to seemingly mitigate their fears. Discussions of structure in particular appear to have become the hostages of the Member States' concerns. Given how key the EPPO's structure is likely to be to its proper functioning, this is unfortunate. It would also not appear to be the appropriate way to deal with the core issues involved. These impact well beyond the working efficiency of the EPPO.

There can be no doubt that the prospect of a supra-national criminal justice institution—no matter what its structure—raises serious issues. These relate not only to the surrender of sovereignty and the transfer of powers to the EU but they go to the heart of issues dogging the EU as a whole. The fundamental need to provide for democratic legitimacy, continuous and effective scrutiny of and

---

[19] As it was at the time the TFEU was drafted, it is now an agency.

[20] See e.g. Hecker (2012), § 5 C III 6.

accountability (in this case for the EPPO's work) is raised. At the heart of this discourse a discussion of what kind of Union we want the EU to be should have been raised. In the frenzy of activity which has ensued in the 4 years since the Commission proposal was tabled, we shall see, however, that such central debate was avoided and a shadow debate pursued.

2.2 Structural Proposals for the EPPO

The nightmare-vision of those fearing the creation of an European Public Prosecutor's Office, even "from Eurojust" was doubtlessly a vision of a centralised agency, sitting in the midst of Brussels (though a seat in Luxemburg is foreseen) issuing orders to and making demands upon national criminal justice institutions or worse, sending or resulting in an independent prosecutor empowered to investigate crimes upon national territory. The Commission knowingly always avoided such a proposal.

The 2013 or Commission Version of the Regulation to create an EPPO foresaw the following[21]:

> There shall be at least one European Delegated Prosecutor in each Member State who shall be an integral part of the EPPO. The EDPs shall act under the exclusive authority of the EPP and follow only his/her instructions, guidelines and decisions when they carry out investigations and prosecutions assigned to them.

The structure foreseen can be summarised in Fig. 1.

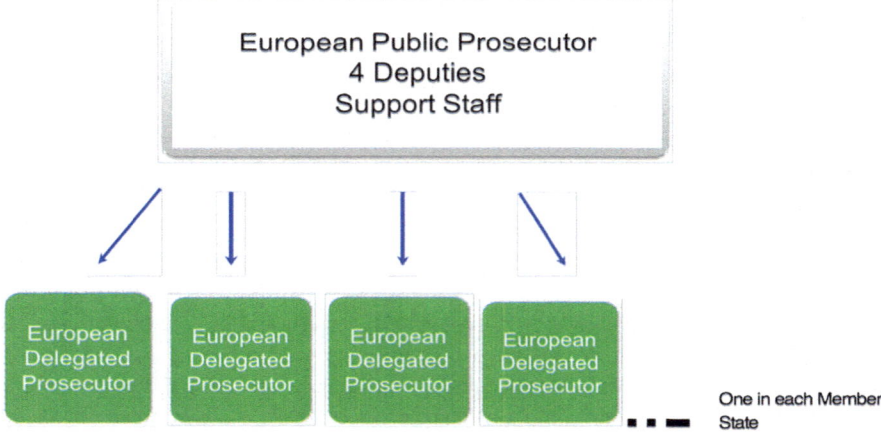

Fig. 1 The EPPO structure as envisaged in the Commission proposal

---

[21]In Article 6 (5).

In other words, the Commission foresaw a fairly simple structure with delegated European prosecutors operating in the Member States and thus in full compliance with article 86 TFEU. Nevertheless, the proposal foresaw a clear centralised focus of power. Simple lines of direction and accountability from the European Prosecutors on the ground, to the European Prosecutor in Luxembourg was foreseen. The detail of work allocation had to be left to be hashed out in working rules to be developed later.[22] However, it is clear that after years of identifying the lack of European priority being lent to the protection of the EU's financial interests, the Commission wishes to ensure this was front, left and centre of all European Prosecutor's minds[23] and the structure proposed, including the hierarchy of the Office—even across borders—reflected this.

Unsurprisingly the Regulation was subject to intense and complicated debate in the Council. The many Council documents relating to it reveal a multitude of concerns and issues requiring painstaking work to reach compromise. Footnotes in intermediary version of the Regulation often reveal contradictory, principled positions amongst the Member States.[24] The deference to the Member States, their substantive laws, procedure and criminal justice structures demonstrated as expected from the EPPO in this context, belies the fundamentally European nature of this revolutionary project. In creating the EPPO, Member State representatives appear guided exclusively by the experiences of their domestic systems and to give little thought to the novelty of the Office they were creating.

In relation to the EPPO's structure, the final Council version of the Regulation[25] features articles 7–12 devoted to the structures of the EPPO. This is obviously a sharp contrast to the simplicity of the Commission version's article 6. The Council version can be seen portrayed (in a simplified manner) in Fig. 2.

It is important to note that, as was true for Fig. 1, every level of governance beyond the European Chief Prosecutor (and his/her deputies who are omitted from the diagram but constitute the European core of the EPPO[26]) is replicated for every participating Member State. In other words the EPPO College will contain

---

[22]In the internal rules foreseen by article 7 of this version of the Regulation.

[23]As Preamble 3.2. stated *"There is a need for the Union to act because the foreseen action has an intrinsic Union dimension. It implies Union-level steering and coordination of investigations and prosecutions of criminal offences affecting its own financial interests, the protection of which is required both from the Union and the Member States by Articles 310 (6) and 325 TFEU. In accordance with the subsidiarity principle, this objective can only be achieved at Union level by reason of its scale and effects. As stated above, the present situation, in which the prosecution of offences against the Union's financial interests is exclusively in the hands of the authorities of the Member States is not satisfactory and does not sufficiently achieve the objective of fighting effectively against offences affecting the Union budget."*

[24]See e.g. article 29 in the version produced in June 2016.

[25]Still pending at the time of writing with the version of the 17th of January 2017 available—see Council of the EU (2017c) and EUCO 4/17 of the 14th of February 2017.

[26]Though note Deputies are appointed by the College from its members—Preamble 35.

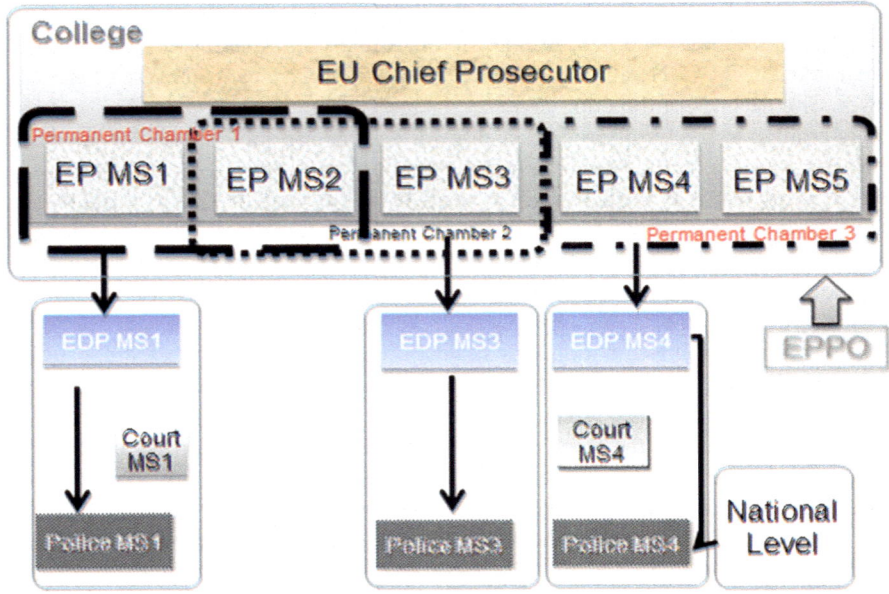

Fig. 2 The EPPO structure post Council negotiations

20 European Prosecutors and there will be at least 40 European Deputy Prosecutors active within the Member States as we shall see.

The Council conceives expressly of the EPPO as "*an indivisible Union body operating as one single Office with a decentralised structure.*"[27] The Council's sentiment that this requires expression is perhaps an acknowledgement that the changes made, mean such a statement is required. The Commission version of the Regulation contained only a simple statement that the EPPO consisted of all the roles to be created. The Council version then goes on to explain that the EPPO "*shall be organised at a central level and at a decentralised level.*"[28] From the offset, the EPPO's foreseen structure is recognised as split (and thus perhaps inherently divisible).

Article 7 of the Regulation as finalized by the Council (and now passed by the European Parliament[29]) lays down that the EPPO Central Office is made up of the College, the Permanent Chambers, the European Chief Prosecutor and his/her Deputies as well as the European Prosecutors. The Decentralised level consists of the European Delegated Prosecutors.

Article 8 regulates the EPPO College which is to be "be responsible for the general oversight of the activities of the Office" it "shall not take operational

---

[27]Council of the EU (2017c) article 7(1).

[28]Council of the EU (2017c) article 7(2).

[29]See European Parliament (2017).

decisions in individual cases."[30] The College consists of the European Chief Prosecutor (ECP) and one European Prosecutor per Member State. In addition the College appoints the Permanent Chambers.[31]

The Permanent Chambers are provided for in article 9 which states the *"Permanent Chamber shall be chaired by the European Chief Prosecutor or one of his/her Deputies, or a European Prosecutor appointed as Chair in accordance with the internal rules of procedure. In addition to the chair, the Permanent Chamber shall have two permanent Members."* Article 9 then further states that the number of these will "take due account of the functional needs of the Office."

Articles 9(3) and (3a) make clear that these Permanent Chambers constitute the working heart of the EPPO. They are tasked with the random, even distribution of workload, the direction of investigations and prosecutions, the review of European Delegated Prosecutors' draft proposals relating to the *"bringing [of] cases to justice,"* case dismissals and use of simplified prosecution. They can instruct case initiation and so-called evocation, allocate and reallocate cases and can *"through European Prosecutor who is supervising … give instructions in compliance with applicable national law"* to ensure the efficient handling of an investigation or prosecution, in the interest of justice and to ensure the "coherent functioning of EPPO."[32] Decisions are taken in Permanent Chambers by simple majority voting.[33]

Article 10 regulates the European Chief Prosecutor stating *"European Chief Prosecutor shall be the head of the European Public Prosecutor's Office. The European Chief Prosecutor shall organise the work of the Office, direct its activities, and take decisions in accordance with this Regulation and the internal rules of procedure."*

According to article 11, the European Prosecutors shall *"On behalf of Permanent Chamber… supervise the investigation and prosecution for which the European Delegated Prosecutors handling the case in their Member State of origin are responsible."* As article 9 does for the Permanent Chambers, article 11 goes on to lay down some detail as to when and how European Prosecutors may delegate their powers.

Article 12 makes provision for the European Delegated Prosecutors (EDPs), who it states *"shall act on behalf of the European Public Prosecutor's Office in their respective Member States and shall have the same powers as national prosecutors in respect of investigations, prosecutions and bringing cases to judgment, in addition and subject to the specific powers and status conferred on them, and under the conditions provided, for in this Regulation."* According to article 12(2) 2 or more per of these EDPs are to be approved per Member State by the ECP "after consulting and reaching an agreement with the relevant authorities of the Member States."

---

[30]Article 8(2).

[31]Article 8(3).

[32]Article 9(4).

[33]Article 9(5).

These EDPS are the frontline workers of the EPPO bearing responsibility for investigation and prosecution of its cases. This is true for cases they initiate, those allocated to them and taken over via the "right of evocation." They are funded by the EU and appointed according to proceedings laid down in the Regulation which states *"Their independence shall be beyond doubt."*[34] They do, however, remain members of their national prosecution services and they are expressly permitted to work national cases[35] if this can be undertaken without disrupting their role within the EPPO.

3 The EPPO Structure: Controversy Expressed in Structure

As the above overview of the structure of the EPPO now created, particularly when contrast with the initial structure proposed by the European Commission, makes clear; the EPPO is an institution burdened by the controversy of its own existence. Although the Council has delivered a legal revolution; a supra-national criminal justice body at the EU level—the form in which it has delivered it demonstrates that it has been loath to do so and, at least in part, attempts to shackle its revolutionary character.

Although this is a European body, every conceivable attempt has been made to ensure its working is infused with and marked by the characteristics of all the national systems of the participating Member States. The EPPO power lies not with the ECP but with the College and above all the Permanent Chambers. Like the College, the Permanent Chambers are dominated by prosecutors appointed as representatives of their Member State. They are the oxymoronic European Prosecutor for their Member State. The ECP can always be outvoted. Although s/he can doubtless exercise influence and power, her/his ability to do so is dependent upon not being blocked by prosecutors still rooted in their Member States. This may not hinder the work of the EPPO. Given the inadequacy of the enforcement situation so far which was dependent upon them, there are, however, more than reasonable grounds to be pessimistic.

At every turn there is indication of the Council (i.e. the Member States)'s desire that the EPPO be deferential to and dependent upon the Member States and their authorities. As seen above, the need for cooperation is inherent in article 86 TFEU. This Regulation increases this exponentially to the point of dependency. Alone the complex structure which has now emerged, ensures there is no direct European line to the frontline professional dealing with the case. Whilst there is certainly more potential for EU-oriented motivation, the influence of the ECP and deputies falls far short of what the Commission intended (and one might expect from the head of any

---

[34] Article 15.

[35] Article 12(3).

organisation); namely that the ECP—as head of an institution—can directly steer the specific work of his/her organisation.

The Regulation now passed is littered with illustrations of the EPPO's dependency on the goodwill of the Member States and their institutions well beyond what is outlined above. For example, the availability of a Union funded prosecutor to work national cases does not end with an indication that such work must occur in deference to the needs of the EPPO. The Regulation states in article 12(3) that if such national work has been undertaken and prevents the EDP from taking on an EPPO case, consultation with the Member State must be entered into to decide which work takes priority. This provision is not guaranteed to hinder the work of the EPPO but it ensures smooth functioning depends upon the goodwill of the Member State.

It is interesting to note, of course, that the Regulation specifies the need for at least 2 EDPs. Given that it also specifies they can undertake national work (but not that there may be less than 2 such prosecutors in post) if it emerges they are doing the latter as a matter of routine, one must recognise that some Member States are apparently hoping to benefit from the presence of these EU funded prosecutors within their systems.

Furthermore, as European Deputy Prosecutors remain members of their national prosecution services they, naturally, also remain subject to dismissal from it on those grounds. Article 15(4) states that if a prosecutor is dismissed due to reasons outside of those regulated in the Regulation, the ECP must merely be informed. If the reasons for dismissal pertain to a matter within the scope of the Regulation, the ECP's consent must be sought. Should the ECP, however, refuse to give this consent, the Member State can request a review of this by the EPPO College. The latter is, of course, a constituent of the EPPO i.e. a European body. It is, however, a body dominated by members appointed based upon their identity as practitioners of that Member State. Eurojust can certainly be pointed to as demonstrating that this must not undermine the body's ability to act in a "European" manner. It equally houses examples, however, of Member State priorities overriding.[36]

The heart of EPPO power lies in Member State dominated structures always operating in deference to national law.[37] The consistent and ever-repeated subservience to national law and structures alongside the convoluted hierarchy associated with the European level cannot be taken as a sign of anything other than the Council's desire to ensure this EU body remains permeated by the Member States. This means they will likely remain hampered by the hurdles which have always stood in the way of the latter's co-operation. The concerns and skepticism expressed over decades in debates over a European Public Prosecutor strongly characterise the structure of EPPO now created.

---

[36]See Wade (2011).

[37]See articles 9(4) and 11(2) for example.

4   The EPPO and the Future

The deep controversy surrounding the EPPO was naturally not only expressed via the structure created. The EPPO has come into existence not with the unanimity in Council article 86 foresaw. It presciently always foresaw an alternative. The EPPO has been born as the child via so-called enhanced cooperation.[38]

From the point of entry into the Treaty, the very notion of a European Public Prosecutor was associated with an exceptional and particularly stringent procedure, article 86 (1) requiring that *"The Council shall act unanimously after obtaining the consent of the European Parliament"*. With this requirement, the TFEU seemed to highlight the fundamental wish that such a step be undertaken only in agreement between all constituent Member States. The relative importance of the Council and each Member State in this exceptional procedure could be regarded as acknowledgement that this would be a step of political import affecting in particular the Member States. The creation of a European Public Prosecutor is declared so game-changing it should not be undertaken against the will of any Member State. It was for them together—and not for the other organs of the Union—to undertake this revolutionary step towards closer Union. The need for broad debate resolving differences, is signposted as legitimate and necessary before such an office could be created.

If that was the ideal it was, however, closely followed by realistic pragmatism. Article 86(1) continues:

> In the absence of unanimity in the Council, a group of at least nine Member States may request that the draft regulation be referred to the European Council. In that case, the procedure in the Council shall be suspended. After discussion, and in case of a consensus, the European Council shall, within four months of this suspension, refer the draft back to the Council for adoption.
>
> Within the same timeframe, in case of disagreement, and if at least nine Member States wish to establish enhanced cooperation on the basis of the draft regulation concerned, they shall notify the European Parliament, the Council and the Commission accordingly. In such a case, the authorisation to proceed with enhanced cooperation referred to in Article 20(2) of the Treaty on European Union and Article 329(1) of this Treaty shall be deemed to be granted and the provisions on enhanced cooperation shall apply.

Given the presence of the (post European Union Act 2011) UK Government at the negotiating table in 2013, no one can seriously have believed the EPPO could be created via the unanimity route. Negotiations over 4 years have still been unable to carry all committed EU Member States and the EPPO is now set to come into existence via the enhanced cooperation of 20 Member States.[39] As this brief examination has shown, the EPPO created has been structured in what appears to be ways intended to hamper and even deny its revolutionary nature.

Indeed article 6a of the Regulation hands Member States a further means to busy the truly European level of the EPPO. It describes the European Chief Prosecutor's

---

[38]See Council of the EU (2017a) and Council of the EU (2017b).

[39]Member States have now committed themselves to the EPPO see Council of the EU (2017a). Council of the EU (2017b) commits 20 Member States to the creation of the EPPO via this route.

duty to prepare an annual report to be submitted to the European Parliament, Member States' Parliaments, Council and Commission. Article 6a continues to outline that the ECP (or her/his 2 Deputies) are expected for an annual appearance before European Parliament, Council and "upon request" Member States' Parliaments. In other words, if Member States are in any way dissatisfied with the performance of the EPPO, they can tie its European level in requirements to answer to their political organs. Given the increased presence of Eurosceptic forces in national Parliaments, this can be expected to entail a number of challenges for any ECP. This will be a high-profile prosecutor with few powers to direct his/her agency but dozens, in fact hundreds, of masters to answer to for its work.

The practicalities of an EPPO's work aside, this must be recorded also as an opportunity missed. Whatever its structures, the worries, ifs and buts, the fact is a European Public Prosecutor has been created, the EU now features a genuine criminal justice body. Even if it has been created to work slowly and under Member State control, this does not mean it cannot be reformed into an efficient body nor indeed that the professionals within it cannot resolve to work cooperatively towards the envisaged European ends the Commission—and all who recognize the legitimacy of its arguments calling for an EPPO—hope for.

Alone the creation of an EPPO is a revolutionary and brave step and ultimately the expression of the Member States' willingness to protect the Union's interests. The form into which it was moulded at birth seems, however, to have been born of the Member States' worst instincts and fears. The EPPO must be described as a severely mutilated birth. Only time will tell whether it can recover from its injuries. It seems fair to remark that the structures created are pretty much as far from a workable and effective EPPO as one might be able to imagine. With the right professionals engaged, it can perhaps be made to work. If, however, any relevant individual wishes to ensure the EPPO's hands are tied, the Member States have plenty of opportunity to facilitate this.

It is perhaps a sign of the desperation at the EU level that the Regulation was still pursued once the Council version emerged. Presumably the hope was, and remains, that more good than ill will come of it, The current enforcement situation is bleak and so one can hope that dedicated practitioners will find a level to cooperate upon and advance the criminal justice responses they are tasked with. It must, be recognised, however, that the structure put in place at the behest of the Council, bears the dangers of playing to all the stereotypes regularly hurled against the EU. If one wanted to create a beurocratic, expensive and immovable institution achieving little with tax-payers money (after controversial constitutional reform in the name of an EU-related goal), the structure described above would seem a good concept with which to start. If this ammunition is utilized against it, and proves in any way accurate, there is a danger the Council has—fatally—set the EPPO up to fail. And in doing so, some Member States have perhaps even provided themselves with a potential resource at the EU's expense. That would be a deeply cynical and wasteful thing to have done. And it seems a deeply cynical thing to suggest has happened. But is it really beyond how we can imagine our governments operating at the EU level? From a British perspective the answer is clearly no to that question. This Regulation is, however, not the UK's making.

5   The Key Opportunity Missed

Beyond the loss of a chance to create an efficient EU body to fight crime that requires fighting or indeed to decide against the supra-nationalisation of this task and begin working towards a viable, co-operation based alternative, the opportunity missed is far-reaching. This was the appropriate point in time and a golden opportunity to discuss the issues at stake. And they reach beyond the EPPO.

The creation of a supra-national criminal justice body is revolutionary because it brings a number of fundamental issues into sharp relief. Questions arise as to whether the EU is an instance of governance with legal goods worthy of protection by the criminal law or (in common law language) against which harms can be perpetrated that justify culpability under criminal law; whether the principle of subsidiarity does not hold against such a creation because adequate protection can be achieved by the Member States; whether the existence of the Schengen area or the Eurozone do not also carry with them the moral necessity of equivalents to counteract the criminal phenomena they encourage (and indeed facilitate). Such fundamental legal questions have knock-on effects for more practical issues, above all concerning how legal protection in investigations and court review of prosecutorial acts can be secured. The permanent insistence that such issues can be tackled adequately within domestic systems ignores the experiences of mere transnational cooperation within the EU context.[40] Prosecutorial work at the EU level is not merely a sum of its national parts even then. This should be all the more true for such powers when supra-nationalised.

Adequate acknowledgement of these technical, criminal justice-related questions should inevitably have called forth concern about political accountability. National prosecution services do not operate in a vacuum, they are subject to considerable political control and rightly so, as they implement sensitive policies. Prosecutors working under the EPPO roof have a full arsenal of prosecutorial powers but only internal guidelines are foreseen to guide them in their use. The European Parliament stands before manifold challenges (beyond those indicated above) to step into the role of holding this Office to effective but constructive political account.

The EPPO is born. It features complex and tangled structures likely to be at least inefficient, if not ineffective. The same can, however, also be said for the multitudinous accountability structure within which it has been placed. That bears potential for the Member States to disrupt the work of the EPPO, but also for the EPPO to avoid any genuine, concentrated scrutiny. For any criticism leveled at it, the ECP can likely point to another EPPO "master" who wants precisely that. Particularly given the vehement disagreements during Council negotiations,[41] this potential seems all the greater. For all the energy seemingly devoted by the Council to ensuring the EPPO cannot work easily, little thought seems to have gone into holding it

---

[40]See https://www.fairtrials.org/campaigns/eu-defence-rights/cases-of-injustice/.

[41]E.g. over transaction powers—with some Member States calling for straight plea-bargaining powers whilst others abhor any transactional powers at all.

effectively accountable. Considering this will be a revolutionary body, impacting in the strongest terms on individual liberties (from a governance level devoid of the usual structures that hold prosecution services to account), pursuing aims and policies as it goes about its business, this is a considerable lacunae.

The gaps and oversights relate also to other forms of accountability and control. Above all the long-overdue, broader debated as to as to the developing nature of the Union and what it ought to be, should have been undertaken. The creation of an EPPO represents, in a concrete way, the beginnings of a European criminal justice system. In an age in which any such systems face great challenges due e.g. to caseload and prison over-crowding, any debate preceding such an event should have taken conscious stock of what criminal justice systems are. National ones encompass the potent sword of Justicia aiming for the efficient prosecution and conviction of the guilty, but they are fundamentally connected also to her shield. At their hearts, domestic criminal justice systems acknowledge that an innocent person may become subject to criminal proceedings and indeed that even a person guilty of a crime is deserving of adequate due process protection. At the European level such processes take on a daunting scale and the protection of individual rights has proved difficult. The introduction of a new repressive body at the supra-national level—fudged by constant reference to everything national law and courts can apparently manage—fails to recognize that these cannot gain oversight of supra-national processes. In so doing, it thus further fails to convince that the members of the Council have taken due consideration of all the interests of their (Member States') citizens. The Council seemingly failed to recognise that, despite their better efforts, they have taken an enormous step towards a new criminal justice system. Or alternatively in so doing they continued to do so aiming only to strengthen the arsenal of prosecutors. The failure to address the need for equivalent defence structures is a considerable one of long-standing tradition within the EU. If only the Council had fully acknowledged the nature of its undertaking, it should have heeded further words of the Court of Justice of the EU, and drawn "inspiration from the constitutional traditions common to the Member States and from the guidelines supplied by international instruments for the protection of human rights on which the Member States have collaborated or to which they are signatories."[42]

This is cause for particular regret. Precisely at this moment with Brexit looming, this was a golden opportunity to frame the European Union and its developments more positively. Perhaps the passing alone of this Regulation should be regarded as the Member States doing something and therewith demonstrating their loyalty to the European Union. That is not how it appears, however. Instead this Regulation bears witness to an apparent unwillingness to commit fully to what is considered right and to stand up for the need to support and protect the EU and the valuable work it performs. Doubtlessly this would have made for even more arduous, and indeed at times painful, discussion and debate. Instead the issues really at stake were buried and the opportunity to engage citizens in the discussion of them was lost. Hopefully the EPPO is not.

---

[42]Court of Justice of the EU (2008) para. 283.

References

Council of the EU (2017a) Press Release 580/17, 12/10/2017 20 Member States confirm the creation of an European Public Prosecutor's Office

Council of the EU (2017b) Council Regulation (EU) 2017/1939 implementing enhanced cooperation on the establishment of the European Public Prosecutor's Office ('the EPPO')

Council of the EU (2017c) Proposal for a Regulation on the establishment of the European Public Prosecutor's Office - Draft Regulation. Brussels, 5766/17, 31 January 2017

Court of Justice of the EU (2008) Yassin Abdullah Kadi and Al Barakaat International Foundation v Council of the European Union and Commission of the European Communities JUDGMENT OF THE COURT (Grand Chamber) 3 September 2008 para. 283

Delmas-Marty M (ed) (1998) Corpus Juris der strafrechtlichen Regelungen zum Schutz der finanziellen Interessen der Europäischen Union. Köln/Berlin/Bonn/München

European Commission (2000) Corpus Juris. Available at https://ec.europa.eu/anti-fraud/policy/european_public_prosecutor/academic_studies_en (last download 2 November 2017)

European Commission (2001) Green Paper on criminal-law protection of the financial interests of the Community and the establishment of a European Prosecutor, COM (2001) 715 final

European Commission (2013a) Proposal for a COUNCIL REGULATION on the establishment of the European Public Prosecutor's Office, COM/2013/0534 final

European Commission (2013b) Impact Assessment accompanying the Proposal for a Council Regulation on the establishment of the European Public Prosecutor's Office, {COM(2013) 534 final} {SWD(2013) 275 final}

European Parliament (2017) Legislative observatory. Available at: http://www.europarl.europa.eu/oeil/popups/ficheprocedure.do?lang=en&reference=2013/0255%28APP%29

Hecker B (2012) Europäisches Strafrecht, 4th edn. Springer, Berlin

Jehle JM (2006) Introduction. In: Jehle JM, Wade M (eds) Coping with overloaded criminal justice systems. Springer, Berlin

Robledo A, Cajani F (2009) Public Prosecution Office Milano Courtroom – Italy. In: Policy Department on Budgetary Affairs: Committee on Budgetary Control – The follow-up of the European Anti-Fraud Office's (OLAF) administrative investigations in Member States, 19 February 2009, 25–27

Sensburg PE (2008), Kriminalistik, 661–665

Wade M (2011) EuroNEEDS – Determining the Needs of and the Need for a European Criminal Justice System - preliminary report. Available online at: http://www.mpicc.de/ww/en/prs/forschung/forschungsarbeit/strafrecht/euroneeds.htm

Wade M (in print) Part 3 The Present Criminal Justice Structures at the National Level, Executive Summary in Sieber/Wade/Meyer, Rethinking European Criminal Justice

Eurojust and the European Public Prosecutor's Office. Introduction to a Historic Reform

Francesca Ruggieri

Contents

Abstract The Author examines the ambiguous relationship between Eurojust and the recently established European Public Prosecutor's Office (EPPO), by retracing the history of these two bodies. While Eurojust has for a long time been the most serious alternative to a supranational investigation authority, although with an exclusively coordinating task, it is now destined to coexist with EPPO. An analysis of this relationship, mainly based on mutual cooperation and the development of operational, administrative and management links between them, will be carried out.

1   Introduction

As is known, almost 3 years have elapsed since the Commission licenced its proposal for a Regulation on the establishment of the European Public Prosecutor's Office and the institutions the new Office might in the future cooperate with. The COM measure (2013) 533 with reference to Olaf, the COM measure (2013) 534 with regard to the European Public Prosecutor's Office, and the COM measure (2013) 535 concerning Eurojust, all date back to 17 July 2013.

F. Ruggieri (✉)
University of Insubria, Department of Law, Economy and Cultures, Como, Italy
e-mail: francesca.ruggieri@fastwebnet.it

© Springer Nature Switzerland AG 2019   181
T. Rafaraci, R. Belfiore (eds.), *EU Criminal Justice*,
https://doi.org/10.1007/978-3-319-97319-7_13

While Eurojust and Olaf have strengthened their presence in the European judicial area of freedom, security and justice, the Council has eventually adopted and published in the Official Journal[1] Council Regulation (EU) 2017/1939 implementing enhanced cooperation on the establishment of the European Public Prosecutor's Office ('the EPPO'); twenty Member States have participated to such enhanced cooperation.[2]

It is also known how the EU courses take various directions, especially in highly delicate subjects as criminal law is. The distrust of Member States in welcoming a fair proposal for a European Prosecutor is softened through the acceptance of an institution like Eurojust. This body, although deprived of specific prosecuting functions, plays today an essential coordinating role in cross-border investigations, both in terms of effectiveness and because it favours the relationships among the prosecuting authorities of the Member States. The Olaf plays a similar role, ensuring that the results of its police investigations—however formally administrative—, in defence of the Union's financial interests, circulate in all systems and give rise, where provided, to the consequent criminal proceedings.

Both Eurojust and the European Public Prosecutor—the former 15 years old, the latter just born—are placed in a context which is not at all univocal. Since the coming into force of the Lisbon Treaty (2009), after the abandonment of the "third pillar" and the consequent end of the transitory period characterizing Framework Decisions until 2014, the Union's schemes in criminal procedural matters have evermore become complicated.

The measures issued on the basis of the mutual recognition principle before 2009 have certainly radically changed relationships among Member States with regard to surrender of persons subject to restrictive measures (think of the European arrest warrant) and to movement of evidence (bear in mind the innumerable measures aimed at seizing and/or freezing assets).

However, it is thank to the Directives issued since 2010, according to Arts. 82 ff. of the Treaty on the Functioning of the European Union (TFEU), that the Union has been changing the traditional instruments of judicial cooperation and legal assistance among Member States. The measures issued for implementing the Stockholm *Roadmap* in defence of a suspect's fundamental rights (interpretation, letter of rights, defence right, presumption of innocence) are more and more harmonizing criminal procedures in the different systems. Besides, the adoption of the European investigation order and Joint investigation teams are bound to apply judicial cooperation modalities that, partly anticipated by the 2000 Convention on mutual legal assistance, are inspired to principles that aim at overcoming the old relationships among sovereign entities, in favour of more effective relations among judicial authorities.

---

[1]OJ L 283, 31 October 2017.

[2]Belgium, Bulgaria, Cyprus, Croatia, Finland, France, Germany, Greece, Lithuania, Luxembourg, Portugal, Czech Republic, Romania, Slovakia, Slovenia, Spain, Italy, Latvia, Estonia and Austria.

2 Eurojust

Eurojust is symbolic of the Union's specific tendency to proceed along more than one path, in order to get to an as most shared result as possible. This body, set up following the tragic events of 9/11/2001, first as a "temporary unit", has been the most serious alternative to a European Public Prosecutor's Office. At the time of the Twin Towers' attacks, a definite outline of a public prosecutor's office had already been defined in the study of *Corpus Iuris* (in 2000, at its second release), and a big dispute had arisen just in that period in view of the preparation of the *Green Paper* on that theme, which would come out on December 2001. Back then, Member States, like nowadays, were anyway rather unwilling to give in even the smallest areas of their sovereignty in criminal matters. Only on Eurojust, in February 2002 (and on the contemporary European arrest warrant, in June the same year) did Member States come to an agreement.

In order to improve the effectiveness of actions against the most serious forms of criminal offences, this body, which has no jurisdictional and/or para-jurisdictional functions in the proper sense, has an exclusively coordinating task. Unlike previous experiences of judicial cooperation, it was not only a simple "network", as had happened before with the network of contact points, created in 1996, or the European Judicial Network of 1998. Eurojust is a composite, specifically organised institution. In the Hague's headquarters, all 28 EU Member States are represented. The single national members, which make up the College, create the link with the national systems.

The central body is the instrument that enables the coordination, information exchange, elaboration of common strategies and initiatives, together with the equivalent police organism called Europol (competences are practically the same).

Thanks to Decision 2009/426/JHA, national members' rights have been expanded, the College's competences strengthened and the relations with other cooperating institutions consolidated. Besides, though under different conditions deriving from the single national implementing laws, nowadays each Member State's representative can receive and transmit calls for legal assistance and start initiatives to ease its implementation and/or supply further information; as well as complete or carry out measures based on the principle of mutual recognition; start investigation measures agreed upon during coordination activities set up by Eurojust, where also national authorities are involved; in urgent cases, it can even authorise and supervise controlled deliveries in the Member States. The College, in turn, can today issue non-binding opinions in cases of conflicts of jurisdiction between two or more Member States and make decisions when it is difficult to implement rogatories or measures grounded on mutual trust.

In standard practice, Eurojust's growth is linked to the faster and faster circulation of information about transnational proceedings in various countries. As can be read in several reports retrievable in its institutional website, Eurojust is rapidly expanding in the context of cross-border operations for particularly serious crimes (i.e. drug trafficking) which involve investigations in more than one country. When, as often is the case, joint investigation teams are created (as provided by the 2000 Convention on mutual legal assistance), Eurojust takes also part in the consequent (new) form of circulation of evidence: what the team collects can, as a rule, be used as evidence in the country where criminal proceedings will take place, even though gathered in the executing Member State.

The Treaty of Lisbon has confirmed the importance of this body, to whom Art. 85 TFEU allows to give powers to start investigations and prevent and solve conflicts of jurisdiction: such powers were not, before then, provided for and are hugely important in the struggle against cross-border crime as a whole, for the defence of the Union's financial interests in particular and enforceable also in cases of serious crimes which require a prosecution on common bases.

Eurojust is bound to take on more and more visibility thanks to the new role of national Parliaments, which the Treaty links to the Union institutions in evaluating its work (Art. 85 TFEU), and is also the basis "from which", according to a non-perfectly clear disposition, the new European Public Prosecutor's Office shall originate (art 86, para. 1 TFEU).

By the proposal for a Regulation on the European Union Agency for Criminal Justice Cooperation (Eurojust), and now the new Regulation on the EPPO, the Commission wants to implement Art. 85 TFEU. The proposal, in its original version, aims at further reinforcing and rationalizing (with respect to the College) the position of national members, coordinating their cooperation with the new European Public Prosecutor's Office and defining the control activity of European and national Parliaments. This text, which is still to be approved, contains no indications as to the new powers quoted in the above mentioned Art. 85.

Eurojust's competences should be extended to prosecution *on common bases*. Instead, the cases to be given to the European Public Prosecutor's Office would seem ruled out. National members, in agreement with local authorities, should be able to take investigative measures, also in hypotheses of urgency, if the case be.

The functions of the College should be distinguished whether it carries out operational functions (support or coordination of national investigations) or management functions (as when preparing the annual budget). Some specific administrative functions should be assigned to a new body, the Executive Board. The Commission might be represented in such body and in the College while performing operative functions. A great freedom of action is given to relations with other inquiring "agencies" (Europol in particular) and the European Public Prosecutor's Office, especially as regards mutual exchange of information and meetings with the respective authorities.

Member States have come to a general agreement on the proposal, from which what regards relations with the European Public Prosecutor's Office has been excerpted. The creation of this new agency is still subject to strong opposition. During negotiations, the Commission was excluded from Eurojust College meetings, although it is still represented in the Executive Board. Among the many rules under discussion, there is the re-introduction of the possibility for Eurojust to intervene, whenever required by a Member State, even apart from crimes within its competence.

3 The European Public Prosecutor's Office (EPPO)

A similar, hard situation has regarded the European Public Prosecutor's Office, of which the most significant features can be now outlined, after the adoption of Regulation (EU) 2017/1939.

Reservations that have accompanied Eurojust have accompanied also the European Public Prosecutor's Office, resulting in the establishment of the enhanced cooperation. The low profile which is typical of the coordinating body is replied also in the new prosecution body. Since the public power to start criminal proceedings has for long been expression of the symbolically strongest nucleus of the national identity, the way to a European Public Prosecutor's Office has been particularly uneven. Italy, one of the most convinced sponsors of the EPPO, decided to participate in the establishment of the enhanced cooperation only at the last minute because of the 'minimalist' approach during negotiations on which all the other Member States agreed. As is known, over 20 years have passed since the first draft of *Corpus Iuris* (1995). And over 40 since when Giscard D'Estaing, early in the '70s, started to think about a common European judicial area. The second release of *Corpus Iuris* in 2000 and the *European public prosecutor green paper* in 2001 came shortly after the acknowledgment of mutual recognition by the Tampere's Council (1999). The debate on the proposal for a Regulation on the establishment of a European Public Prosecutor's Office initiated in a scenario where measures tending to harmonization of procedural rights were enormously growing. In this picture, art. 86 TFEU represents the widest licence that Member States have wished to acknowledge to what could be the first and unique "para-jurisdictional" body of the Union.

The points on which Member States have eventually reached a necessary compromise for the creation of the EPPO, however, are similar to 20 years ago. Three, in short, are the questions to which debatable solutions have been found: (1) the organization of the body; (2) the regulation of its investigation activity; (3) rules on prosecution.

Preliminary to all these profiles is the detection of crimes for which the European Public Prosecutor's Office will be competent, namely those that impact the Union financial interests (Art. 86 TFEU). In line with this provision, at the beginning after 3 years following the entry into force of the Regulation, the EPPO will be competent only for cases that involve the Union's financial interests (Art. 86 TFEU), this corresponding to a reduction of Member States' prerogatives on such matter. Details on EPPO's competence can be found under art. 22 of the Regulation, according to which (para. 1): "the EPPO shall be competent in respect of the criminal offences affecting the financial interests of the Union that are provided for in Directive (EU) 2017/1371, as implemented by national law, irrespective of whether the same criminal conduct could be classified as another type of offence under national law".

Member States have manifested large perplexities both in terms of structural choices (1) and of those related to the body functions (2 and 3) because of the inevitable limitation of their sovereignty.

This approach has marked, on a central level, the creation of a very complex, centralised structure which allows Member States to control EPPO's activity through "the Permanent Chambers" (see art. 10 of the Regulation), and, on a local level, the choice of the so called "double hat".

At a central level, under the central authority's control (the EPP, see art. 8 and 9 of the Regulation) and that of a series of its deputies in each of the Member States, the necessary joint functions have been entrusted to Permanent Chambers that will be made responsible for the "euro-investigations". The original idea of the proposal that was for a much smoother central authority has been abandoned. The need for control and/or intervention, also at level of Member States, requires that all be represented and that some "Permanent Chambers" endeavour to follow, verify and monitor euro-proceedings.

At a local level, the choice of the so called "double hat" too is symbolic of such approach. The national representative, more or less free of tasks entrusted to him/her in the domestic system, should act as a European Prosecutor in his/her Member State with powers typical of his/her original qualification.

Despite Art. 86 TFEU does not preclude the possibility to regulate specifically EPPO's activity, the Regulation confines itself to provide for "investigation measures and other measures" (see art. 30) whose existence has to be ensured by Member States in their systems so as to make them available for the EPPO, subject to certain conditions.

The Regulation on this regard recalls the *Corpus Iuris*. Unlike the 2000 project, however, the text in no way competes with any Euro-unitary discipline. The reference to the applicable national law *(lex loci)*, in line with the mutual recognition principle and the evermore developed harmonization among Member States' systems, is instrumental to enabling the EPPO to order and/or request certain measures provided for at national level.

The Union legislator is not interested in introducing provisions on European criminal procedures, anyway limited to the pre-trial phase, according to Art. 86 TFEU (as is known, a Euro-prosecutor does not match with a Euro-judge). Respect for national traditions halts the search for shared provisions. The results of a research by the scholars supervised by Katalin Ligeti and condensed in the renowned *Model Rules* have not influenced the Commission's decisions.

The Regulation has reshaped the rules on prosecution as provided for under the proposal of 2013. While the principle of obligatoriness has been confirmed under Recitals 65 e 66 of the Preamble, with reference to choosing between prosecution and dismissal, the text points out the consistency of evidence needed to propose to bring a case to judgment, and provides for judicial review before the Court of Justice (see art. 42 of the Regulation). "Simplified prosecution procedures" can be applied only "if the applicable national law provides for a simplified prosecution procedure aiming at the final disposal of a case on the basis of terms agreed with the suspect" (art. 40 of the Regulation).

Furthermore, in order to regulate the complex cases of concurrent competence by European and national prosecution (see art. 24 and 25 of the Regulation), the Regulation provides for simplified criteria according to which allocating jurisdiction, with the involvement of the Permanent Chambers (art. 26 of the Regulation).

4 Eurojust and the EPPO

What comes out of the quickly described scenario with regard to the two bodies, Eurojust and the EPPO, is the preeminence of operative solutions.

Both Eurojust and the EPPO integrate a "vertical" cooperation model. Both aim at creating a judicial assistance and cooperation system that goes beyond traditional rogatorial forms, which are bi- or multi-lateral and therefore "horizontal" among Member States, allowing to carry out investigations coordinated by a unique superior body.

Although, or perhaps just because, according to art. 86 TFEU, the EPPO may have been established *from* Eurojust, the Regulation contains only one specific provision, art. 100, on the "Relations [of the EPPO] with Eurojust".

According to art. 100, para. 1 of the Regulation, "the EPPO shall establish and maintain a close relationship with Eurojust based on mutual cooperation within their respective mandates and on the development of operational, administrative and management links between them as defined in this Article. To this end, the European Chief Prosecutor and the President of Eurojust shall meet on a regular basis to discuss issues of common concern".

Eurojust is also a supportive body in operational matters, especially in relations with EU countries that are not parties to the EPPO and non-EU countries. Art. 100, para. 2 affirms that: "in operational matters, the EPPO may associate Eurojust with its activities concerning cross-border cases, including by: (a) sharing information, including personal data, on its investigations in accordance with the relevant provisions in this Regulation; (b) inviting Eurojust or its competent national member (s) to provide support in the transmission of its decisions or requests for mutual legal assistance to, and execution in, Member States of the European Union that are members of Eurojust but do not take part in the establishment of the EPPO, as well as third countries".

The two bodies share the same information so that the EPPO may enjoy the *know how* of Eurojust. According to art. 100, para. 3: "the EPPO shall have indirect access to information in Eurojust's case management system on the basis of a hit/no-hit system. Whenever a match is found between data entered into the case management system by the EPPO and data held by Eurojust, the fact that there is a match shall be communicated to both Eurojust and the EPPO, as well as the Member State of the European Union which provided the data to Eurojust. The EPPO shall take appropriate measures to enable Eurojust to have access to information in its case management system on the basis of a hit/no-hit system". Lastly, art. 100, para. 4 provides that: "the EPPO may rely on the support and resources of the administration of Eurojust. To that end, Eurojust may provide services of common interest to the EPPO. The details shall be regulated by means of an Arrangement".

This provisions implement that enigmatic affirmation on the establishment of the EPPO "from" Eurojust, by ensuring that the EPPO may benefit from Eurojust's long experience.

5   Some Considerations of the European Parliament, Followed in the Regulation on the EPPO

The above mentioned provisions stem from some considerations delivered by the European Parliament some time before the adoption of the Regulation according to enhanced cooperation.

Since, as is known, the Treaty does not provide for a co-decision with the European Parliament related to the creation of the EPPO, the former could have only accepted or turned down the unanimous compromise of the Council and sent recommendations and (non-binding) suggestions to the Council throughout negotiations.

On the occasion of the preparation of a Resolution project to this end—*Motion for a Resolution further to Question(s) for Oral Answer pursuant to Rule 128(5) of the Rules of Procedure on European Public Prosecutor's office and Eurojust*, "Resolution on European Public Prosecutor's office and Eurojust" [2016/2750(RSP)]—on September 28 2016, the European Parliament, after recalling the relevant provisions of the TFEU, the proposals of the Commission and the Council's works, first of all underlined the losses due to frauds against the Union ["an overwhelming €159.5 billion in Value Added Tax (VAT) revenues were lost across the EU in 2014 according to figures released by the European Commission on the 6th of September"]. The European Parliament therefore stressed the reasons why the EPPO needed to be established.

It then pinpointed the importance that the Union pursues these cases, "thus protecting the taxpayers of all the Member States who contribute to the Union's budget" and the significance of Eurojust (which "has facilitated coordination and cooperation between national investigative and prosecution authorities in dealing with cases affecting a number of Member States, [. . .] helped to build mutual trust and to bridge EU's wide variety of legal systems and traditions, [. . . and] has facilitated the execution of requests for cooperation and the application of mutual recognition instruments, thereby improving cross-border prosecution").

By pleading for the rapid creation of the EPPO, it reaffirmed "the Parliament's long-standing support for the establishment of an efficient and independent EPPO to reduce the current fragmentation of national law enforcement efforts to protect the EU budget, thus strengthening the fight against fraud in the European Union".

The Parliament, besides, wished that the Council succeeded in: providing an unambiguous and clear set of competences and proceedings concerning the EPPO based on the proposed Directive on the fight against fraud to the Union's financial interests by means of criminal law (PIF Directive); clarifying the prosecution competences of the EPPO and national prosecutors (in cases of multiple offences and mixed offences); clarifying the relations between Eurojust and the EPPO, and in particular the implications of the collegiate structure, as well as the EPPO's relation with OLAF, in order to differentiate between their respective roles in the protection of the EU's financial interests.

The Regulation seems to fully address these issues. Now, its effectiveness will need to be tested.

6 Annotated Bibliography

The bibliography on this matter is quite large.

Following are, divided by topic, the latest contributions which also present the "State of the Art" until their publication.

Regarding the novelties of the Lisbon Treaty with reference to the abolition of the third pillar, it is useful to consult, for its manual approach, from the perspective of a constitutionalist, Corleto *La Cooperazione in materia giudiziaria penale nell'Unione europea: tutela giurisdizionale e relazioni inter ordinamentali dopo il Trattato di Lisbona*, 2014, Editoriale Scientifica. For a more strictly procedural vision, Aprile-Spiezia, *Cooperazione giudiziaria penale nell'Unione europea prima e dopo il Trattato di Lisbona*, 2009, Ipsoa, and Kostoris (a cura di), *Manuale di procedura penale europea*, 2015, Giuffrè, 2nd ed.

As to English, see the classic book by Klip, *European Criminal Law*, 2016, Intersentia Ltd, 3rd Revised edition, and the most recent work by Mitsilegas, *EU Criminal Law after Lisbon Rights, Trust and the Transformation of Justice in Europe,* 2016, Hart Publishing.

As to the analysis and history of Eurojust, see in particular Spiezia, *I cambiamenti in corso nello spazio europeo di libertà sicurezza e giustizia: quale futuro per Eurojust?*, 2015, available at http://www.penalecontemporaneo.it and in *Cassazione penale* 2015, pp. 1614 ff.

Reflections in the light of negotiations on the proposal for a Regulation by the European Commission COM(2013) 535 of July 17th 2013 can be found in Gutiérrez Zarza *Eurojust* (ed.), *Exchange of Information and Data Protection in Cross-border Criminal Proceedings in Europe,* 2015, Springer-Verlag (p. 50 ff.). Previously, see also Monar, *Eurojust's present and future role at the frontline of European Union criminal justice cooperation*, ERA Forum, 2013-14, 187.

On the EPPO, see Erkelens, Meij, Pawlik (eds.), *The European Public Prosecutor's Office. An extended arm or a Two-Headed dragon?*, 2015, T.M.C. Asser Press, where all the features of the proposed Regulation are discussed: from the body structure to its relations with Eurojust, until the provisions on its activity. The volume Ligeti (ed.) *Toward a Prosecutor for the European Union, Comparative Analysis*, Volume 1 (Modern Studies in European Law), 2012, Hart/Beck collects and discusses all national reports regarding the pre-trial phase of criminal proceedings of Member States, in view of the predisposition of the *Model Rules* (available on the Luxembourg University website).

A first comment on the Regulation establishing the EPPO, with a historic reconstruction of its origin, has been recently published by Salazar, *Habemus EPPO! La lunga marcia della Procura europea*, in Archivio penale, 2017-3, p. 1 ff.

Judicial Control of the European Public Prosecutor's Office

Martin Böse

Contents

Abstract According to the recently adopted EU Regulation on the establishment of the European Public Prosecutor's Office (EPPO), the new supranational body shall be subject to judicial control not only by Union courts, but first and foremost by national courts of the Member States. The particular role of national courts is rooted in the hybrid structure of proceedings that are initiated by the EPPO, but will result in a trial before a national criminal court. This paper, however, argues that judicial control of a Union institution should be exercised by a Union court and that the treaty system of judicial protection does not allow for a delegation of jurisdiction to national courts.

A German version of this article has been published in Böse M (2017) Die Europäische Staatsanwaltschaft 'als' nationale Strafverfolgungsbehörde – Kritik eines neuen Rechtsschutzmodells. JuristenZeitung 72(2):82–87.

M. Böse (✉)
University of Bonn, Department of Law, Bonn, Germany
e-mail: boese@jura.uni-bonn.de

© Springer Nature Switzerland AG 2019
T. Rafaraci, R. Belfiore (eds.), *EU Criminal Justice*,
https://doi.org/10.1007/978-3-319-97319-7_14

1 Introduction

As a supranational body responsible for criminal investigation and prosecution, the European Public Prosecutor's Office (EPPO) will take measures seriously interfering with fundamental rights. Thus, an effective judicial control of the EPPO will be of crucial importance. The complex structure of the EPPO, the 'double hat model' in particular,[1] has raised a number of questions on how to organize judicial review and to delimit the jurisdiction of national courts from that of the European Court of Justice. The following contribution will focus on these institutional aspects, i.e. the question which court shall be competent for judicial control.

This focus requires some preliminary remarks on function and scope of judicial control (Sect. 2) before the provision on judicial review in recently adopted Regulation on the establishment of the European Public Prosecutor's Office[2] shall be addressed (Sect. 3). In a second step, the article will outline general treaty framework of judicial review and the division of powers between national courts and Union courts (Sect. 4) and then discuss whether the treaty basis for the establishment of the EPPO (Art. 86 TFEU) provides or allows for a particular role of national courts in this context (Sect. 5).

2 Function and Scope of Judicial Control

Judicial control shall ensure that the law is observed (Art. 19 para. 1 sent. 2 TEU). Thereby, it has an objective function which is deeply rooted in the rule of law (Art. 6 para. 1 TEU), and a subjective function aimed at the protection of fundamental rights.[3] According to Art. 47 para. 1 of the EU Charter of Fundamental Rights (EU-CFR), everyone whose rights and freedoms are violated has the right to an effective remedy before a tribunal.

So, judicial control means first of all judicial review of an act that has been challenged by an individual claiming a violation of his/her rights, e.g. an investigative measure interfering with fundamental rights (home searches), a procedural act (e.g. the denial of access to the file) or a prosecutorial decision (e.g. dismissal of the case).[4] The key question in this regard is whether the EPPO's decision directly

---

[1]See Ligeti and Weyembergh (2015), p. 62; see also with regard to the general risks of a semi-decentralized model: Kaiafa-Gbandi (2015), pp. 236–237.

[2]Regulation (EU) 2017/1939 of 12 October 2017 implementing enhanced cooperation on the establishment of the European Public Prosecutor's Office (O.J. L 283/1).

[3]See with regard to these functions: Sauer (2008), p. 32 et seq.

[4]Đurđević (2013), pp. 1003–1004; Wasmeier and Killmann (2015), Art. 86 AEUV para. 152; see also Art. 11 Directive 2012/29/EU of 25 October 2012 establishing minimum standards on the rights, support and protection of victims of crime (O.J. No. L 315/57): The right to a review of a decision not to prosecute, however, does not require review by a court.

affects individual rights. This may be questioned for intermediate decisions (e.-g. the initiation of an investigation).[5] Nevertheless, any decision whereby the EPPO exercises its competence triggers the supranational procedural framework and, thereby, does affect the status of the defendant; this seems obvious for decisions on case allocation and forum choice (see also recital (87) of the Regulation).[6]

Besides, judicial control can be exercised *ex officio*, i.e. without an individual complaint. The decision to file an indictment and to commit the case to trial is subject to court review whether there is sufficient evidence for charges.[7] A settlement or transaction may require the court's consent, too.[8] Furthermore, judicial control may also serve as procedural safeguard, providing judicial protection *ex ante* (e.g. an arrest warrant or a search warrant). Thereby, judicial control is exercised in a stage of proceedings where judicial review is not yet available because the person concerned is not aware of the investigation and, thus, cannot challenge the corresponding acts.[9]

In the treaty framework of judicial protection, the jurisdiction of the Court of Justice mainly focuses on judicial review. By contrast, judicial control *ex officio* is not explicitly foreseen in the treaties and seems to be a matter for national courts only. This institutional setting also corresponds to the hybrid structure of criminal proceedings triggered by the EPPO, namely a supranational pre-trial phase and a national trial-phase.

The lacunae of the jurisdiction of the Court of Justice have provoked the question whether both judicial control of the EPPO and judicial review of its decisions should be exercised by national courts especially because the EPPO's decisions will be mainly based upon national law. At first sight, this holistic approach is appealing, and, thus, it takes no surprise that it has been followed in the Commission's proposal as well as the final version of the regulation on the establishment of the EPPO.

---

[5]Larsen (2013, unpublished), presentation at a conference on "The European Public Prosecutor's Office – A constructive approach towards the legal framework", Vilnius 16–17 September 2013, as summarized in Council-Document 13863/13, pp. 16, 19; for the contrary view see Erbežnik (2015), p. 216; see also Đurđević (2013), pp. 1002–1003.

[6]Luchtman and Vervaele (2014), pp. 145–146.

[7]Đurđević (2013), pp. 1001–1002; see with regard to an action for annulment Wasmeier and Killmann (2015), Art. 86 AEUV paras. 150–151.

[8]See e.g. section 153a para. 1 German Code of Criminal Procedure (Strafprozessordnung); see for the function of this requirement (judicial control of the prosecutor): Federal Court of Justice (Bundesgerichtshof), decision of 29 October 1992 – 4 StR 353/92, official court reports (BGHSt) vol 38, pp. 381, 382.

[9]Luchtman and Vervaele (2014), p. 146; Böse (2012), p. 175.

3   The Commission's Proposal and the Negotiations in the Council

According to the Commission's proposal for a regulation on the establishment of the EPPO,[10] judicial review of the EPPO's decisions should be a matter for national courts: By means of legal fiction, the EPPO should be considered as a national authority so that its decisions would be subject to judicial review by national courts (Art. 36 para. 1). The Commission argued, that the procedural acts and investigative measures of the EPPO will be executed in the national criminal justice systems on the basis of national law, and, thus, it seemed more appropriate to provide for judicial review by national courts; thereby, suspects and lawyers can work within an institutional and procedural framework they are familiar with.[11] Nevertheless, the Court of Justice should remain competent to give preliminary rulings on the interpretation and validity of EU law, the regulation on the establishment of the EPPO in particular.[12] The preliminary ruling procedure, however, should not apply to national provisions that were rendered applicable by this regulation (Art. 36 para. 2). All in all, the assessment of the legality and validity of the EPPO's decisions fell within the sole jurisdiction of the competent national court.

During the negotiations in the Council, a majority of Member States supported the Commission's view that national courts should be competent to review the legality of the EPPO's decisions. Nevertheless, there was a common understanding that decisions that are by their nature "European" (e.g. on forum choice) should be subject to judicial review by a Court of the Union.[13] These concerns resulted in the idea of splitting up the competence for judicial review between national courts and the European Court of Justice, depending on whether the relevant decision of the EPPO is taken on the centralized (e.g. initiation of an investigation, referral of the case to national authorities) or the decentralized level (e.g. investigative measures).[14] Under the Dutch presidency, the remaining competences of the Union's Court of Justice were clarified, in particular in the areas that have been discussed at the very end of the negotiations (e.g. data protection).[15]

In the end, the final provision on judicial review (Art. 42) has become quite complex.[16]

---

[10]COM (2013) 534 final of 17 July 2013.

[11]COM (2013) 534 final of 17 July 2013, p. 7; see also recital (87) of the Regulation.

[12]COM (2013) 534 final of 17 July 2013, p. 20.

[13]Council Document 6490/14, p. 5.

[14]Council Document 11045/15 - Annex, p. 27; see also Option 2 in Council Document 15862/1/14 REV 1 - Annex II, p. 48; see also the European Parliament's resolution of 29 April 2015 - P8_TA (2015)0173, paras. 24–25.

[15]Council Document 10266/16 - Annex, pp. 3–4.

[16]See for an earlier version of Art. 36 resulting from the council negotiations: Council Document 12774/1/16 REV 1, p. 57; see also Council Document 11350/1/16 REV 1, p. 72.

The general rule still is that procedural acts of the EPPO shall be subject to judicial review by the competent national courts according to the rules and procedures laid down by national law (Art. 42 para. 1). In order to meet the concerns that judicial review of the validity of acts of a Union institution falls within the exclusive competence of Union courts, Art. 42 para. 2 lit. a states that the Court of Justice shall have jurisdiction to give preliminary rulings on the validity of procedural acts of the EPPO insofar as the validity is questioned directly on the basis of Union law. Thus, Union courts are competent for judicial review on the basis of Union law whereas review on the basis of national law falls within the exclusive competence of national courts (Art. 42 para. 1). Thus, the act is valid until it is declared void either by the national court or by the European Court of Justice—in the latter case, the preliminary ruling of the Court will not be preliminary, but more or less final.[17]

This concept of shared judicial review is based upon the assumption that the assessment of the legality of an act can be split up in legality under Union law and legality under national law. This assumption, however, ignores the interaction of Union law and national law.

Let me illustrate this by an example: According to Art. 30 para. 1 lit. b of the Regulation, the European Delegated Prosecutor shall be entitled to issue production orders according to national law. As Art. 30 para. 3 suggests, this investigative power must not be subject to further conditions under national law. If national provisions, however, do not allow for a production order against the suspect because this is considered to be in breach with the privilege against self-incrimination, a production order issued by the EPPO would be illegal under national law.[18] If, however, the protection of the suspect is considered to be incompatible with Art. 30 para. 1 of the regulation, the primacy of Union law will render this provision inapplicable and the production order is to be considered perfectly legal. So, the million dollar question is which court shall be competent for this assessment. According to its wording, Art. 42 para. 2 lit. a does not apply because the validity of the order is not questioned on the basis of Union law, but of national law. On the other hand, Union law has a significant impact on the judicial review of the production order, and there is no reason to make the jurisdiction of the Court of Justice dependent upon whether Union law is applied to annul or to uphold the EPPO's decision. In both constellations, the interpretation and application of Union law may result in an annulment of the EPPO's decision and, if taken by a national court, jeopardize the uniform application of Union law. It does not take a prophet to

---

[17]Due to the preliminary ruling procedure, however, court proceedings will take a long time and, thereby, hamper an effective investigation, see Wasmeier and Killmann (2015), Art. 86 AEUV paras. 149.

[18]See for criminal investigations in Germany: Constitutional Court (Bundesverfassungsgericht), decision of 29 November 2004 – 2 BvR 1034/02, Neue Juristische Wochenschrift 58(23):1640, 1641; see also the compromise in Ligeti et al. (2012), Rule. 50 para. 5 of the "Model Rules for the Procedure of the EPPO", available at http://www.eppo-project.eu/index.php/EU-model-rules (8 Nov 2017).

foresee various potential conflicts between national law and Union law in this respect because the applicable national law has to abide by the Charter of Fundamental Rights (Art. 51 para. 1 EU-CFR) on the one hand,[19] and it must allow for an effective investigation and prosecution by the EPPO on the other. As we have learned from the Taricco-judgment, the latter requirement may take precedence and set aside national rules on criminal proceedings.[20]

The action of annulment is subject to a similar regime: The decision to dismiss a case shall be subject to an action of annulment only as far as it is contested directly on the basis of Union law (Art. 42 para. 3). Since the protection of personal data, public access to documents and the dismissal of European Delegated Prosecutors are governed by Union law, the Court of Justice shall be competent for judicial review in this respect, too (Art. 42 para. 8). Again, judicial review of the EPPO's decision on the basis of national law shall fall within the exclusive competence of national courts. This provision meets the same concerns as the corresponding provision on preliminary rulings. Furthermore, the plaintiff has to challenge the EPPO's decision before both the competent national court and the Union court if the validity of the relevant act is contested on the basis of national and Union law. On the other hand, the subject matter of the assessment will overlap to a significant extent (e.g. sufficient evidence, public interest in prosecution, proportionality[21]), and this will obviously result in a waste of resources.[22] Finally, the list of decisions to be challenged before Union courts does not appear to be properly considered as there are several other decisions that are mainly based upon Union law (case allocation, forum choice)[23] or significantly overlap with the decision subject to the jurisdiction of the Union courts (e.g. access to the file under Art. 41 para. 2 lit. b, and access to personal data under Art. 59).

Finally, the jurisdiction of the Court of Justice on compensation claims (Art. 268 TFEU), staff-related matters (Art. 270 TFEU) and pursuant arbitration clauses (Art. 272 TFEU) is explicitly reaffirmed (Art. 42 paras. 4 to 6) although in these proceedings, Union courts may be called upon to apply national law as well, e.g. in order to establish the illegal act of the EPPO that has caused the damage (whereas Union courts shall not have jurisdiction to rule on the legality of this act under Art. 263 TFEU). To some extent, the EU legislator seems to rely on the treaty system of judicial control (see recital [89]) whereas it has no concerns about cutting down the Court's jurisdiction over the action for annulment (Art. 263 TFEU) and the preliminary ruling procedure (Art. 267 TFEU).

---

[19]Inghelram (2015), pp. 128–129; Larsen (2013, unpublished) (note 5), p. 18.

[20]CJEU, Judgment of 8 September 2015, Case C-105/14, Taricco and others, paras. 49 et seq.

[21]See for proportionality checks under national law recital (88) of the Regulation.

[22]See with regard to parallel problems in prior authorization procedures: Inghelram (2015), p. 132.

[23]See the former version of Art. 36, Council Document 13227/15 - Annex, p. 15.

4 The Treaty Framework of Judicial Review in the Union

So, the final version of the regulation on the EPPO seems to follow a piecemeal approach, making its own choices where jurisdiction of the Union courts shall be maintained and where not. The question, however, is whether this legislative approach of jurisdiction *à la carte* complies with the treaty framework and its rules on jurisdiction of Union courts.

The application and enforcement of EU law is not a matter for EU institutions only (direct enforcement), but also for the competent authorities of the Member States (indirect enforcement). Accordingly, judicial review of this enforcement is a responsibility of both European and national courts (Art. 19 para. 1 sent. 3 TEU). Thus, rules and criteria are needed to determine the jurisdiction of national courts and Union courts. Basically, this delimitation can be based upon two criteria: the act subject to judicial review (1.) and the law to be applied (2.).

4.1 The Validity of Supranational Acts: Exclusive Jurisdiction of Union Courts

Even though national courts interpret and apply EU law, they do not have jurisdiction to determine acts of EU institutions invalid.[24] According to the well-established case-law, it is rather upon the Court of Justice to rule on the validity of EU law. This exclusive jurisdiction is mainly based upon two reasons[25]: First, EU law shall be applied in a uniform manner throughout the Union, and different judgments of national courts on the validity of an act of the Union would seriously undermine the uniform application of EU law and the requirement of legal certainty.[26] Secondly, jurisdiction of national courts to rule on the validity of Union acts is incompatible with the treaty system of judicial protection. By the action for annulment (Art. 263 TFEU) and the preliminary ruling procedure (Art. 267 TFEU), the treaty has established a complete and coherent system of procedures to review the legality of acts of EU institutions that does not allow for concurrent jurisdiction of national courts.[27]

---

[24]Inghelram (2011), pp. 227–228, 265; Meij (2015), p. 114.

[25]CJEU, Case C-314/85, Foto-Frost, [1987] ECR 4199 paras. 15–17.

[26]The decision of national court on the validity of an act adopted by a Union body will not have effect throughout the Union, see AG *Mengozzi*, opinion of 26 October 2006, C-354/04, Gestoras Pro Amnistia, [2007] ECR I-1583 paras. 120.

[27]Since the Lisbon-Treaty has integrated the cooperation in criminal matters into the supranational structure of the Union, the Court of Justice has exclusive jurisdiction to rule on the legality and validity of acts adopted in this framework. See, by contrast, with regard to the pre-Lisbon era: AG *Mengozzi* (2006) (note 26), paras. 118 ff.

4.2 The Application of National Law: Exclusive Jurisdiction of National Courts?

So, the EPPO is a supranational Union body and, thus, should be subject to judicial control by Union courts. On the other hand, according to the corresponding provisions of the Regulation, the investigative and prosecutorial decisions of the EPPO are mainly based upon the national law of Member States (Art. 28 paras. 1 and 2, Art. 29 para. 1, Art. 30 paras. 2, 3 and 4, Art. 32, Art. 33 para. 1, Art. 39 para. 1, Art. 40 para. 1). Thus, judicial review by national courts might appear more appropriate, if not mandatory because Union courts would lack a competence to assess whether these acts are in conformity with national law.[28]

The treaty provisions on the Court of Justice indicate indeed that the jurisdiction of the court is limited to the interpretation of Union law (e.g. Art. 263 para. 2: "infringement of the Treaties or of any rule of law relating to their application", Art. 267 para. 1 lit. a and b TFEU: "the interpretation of the Treaties", "the validity and interpretation of acts of the institutions … of the Union").[29] Besides, national courts are in a far better position to interpret and to apply their domestic law.

Nevertheless, even though the interpretation of national law is a genuine task of national courts, the treaty framework of judicial protection does not prohibit Union courts from interpreting and applying national law, but even may require them to do so.[30] According to Art. 272 TFEU, the Court of Justice has jurisdiction to give judgment pursuant to any arbitration clause in a contract concluded by the Union; in exercising its jurisdiction, the court has to interpret the national law that applies to that contract.[31] Furthermore, Art. 268 TFEU establishes the Court's jurisdiction in disputes relating to compensation for damages caused by illegal acts adopted by the Union's institutions. In that respect, the Court of Justice has expressly stated that a claim for compensation can be based upon a breach of national law where EU law requires the Union institution to abide by the relevant national legislation.[32] As far as Union law refers to and, thereby, incorporates national law, the Courts of the Union must take the latter into account when assessing the legality of a measure adopted by a Union institution. If Union courts were not allowed to interpret and to apply national law, this would seriously undermine the right to effective judicial review (Art. 47 para. 1 EU-CFR).[33] So, if decisions of the EPPO are—at least in part—based upon national law, judicial review of these decisions by Union courts must

---

[28]Larsen (2013, unpublished) (note 5), p. 21.

[29]See with regard to the action for annulment: ECJ, Case C-50/00, Unión de Pequeños Agricultores, [2002] ECR I-6677 para. 43; see with regard to the preliminary ruling procedure: ECJ, Case C-222/04, Cassa di Risparmio di Firenze, [2006] ECR I-289 para. 63, with further references.

[30]AG *Mengozzi*, opinion of 27 January 2011, Case C-401/09, Evropaïki Dynamiki, [2011] ECR I-4911 paras. 68–70.

[31]CJEU, Case 109/81, Porta, [1982] ECR I-2469 paras. 11 et seq.

[32]CJEU, Case C-308/87, Grifoni, [1990] ECR I-1203 paras. 8–9.

[33]AG *Mengozzi* (2011) (note 30), paras. 72–75.

consequently extend to compliance with the relevant national law. Thus, the treaty system of judicial review does not exclude judicial control of the EPPO by Union courts because the EPPO's decisions are mainly based upon national law.

In short, jurisdiction to rule on the validity of an act depends upon the institution that has adopted the act: Decisions of Union bodies are reviewed by Union courts, decisions of national authorities are reviewed by national courts.[34]

5 The EPPO and Its Relationship to National Courts (Art. 86 TFEU)

As we have seen so far, the treaty system of judicial protection supports the view that the EPPO should be subject to judicial control by the courts of the Union. The legal basis for the establishment of the EPPO (Art. 86 TFEU), however, might provide for an exception from this general rule and allow for judicial review by national courts.

5.1 The Competence of National Courts Under Art. 86 Para. 2 TFEU

According to Art. 86 para. 2 second sentence TFEU, the EPPO 'shall exercise the functions of prosecutor in the competent courts of the Member States'. This wording might give rise to the interpretation that national courts may be competent for judicial review of the EPPO's measures. A closer look, however, reveals that Art. 86 para. 2 TFEU does not deal with the competence of national courts, but the functions of the EPPO. The first sentence defines the EPPO's functions in the pre-trial stage of proceedings (investigating, prosecuting and bringing to judgment) whereas the second sentence determines the functions of the EPPO in the trial phase. Since the treaty does not provide for a competence to establish a European Criminal Court, the trial is held before a national court.[35] This is why the second sentence refers to the competent courts of the Member States, but neither wording nor systematic context of Art. 86 para. 2 TFEU allow for any conclusion that judicial review in the pre-trial stage should be exercised by national courts as well.

---

[34]Meij (2015), p. 114.

[35]See the former German version of the corresponding provision in the European Constitutional Treaty (Art. III-170 para. 2 sent. 2), CONV 727/03 of 27 May 2003, p. 46 ("zuständig für die Erhebung der öffentlichenm Anklage"); for a detailed analysis see Böse (2012), pp. 190–191.

5.2 The Scope of the Power to Regulate Judicial Review (Art. 86 Para. 3 TFEU)

Even though the treaty has not established a competence of national courts to control the EPPO in the pre-trial stage, it might have empowered the Union legislator to do so. Art. 86 para. 3 TFEU provides a legal basis to adopt 'the rules applicable to the judicial review of procedural measures' of the EPPO. Thereby, Art. 86 para. 3 TFEU might provide a legal basis to limit (or even exclude) jurisdiction of Union courts and to delegate judicial review to the national courts.[36] Thus, the Union legislator would modify the treaty framework of judicial protection and draw up a special regime for judicial control of the EPPO.

The Union legislator, however, does not have a power to amend the treaties. It follows from the hierarchy of norms and the primacy of the treaties over secondary legislation that any regulation adopted by the Council and the Parliament must comply with the treaty framework of judicial control by the Court of Justice of the European Union. Limiting (or even excluding) the Court's jurisdiction would substantially affect this framework and be tantamount to an amendment of the corresponding treaty provision.[37] That does not mean that the legislator has no power at all to regulate judicial control by Union courts. Art. 263 para. 5 TFEU expressly allows for legislative acts that lay down specific conditions and arrangements concerning the action for annulment against acts of Union bodies such as the EPPO. This provision, however, does not provide a basis to abolish the Court's jurisdiction on actions for annulment brought by private parties and to establish a new regime for judicial review.[38] All the more, the Court's jurisdiction with regard to other proceedings (e.g. the preliminary ruling procedure) must not be excluded where modifications by secondary legislation are not foreseen.

The only way to overcome these objections is to interpret Art. 86 para. 3 TFEU as an implicit and comprehensive derogation from the treaty framework of judicial review. Since the treaty provisions only exceptionally provide for modifications by secondary legislation (Art. 263 para. 5; see also Art. 261 TFEU), such an understanding seems hardly acceptable. Furthermore, it stands in sharp contrast to the settled case-law of the Court of Justice on exclusive jurisdiction over the validity of EU law and the acts of Union institutions (supra, Sect. 4.1). The Court has left no doubt that the scope of its jurisdiction under the current treaty framework must not be affected by secondary legislation. In its opinion on the accession of the European Union to the European Convention on Human Rights, the Court highlighted the role of the treaty system of judicial protection to ensure consistency and uniformity in the

---

[36]Wasmeier and Killmann (2015), Art. 86 AEUV paras. 145, 147.

[37]See also Inghelram (2015), pp. 132–133.

[38]Gärditz (2013), § 24 para. 52; German Bar Association (Bundesrechtsanwaltskammer) (2013), p. 9.

interpretation of Union law.[39] In the end, the draft agreement on the accession of the Union to the ECHR was held incompatible with this system, *inter alia* because it could affect the autonomy and effectiveness of the preliminary ruling procedure.[40] Although the legal basis for the accession to the European Convention on Human Rights (Art. 6 para. 2 TEU) clearly involves rules on judicial review (namely a mechanism to coordinate the jurisdictions of the Courts in Strasbourg and Luxembourg),[41] it was not considered a legal basis for derogations from the treaty system of judicial review. So, Art. 86 para. 3 TFEU cannot be interpreted as legal basis to abolish the Court's jurisdiction to rule on the legality of the EPPO's decisions, either.[42]

6 Conclusion

Judicial review of the EPPO's decisions falls within the competence of the Union courts. The rule on judicial review Regulation on the establishment of the EPPO is not compatible with the treaty system of judicial control because this system does not allow for a delegation of jurisdiction to national courts that turns the judicial system upside down.[43] Judicial review by Union courts is the logical consequence of establishing a supranational body vested with investigative and prosecutorial powers, and the treaty clearly states that any question of the validity of acts adopted by Union institutions must be brought before the Court of Justice (Art. 267 para. 1 lit. b, para. 3 TFEU).[44]

So, what options are left for organizing judicial control of the EPPO?

The first option might be to assign judicial control of the EPPO to Union courts even where not explicitly foreseen by the treaty, in particular with regard to *ex ante* authorization by a Union court (e.g. a pre-trial chamber).[45] However, a smooth functioning of judicial control by Union courts would require supranational rules on

---

[39]CJEU, Opinion No. 2/13 of 18 December 2014, para. 174; see also with regard to the Court's monopoly on reviewing the legality of acts of the institutions the opinion of AG *Kokott* of 13 June 2014, *ibid.*, para. 121.

[40]CJEU, *ibid.*, paras. 174, 197–198.

[41]See Art. 1 of the Protocol No 8 to the TEU and to the TFEU.

[42]Similarly Inghelram (2015), p. 266, 267; Meij (2015), p. 114.

[43]Meij (2015), p. 112.

[44]The argument that the Court of Justice lacks the capacity to exercise judicial control (Alexandrova [2015], p. 19) seems odd where decisions of the EPPO are taken by chambers of several prosecutors. If the Union can afford an institution for investigation and prosecution, there is a duty to provide judicial protection as well.

[45]Delmas-Marty (2000), pp. 52–53; for a detailed analysis of the treaty framework see Böse (2012), p. 172 et seq.; Rheinbay (2014), p. 248 et seq.; for the contrary view see Inghelram (2011), pp. 264–265; see also Luchtman and Vervaele (2014), p. 146.

pre-trial proceedings (e.g. investigative measures).[46] For the time being, it comes as no surprise that the Member States did not agree upon such a model.

The alternative model would be a truly decentralized structure with national prosecutors acting as EPPO counterparts in each Member State. These counterparts would be national authorities subject to judicial review by national courts. The jurisdiction of Union courts would be limited to decisions taken by the EPPO on the central level. This alternative model would abandon the 'double hat model' of the EPPO with its inherent contradiction that the EPPO is an 'indivisible Union body operating as one single office with a decentralized structure' (Art. 8 para. 1) where the European Delegated Prosecutor (i.e. the decentralized level) exercises the powers of a national prosecutor (Art. 13 para. 1). The final version of judicial review clearly reveals the conceptual deficit of the double hat model and its ambiguity: Splitting up jurisdiction over the acts of an indivisible body between national and Union courts will inevitably result in a shell game[47] on judicial protection leaving the defendant in a jurisdictional limbo.[48]

References

Alexandrova V (2015) Presentation of the Commission's proposal on the establishment of the European Public Prosecutor's Office. In: Erkelens LH, Meij AWH, Pawlik M (eds) The European Public Prosecutor's Office: an extended arm or a two-headed dragon?. Springer, Berlin, pp 11–20

Böse M (2012) Ein europäischer Ermittlungsrichter – Perspektiven des präventiven Rechtsschutzes bei Errichtung einer Europäischen Staatsanwaltschaft. Rechtswissenschaft 3(2):172–196

Delmas-Marty M (2000) Necessity, legitimity and feasibility of the Corpus Juris. In: Delmas-Marty M, Vervaele JAE (eds) The implementation of the Corpus Juris in the Member States, vol 1. Intersentia, Antwerp, pp 11–104

Ðurđević Z (2013) Judicial control in pre-trial criminal procedure conducted by the European Public Prosecutor's Office. In: Ligeti K (ed) Towards a prosecutor for the European Union, vol 1, a comparative analysis. Hart, Oxford, pp 986–1010

Erbežnik A (2015) European Public Prosecutor's Office (EPPO) – too much, too soon, and without legitimacy? Eur Crim Law Rev 5(2):209–221

Gärditz K-F (2013) § 24 Rechtsschutz. In: Böse M (ed) Europäisches Strafrecht. Nomos, Baden-Baden, pp 887–921

---

[46]Zwiers (2011), p. 408. This approach has been taken in the "Model Rules for the Procedure of the EPPO" (note 18).

[47]In German, the term "Hütchenspiel" (shell game, thimblerig) corresponds to the notion of the double hat model ("Doppelhut-Modell").

[48]See also Meij (2015), p. 104 (transparency of organization and procedure as a pre-condition for effective judicial review). Even where judicial review is assigned to national courts, it is far from clear which Member State will be competent. For instance, which Member State respectively court shall be competent to review the decision to reallocate a case to a European Delegated Prosecutor in another Member State (Art. 22 paras. 4 and 5): the Member State of the European Delegated Prosecutor who has taken over the case or that of the one who has conducted the investigation before?

German Bar Association (Bundesrechtsanwaltskammer) (2013) Opinion 22/2013. http://www. brak.de/zur-rechtspolitik/stellungnahmen-pdf/stellungnahmen-deutschland/2013/oktober/ stellungnahme-der-brak-2013-22-und-des-dav-2013-48.pdf. Accessed 15 Nov 2017
Inghelram JFH (2011) Legal and institutional aspects of the European Anti-Fraud Office (OLAF). Europa Law Publishing, Groningen
Inghelram JFH (2015) Search and seizure measures and their review. In: Erkelens LH, Meij AWH, Pawlik M (eds) The European Public Prosecutor's Office: an extended arm or a two-headed dragon?. Springer, Berlin, pp 121–138
Kaiafa-Gbandi M (2015) The establishment of an EPPO and the rights of suspects and defendants: reflections upon the Commission's 2013 proposal and the council's amendments. In: Asp P (ed) The European Public Prosecutor's Office: legal and criminal policy perspectives. Juridiska fakultetens skriftserie, Stockholm, pp 234–254
Ligeti K, Weyembergh A (2015) The European Public Prosecutor's Office: certain constitutional issues. In: Erkelens LH, Meij AWH, Pawlik M (eds) The European Public Prosecutor's Office: an extended arm or a two-headed dragon?. Springer, Berlin, pp 53–78
Luchtman M, Vervaele J (2014) European agencies for criminal justice and shared enforcement (Eurojust and the European Public Prosecutor's Office). Utrecht Law Rev 10(5):132–150
Meij AWH (2015) Some explorations into the EPPO's administrative structure and judicial review. In: Erkelens LH, Meij AWH, Pawlik M (eds) The European Public Prosecutor's Office: an extended arm or a two-headed dragon?. Springer, Berlin, pp 101–120
Rheinbay S (2014) Die Errichtung einer Europäischen Staatsanwaltschaft. Duncker&Humblot, Berlin
Sauer H (2008) Jurisdiktionskonflikte in Mehrebenensystemen: Die Entwicklung eines Modells zur Lösung von Konflikten zwischen Gerichten unterschiedlicher Ebenen in vernetzten Rechtsordnungen. Springer, Berlin
Wasmeier M, Killmann B-R (2015) Europäische Staatsanwaltschaft. In: von der Groeben H, Schwarze J, Hatje A (eds) Europäisches Unionsrecht, 7th edn, vol 2. Nomos, Baden-Baden, Artikel 86 AEUV
Zwiers M (2011) The European Public Prosecutor's Office. Intersentia, Antwerp

Defence Areas and Limits in the Investigations of the European Public Prosecutor

Ezechia Paolo Reale

Contents

Abstract The creation of a European Public Prosecutor's Office stems from a need extraneous to defence guarantees. However, the Author tries to draw a map of the provisions from which a guarantee statute can be extracted for those who will be subject to investigation and actions by the European Public Prosecutor's Office. The Author concludes with an altogether positive assessment about the defence statute before the European Public Prosecutor's Office but underlines that some critical points still remain, above all the risk that relying on provisions and principles in diverse normative texts may undermine accessibility to such a statute, known to only a small number of experts.

1 Introduction

The creation of a European Public Prosecutor's Office stems from a need extraneous to defence guarantees from all viewpoints, namely from the need to safeguard EU financial interests from criminal offences which generate significant financial damages, not sufficiently investigated and prosecuted by the relevant national authorities, as from paragraph 3 of the Preamble to the Council Regulation (EU) 2017/1939 of

E. P. Reale (✉)
The Siracusa International Institute for Criminal Justice and Human Rights, Siracusa, Italy
e-mail: ep.reale@siracusainstitute.org

© Springer Nature Switzerland AG 2019
T. Rafaraci, R. Belfiore (eds.), *EU Criminal Justice*,
https://doi.org/10.1007/978-3-319-97319-7_15

12 October 2017 (Official Journal of the European Union of 31 October 2017) which provides for the institution of this body.

No wonder, then, that the respect of defence rights finds a place only in the last paragraphs of the Preamble, from 83 to 85, by references to external measures which are fully operative in the EU system and recall minimum rules that would have been applicable to the European Public Prosecutor's Office activity anyway, given its nature of EU organism.

My contribution might then come to an end here, highlighting how there is no indication whatsoever of a statute dedicated to defence before the European Public Prosecutor's Office, for this being necessary to refer to basic rights and principles granted by Article 6 TEU and the Charter of Fundamental Rights of the European Union, specifically Title VI, as well as by the European Convention for the Protection of Human Rights and Fundamental Freedoms, implemented by the Directives adopted under Article 82, paragraph 2, TFEU, which, as is known, allows the EU to establish "minimum rules on the rights of individuals in criminal procedure".

However, let me make a logical map of the provisions from which a guarantee statute can be extracted for those who will be subjected to investigation and actions of the European Public Prosecutor's Office, being sure that, by the end of such recognition, the firstly negative impact of the assessment becomes fairly weaker.

First of all, I wish to underline that we reflect today on a final text, quite distant from the Proposal for a Council Regulation on the establishment of the European Public Prosecutor's Office, resulting from the European Commission on 17/7/2013 (COM 2013/0534), which, after the early warning system started by some national Parliaments under Article 7, paragraph 2, of Protocol 2 attached to the Treaties, had been the basis of negotiations which took place inside the Council.

Following developments are well known: from the provisional version of the consolidated text of the draft Regulation (11350/1/16), as updated by the Working Party on Cooperation in Criminal Matters of the Council of the EU, after the meeting of 19 and 20 July 2016 (11350/1/16 REV 1), to resolution (2016/2750 RSP) adopted on 5 October 2016 by the European Parliament containing even strong criticism on the central theme of competence of the European Public Prosecutor's Office, but also not less important doubts on the jurisdictional control of the European Public Prosecutor's Office measures and the safeguard of rights of suspects and accused; from the update of the consolidated text carried out (11350/1/16 REV 2 CORR1) after another meeting on 13 and 14 October 2016 to the general reservation expressed by the Commission on the Chapter entitled "Procedural Safeguards", namely in the article filed as "Scope of the Rights of the Suspected and Accused persons".

This is not surprising, given the diversity between the final text and the original one proposed by the Commission, which on Chapter IV on "Procedural Safeguards" featured 4 Articles (from 32 to 35).

At the end of negotiations the only provision in the final text, Article 41, is composed of three paragraphs (compared to the six of the related Art. 32 in the Commission's proposal), of which two of general tenor and one that can be defined additional.

2 Guarantees of National Systems

Paragraph 3 of Article 41 contains the general provision by which "suspects and accused as well as other persons involved in the proceedings of the European Public Prosecutor's Office shall have all the procedural rights available to them under the applicable national law, including the possibility to present evidence, to request the appointment of experts or experts examination and hearing of witnesses, and to request the EPPO to obtain such measures on behalf of the defence".

In its *incipit*, the provision presents the safeguard clause "without prejudice to the rights provided in this Chapter", which shows that, even in case a national procedure contains no minimum guarantees provided for on Chapter VI, these are anyway applicable to procedures for which the European Public Prosecutor's Office is competent. This clause upturns the perspective of the provisions proposed by the Commission, which subordinated the application of these guarantees to their being acknowledged within the national applicable law.

The apparently fair and appeasing provision will really become such in so far as the knotty questions connected with the *forum shopping* exercisable by the European Public Prosecutor's Office are resolved, in compliance with Articles 26 and 36, to which the innovative *law shopping* has to be added, well known in international arbitrations, that stems from the formulation of Articles 5 and 13.

If it is true that, ideally speaking, the principle of mutual trust that characterizes European legal orders should render unimportant which jurisdiction and national law are to be applied, it is also true that, shifting from the abstraction of principles down to reality, there are still substantial differences between procedural guarantees in the various national European systems; then the real extension of the rights of suspects and accused risks to be largely dependent on the national competent jurisdiction and the applicable law, the choices of which in turn depend on internal decision of the European Public Prosecutor's Office.

The referability of defence rights to domestic laws, however, together with the safeguard clause that ensures minimum *standards* of guarantee, is an important element anyway, namely in relation to those Member States in whose proceedings the safeguard of defence rights is, even during the pre-trial phase, at a more advanced state of development.

Article 42, dealing with judicial review—despite a dramatic modification on its way from Commission proposal to final text, after its significant introduction in the Chapter of "Procedural Safeguards", whereas beforehand it formed by itself the Chapter on "Judicial review",—reaffirms such shareable approach whereby it highlights that the procedural acts of the European Public Prosecutor's Office, which are intended to produce legal effects *vis-à-vis* third parties (Paragraph 87 of the Preamble clarifies that this diction comprehends also the suspect and the victim), are subject to review by the competent national courts in accordance with the requirements and procedures laid down by national law.

In the same way, "Investigation measures" (Art. 30), even though "cross-border" ones (Art. 31), are regulated, as regards their adoption and then in terms of guarantee as well, by the national applicable law. In addition, in this last event, the judicial authority's authorization will be needed even if not required in the State of execution and, *vice versa*, even if it is not required in the European Delegated Prosecutor's State, whose designation determines the national applicable law.

And the same happens for pre-trial detention, disposed or requested in compliance with the law applicable in similar national cases (Art. 33).

3   Minimum Standards in the European Directives

Paragraph 2 of Article 41 says that "any suspect and accused person in the criminal proceedings of the European Public Prosecutor's Office shall, as a minimum, have the procedural rights as they are provided for in Union law, including directives concerning the rights of suspects and accused persons in criminal procedures" and recalls then the European Directives implementing Article 82, paragraph 2, TFEU mentioned in the Resolution of the European Council of 30/11/2009, better known as "Roadmap for strengthening procedural rights of suspected or accused persons in criminal proceedings" (2009/C 295/01), and precisely:

(a) The right to interpretation and translation, in compliance with Directive 2010/64/UE of the European Parliament and the Council of 20/10/2010. Deadline for implementation 27/10/2013. Adopted in Italy through Law Decree no. 32 of 4/3/2014.

According to Article 2 of the Directive, "Member States shall ensure that suspects or accused who do not speak or understand the language of the criminal proceedings concerned are provided, without delay, with interpretation during criminal proceedings before investigative and judicial authorities, including during police questioning, all court hearings and any necessary interim hearings; that interpretation is available for communication between suspects or accused and their legal counsel in direct connection with any questioning or hearing during the proceedings or with the lodging of an appeal or other procedural applications", specifying that "the right to interpretation includes appropriate assistance for persons with hearing or speech impediments".

Interpretation provided under this article shall be of a quality sufficient to safeguard the fairness of the proceedings, in particular by ensuring that suspects or accused are aware of the case against them and are able to exercise their right of defence.

Similarly, under Article 3 of the Directive, it is provided that "Member States shall ensure that suspects or accused, who do not understand the language of the criminal proceedings concerned, are, within a reasonable period of time, provided with a written translation of all documents which are essential to ensure that they are able to exercise their right of defence and safeguard the fairness of the proceedings. Essential documents shall include any decision depriving a person of his liberty, any charge or indictment, and any judgment".

As to the quality of translation, article 5 of the Directive contains a provision similar to that of interpretation.

(b) The right to information, in line with Directive 2012/13/UE of the European Parliament and Council of 5/22/2012. Deadline for implementation 2/6/2014. Adopted in Italy through Law no. 101 of 1/7/2014.

Member States shall ensure that suspects or accused be promptly provided, in simple, accessible language, with information concerning the following procedural rights: (a) the right of access to a lawyer; (b) any entitlement to free legal advice and the conditions for obtaining such advice; (c) the right to be informed of the accusation; (d) the right to interpretation and translation; (e) the right to remain silent.

This guarantee, according to Article 4 of the Directive, is strengthened for persons arrested or in detention who are to receive, in writing, beside the above listed information, even that regarding: (a) the right of access to the materials of the case; (b) the right to have consular authorities and one person informed; (c) the right of access to urgent medical assistance; and (d) the maximum number of hours or days suspects or accused may be deprived of liberty before being brought before a judge and about any possibility of challenging the lawfulness of the arrest; obtaining a review of the detention; or making a request for provisional release.

Finally, at the latest on submission of the merits of the accusation to a court, detailed information is provided about the accusation, including the nature and legal classification of the criminal offence, as well as the nature of participation by the accused and of any changes in the information given to them where this is necessary to safeguard the fairness of the proceedings.

As regards the access to documents of the case, Article 7 of the Directive provides that an arrested or detained person has the right that the documents related to the specific case in the possession of the competent authorities which are essential to challenging effectively, in accordance with national law, the lawfulness of the arrest or detention, are made available to arrested persons or to their lawyers. More generally, access is granted in due time in order to allow the effective exercise of defence rights and at the latest when the merits of the accusation are submitted to the judgment of a court.

As to the right of access, moreover, let me recall a specific provision of the final text of the Regulation, whose coherence with the Directive's provisions seems not at all verified, according to which "access to the case file by suspects and accused as well as other persons involved in the proceedings shall be granted by the handling European Delegated Prosecutor in accordance with the national law of that Prosecutor's Member State" (Art. 45).

(c) The right of access to a lawyer and the right to communicate with and have third persons informed in case of detention in line with Directive 2013/48/EU of the European Parliament and Council of 22/10/2013. Deadline for implementation 27/11/2016. Adopted in Italy through Law no. 184 of 15/9/2016.

Under Article 3 of the Directive, it is provided that suspects and accused have the right of access to a lawyer in such time and manner so as to allow the persons concerned to exercise their rights of defence practically and effectively, [. . .] without undue delay and, in any event, shall have access to a lawyer from whichever of the following points in time is the earliest: (a) before they are questioned by the police or by another law enforcement or judicial authority; (b) upon the carrying out by investigating or other competent authorities of an investigative or other evidence-gathering act, such as identity parades, confrontations, reconstruction of the scene of a crime; (c) after deprivation of liberty; (d) where they have been summoned to appear before a court having jurisdiction in criminal matters".

"Suspects or accused persons have the right to meet in private and communicate with the lawyer representing them, including prior to questioning by the police or by another law enforcement or judicial authority and the right for their lawyer to be present and participate effectively when questioned".

Besides, Member States shall endeavor to make general information available to facilitate the obtaining of a lawyer by suspects or accused persons.

Under Article 4 of the Directive, privacy of communications between suspects or accused and their lawyers is to be respected, including meetings, mail, phone conversations and other forms of communication granted.

Suspects or accused persons who are deprived of liberty have the right to have at least one person, such as a relative or an employer, nominated by them, informed of their deprivation of liberty without undue delay (Art. 5 of Directive).

Under Article 6 of the Directive, suspects and accused deprived of their personal freedom have the right to communicate, without undue delay, with at least a third person, such as a relative indicated by them (Art. 7 of Directive) and, in case they are not citizens of the State where they are detained, they have the right to inform, without undue delay, the consular authorities of their Country about their being arrested and, later on, to communicate with these authorities.

(d) The right to be present at the trial and the enforcement of some aspects of the presumption of innocence, in conformity with Directive 2016/343/EU of the European Parliament and Council of 9/3/2016. Deadline for implementation 1/4/2018.

Under Article 3 of the Directive, Member States shall ensure that suspects and accused persons are presumed innocent until proved guilty according to the law, as well as take (Art. 4 of the Directive) the necessary measures to ensure that, for as long as a suspect or an accused person has not been proved guilty according to the law, public statements made by public authorities, and judicial decisions, other than those on guilt, do not refer to that person as being guilty.

Moreover, under Article 5, the Directive provides that Member States shall take appropriate measures to ensure that suspects and accused persons are not presented as being guilty, in court or in public, through the use of measures of physical restraint.

Finally, Article 7 of the Directive ensures that suspects and accused are granted the right to remain silent in relation to the crime/s they are suspected or accused of having committed, as well as the right not to incriminate themselves, specifying that the exercise of the right to silence or not to incriminate oneself cannot be used against them and is not deemed to be evidence of their having committed the criminal offence ascribed to them.

(e) The right to legal aid, in compliance with Directive 2016/1919/EU of the European Parliament and Council of 26/10/2016. Deadline for implementation 25/05/2019.

4 Fundamental Rights

Paragraph 1 of Article 41 says that "the activities of the European Public Prosecutor's Office shall be carried out in full compliance with the rights of suspects and accused persons enshrined in the Charter of Fundamental Rights of the European Union, including the right to a fair trial and the rights of defence".

Therefore, as expressly stated at paragraph 83 of the Preamble, the right to an impartial judge, defence and presumption of innocence, as established by Articles 47 and 48 of the EU Charter of Fundamental Rights, come to the fore, just like Article 50, which preserves the right not to be judged or punished twice for the same crime (*ne bis in idem*), and guarantees that the criminal action started by the European Public Prosecutor's Office does not lead to a double sentence.

More generally, however, and more clearly, the principles set up by the European Court of Human Rights are called into question, regarding the right to defence in criminal proceedings, provided by Articles 5 and 6 of the European Convention for the Protection of Human Rights and Fundamental Freedoms, which establish the rights of arrested or detained persons and the right to a fair trial, respectively.

It is known, in fact, that since the Lisbon Treaty which modified the Treaty on the European Union came into force, on December 1st 2009, after its signing on December 13th 2007, by its new article 6, as the EU Charter of Fundamental Rights of 7/12/2000 was given equal legal effects as the Treaties, fundamental rights guaranteed by the European Convention for the protection of Human Rights and Fundamental Freedoms have been recognized as fundamental principles of EU law.

It is first of all to be recalled that what, under Article 6 of the Convention, finds application even in the phase prior to criminal proceedings is already a recognized principle.[1] Reflecting quickly on some of the many fundamental rights applicable to the pre-trial phase, I like recalling that a suspect must have the chance to be assisted by a lawyer in the preliminary stage of police questionings,[2] as well as when he/she is arrested, in such case independently of any form of questioning[3] and that these guarantees shall also be applied to witnesses, in the event they are investigated for a

---

[1] ECrtHR November 27th 2008, *Salduz vs. Turkey*, Case no. 36391/02.

[2] ECrtHR, *Salduz v. Turkey*, cited before.

[3] ECrtHR 13/10/2009, *Dayanan v. Turkey*, case no. 73377/03.

crime,[4] since the lack of legal aid for a suspect during the questioning is an infringement of the right to defence.[5]

Furthermore, maximum privacy is to be ensured to conversations between the lawyer and the suspect, as a crucial element for an effective representation of the suspected person's interests.[6]

The content of Articles 5 and, above all, 6 of the European Convention for the Protection of Human Rights and Fundamental Freedoms, in its quality and extension reached thanks to the long and rich revision by the European Court of Human Rights, is, then, a significant foundation of the defence statute before the European Public Prosecutor's Office.

As a matter of fact, it is not to be neglected, obvious though it may be, how the investigation phase is instrumental to a successive verification which will not take place but in a cross-examination, before a national judge and therefore in a friendly or at least familiar context for the defence. Also in this context, Article 37 is not certainly indifferent, since, although it provides that "the evidence presented to a court by the European Public Prosecutor's Office or by the defendant – the term is found in the official text – shall not be denied admission on the mere ground that the evidence was gathered in another Member State or in accordance with the law of another Member State", at the same time it prescribes that in order for the evidence to be accepted, the judge has to verify its being compatible "with Member States' obligations to respect the fairness of the procedure, the rights of defence, or other rights as enshrined in the Charter, in accordance with Article 6 TEU".

5   Conclusions

Getting to a conclusion, an altogether positive assessment can be given about the defence statute before the European Public Prosecutor's Office.

Some critical points still remain. For instance, I would like to highlight that related to the preliminary identification of the competent judge during the investigation phase, a problem which impacts the principle of the "natural judge", as well as that of the right of a person to be questioned before the Public Prosecutor who exercises any legal action towards him/her; a right that, in the Italian system, led to declare as unconstitutional some provisions which did not provide for it as a sole, full right.

Articles 35 and 36, in fact, dealing with the termination of investigation and the prosecution before national courts do not provide for the obligation, on the Public Prosecutor's part, to hear the defendant before deciding which accusation to

---

[4]ECrtHR, October 14th 2010, *Brusco vs. France*, case no. 1466/07.

[5]ECrtHR, December 11th 2008, *Panovits vs. Cyprus*, case no. 4268/04.

[6]ECrtHR, March 13th 2007, *Castravet vs. Moldavia*, case no. 23393/05; ECrtHR, March 27th 2007, *Istratii vs. Moldavia*, case no. 8721/05.

formulate and indict him/her, and here the applicable law does not seem to be of any help, being this a phase which will be totally regulated autonomously by the Regulation's provisions under approval.

The same Article 36, paragraph 5, moreover, provides that "once the Member State where the legal action is to take place is chosen, the competent court of this Member State is determined on the basis of the national law", but a similar provision does not exist for the previous phase, consequently it may seem uncertain which national competent judge is going, for example, to authorize or take investigative or restraining measures.

Besides, let us also consider how the debates which had taken place inside the Council impoverished the defence statute framework, so much that the European Parliament itself, in the Resolution of 10/5/2016 suggested, successfully, reintroducing some defence rights of which there was nothing left at that time in the draft text, whereas they were expressly provided for in the initial text proposed by the Commission.

In particular, I am referring to the right to present evidence and ask the European Public Prosecution to gather evidence useful for the investigations, already provided for under Article 32 lett. f) and Article 35 of the Commission's proposal which, I am pleased to remember, was the offspring of an altogether long, shared and careful work. Be it enough to recall, besides the consultations with many judges, experts and defence lawyers, the huge work carried out, on the European Commission's behalf, to the processing of 1997 *Corpus Juris*, later implemented in 2000 in the so-called "Florence version", followed in 2001 by "the Green Paper on criminal-law protection of the financial interests of the Community and the establishment of a European Prosecutor" and in 2003 "the report on the reactions" to such Green Paper.

It is true that having those rights been deleted from the draft text did not entail their being denied, as they could have always been restored through national applicable laws which provide for them. However, it is an important signal that the European Parliament's preoccupation that their expressed missing provision might have affected practical effectiveness and, still more, the Parliament's desire for them to be acknowledged as minimum guarantees to be applied where they are not provided in the national applicable laws have been taken into consideration with the reintroduction of those rights into the final text.

The creation of a defence statute through reference to provisions and principles present in diverse normative texts, the deep knowledge of which is peculiar only to a small number of experts, will, in my opinion, make it difficult and controversial to apply defence rights in proceedings before the European Public Prosecutor's Office. It is then highly desirable that, with the urgency required by the need, three indispensable measures are taken.

First, the update and detailed analysis—perhaps directed only to defence rights—of that outstanding work dealing with the elaboration of the "Model Rules for the Procedure of the European Public Prosecutor's Office", drawn at the outcome of a research project carried out in 2010–2012 and coordinated by Katalin Ligeti which offers an operative tool, soft though it may be, able to direct the daily work of law operators; secondly, endowing the European Public Prosecutor's Office with suitable IT equipment which may somehow fill the logistic gap for the defence owing to geographical distances, which risks to render any right illusory, as defending lawyers well know from their daily national experience in vast countries like Italy; thirdly, the immediate activation of forensic associations in order to face the need for a highly specific education without which, once again, all that is written and processed in terms of rights will remain unattended due to the inability of its users to avail themselves of it.

Printed by Printforce, the Netherlands